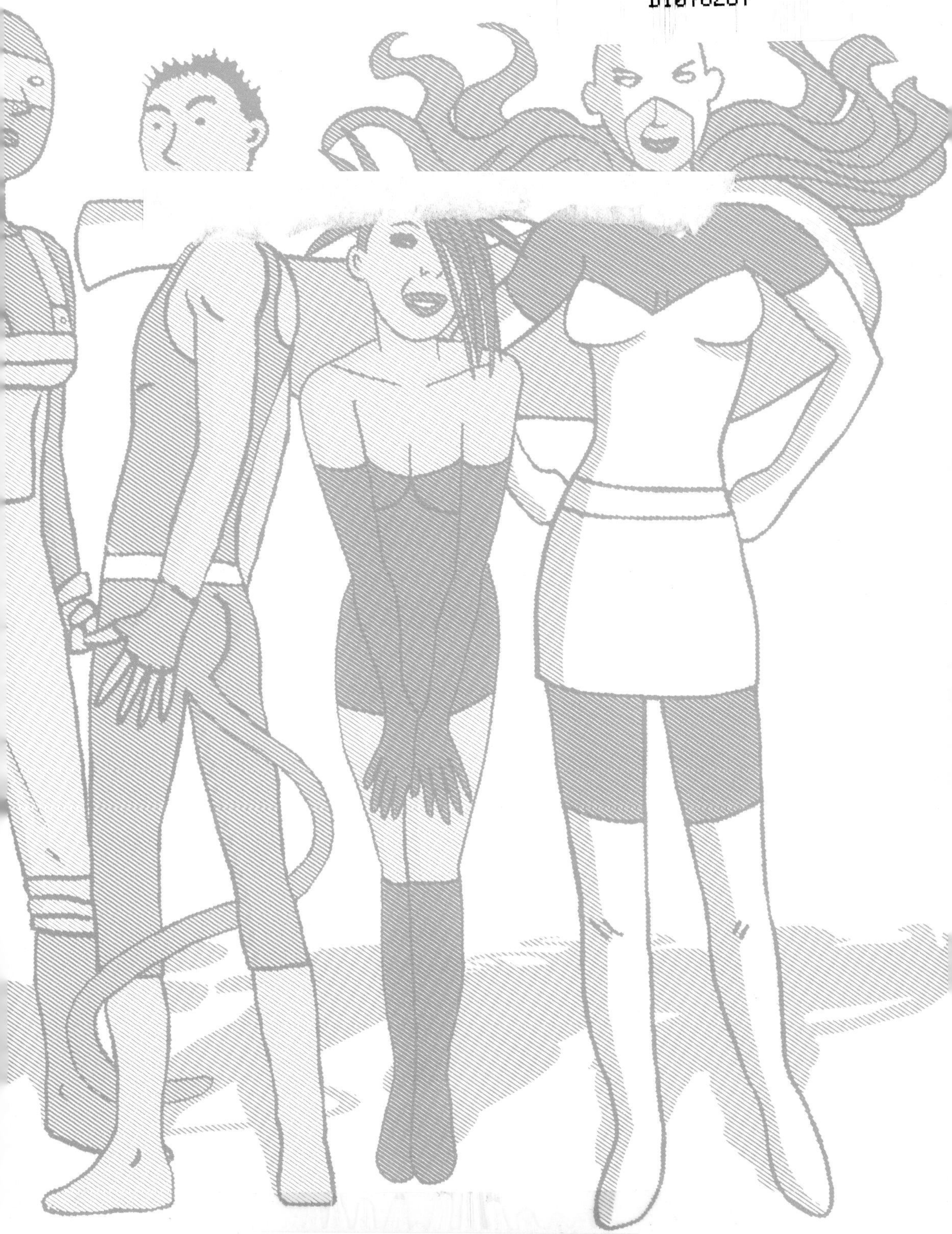

SPANDEX

FAST AND HARD

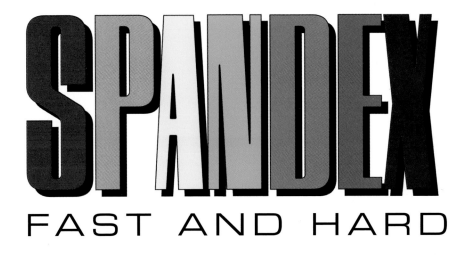

SPANDEX: FAST AND HARD

ISBN: 9780857689733

Published by Titan Books
A division of Titan Publishing Group Ltd.
144 Southwark St.
London
SE1 0UP

A CIP catalogue record for this title is available from the British Library.

First edition: May 2012

10 9 8 7 6 5 4 3 2 1

Printed in China

www.spandexcomic.com

What did you think of this book? We love to hear from our readers. Please email us at: readerfeedback@titanemail.com, or write to us at the above address.

To receive advance information, news, competitions, and exclusive offers online, please sign up for the Titan newsletter on our website: **www.titanbooks.com**

SPANDEX

FAST AND HARD

MARTIN EDEN

TITAN BOOKS

CHAPTER ONE

"ATTACK OF THE 50 FT. LESBIAN"

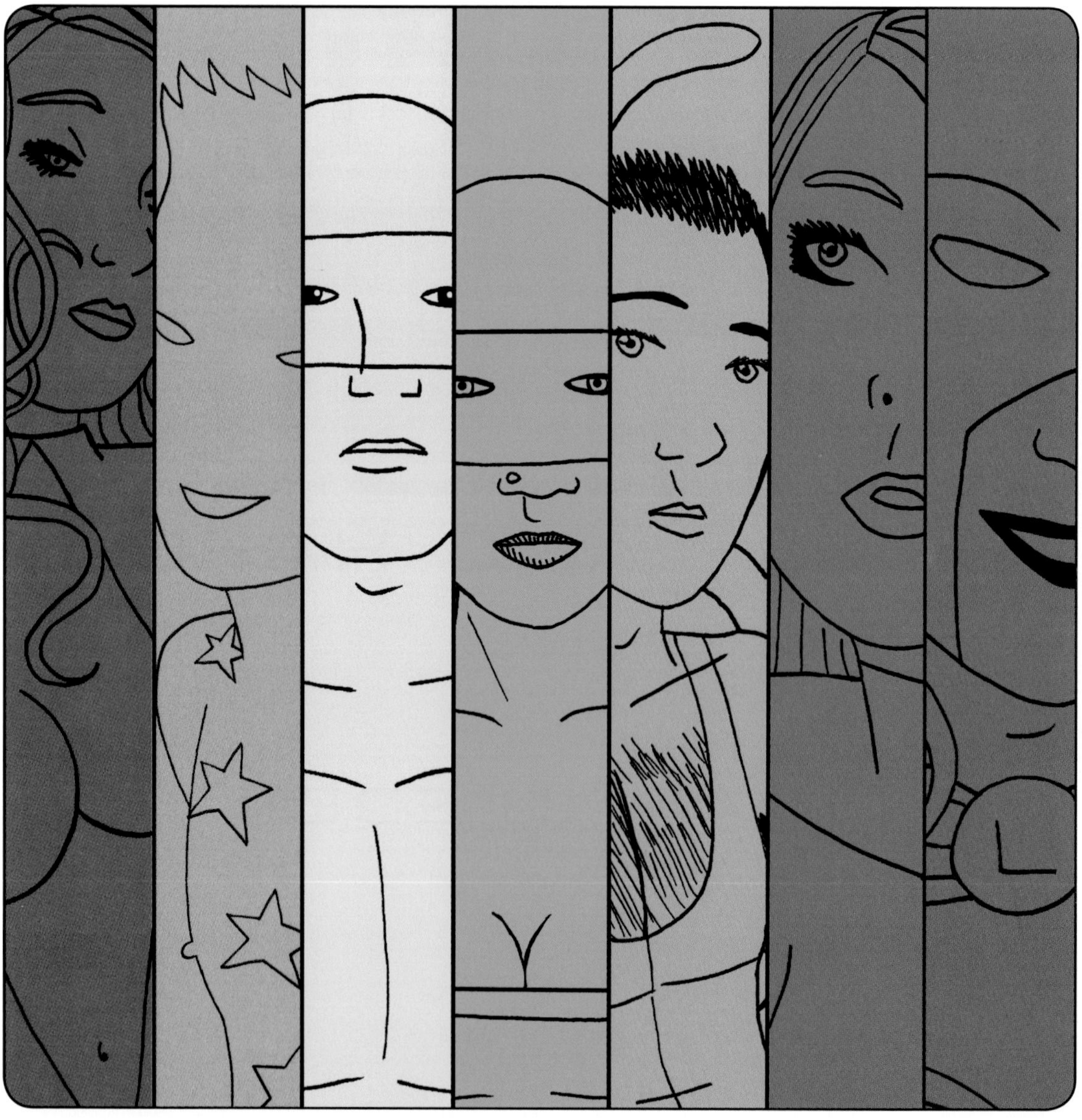

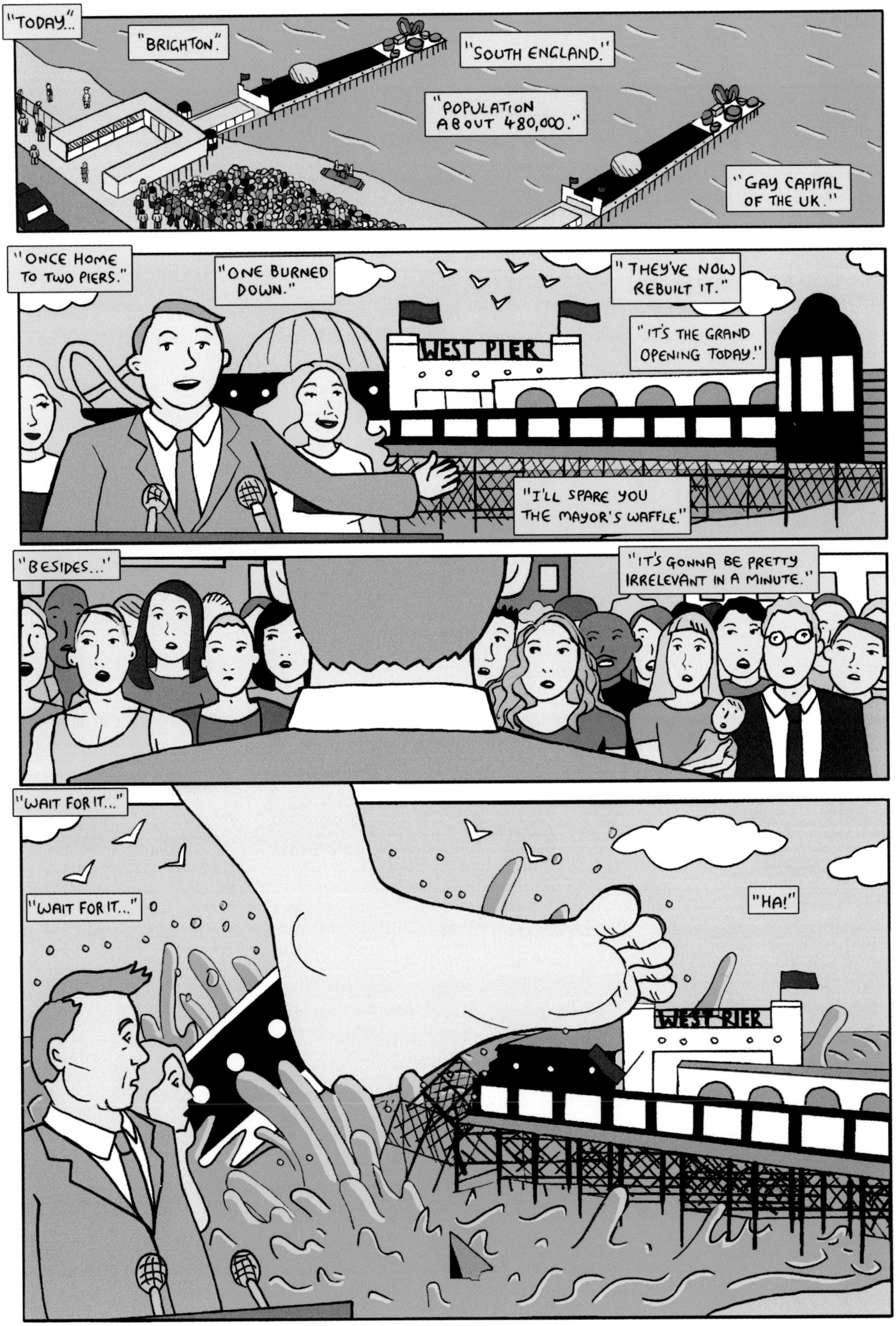
"TODAY..."
"BRIGHTON."
"SOUTH ENGLAND."
"POPULATION ABOUT 480,000."
"GAY CAPITAL OF THE UK."
"ONCE HOME TO TWO PIERS."
"ONE BURNED DOWN."
"THEY'VE NOW REBUILT IT."
"IT'S THE GRAND OPENING TODAY."
WEST PIER
"I'LL SPARE YOU THE MAYOR'S WAFFLE."
"BESIDES..."
"IT'S GONNA BE PRETTY IRRELEVANT IN A MINUTE."
"WAIT FOR IT..."
"WAIT FOR IT..."
"HA!"
WEST PIER

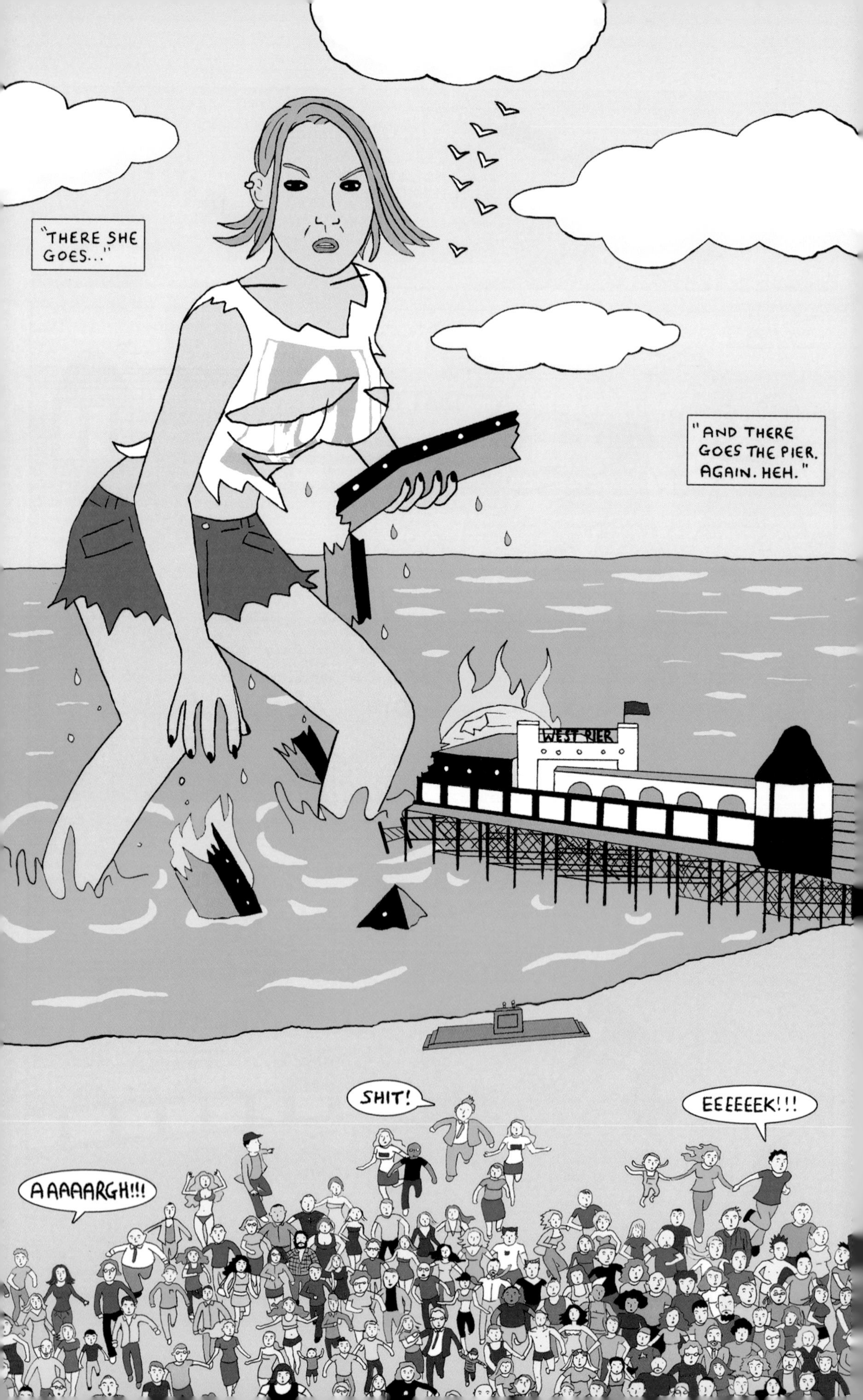
"THERE SHE GOES..."
"AND THERE GOES THE PIER. AGAIN. HEH."
WEST PIER
SHIT!
EEEEEEK!!!
AAAAARGH!!!

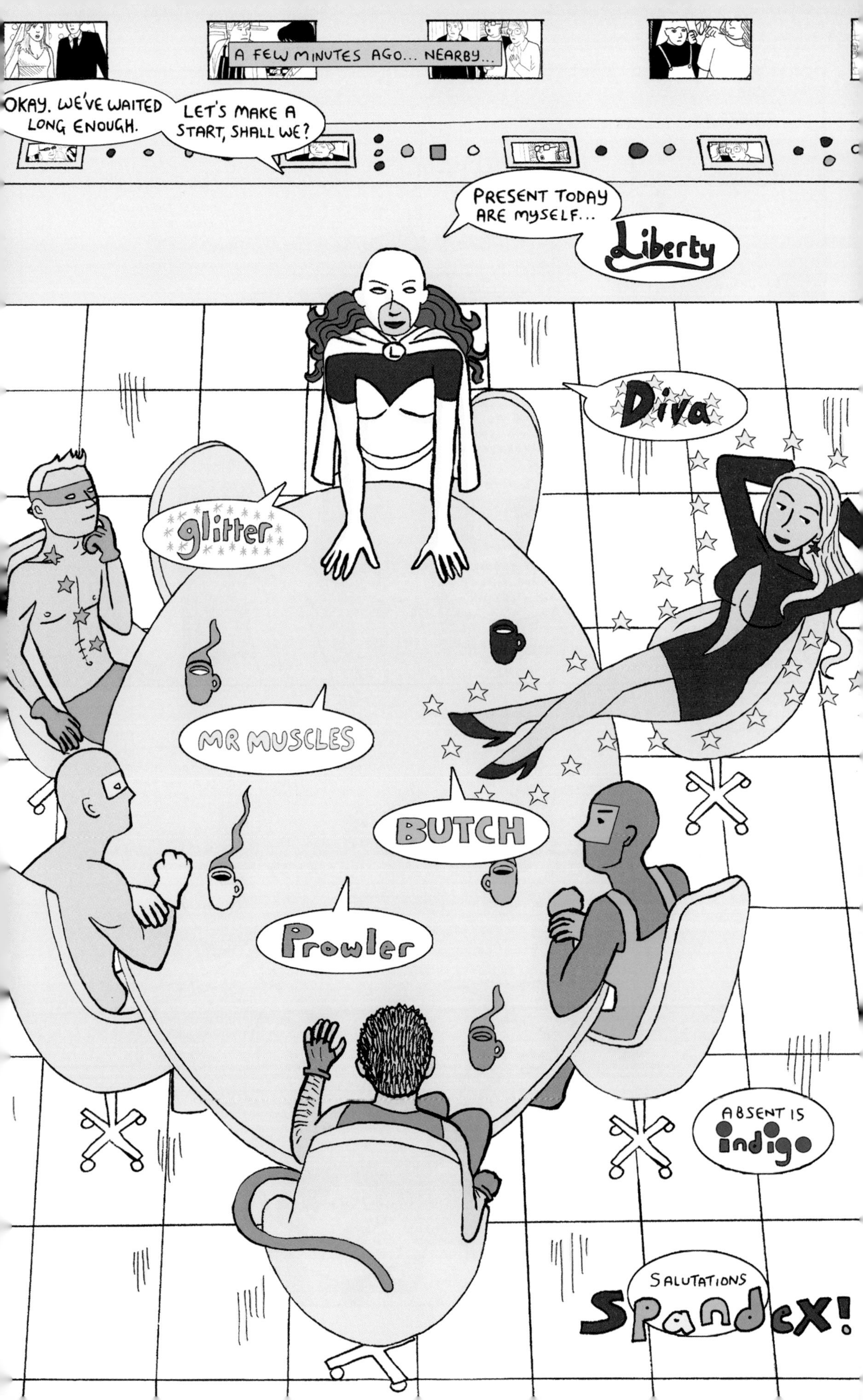
A FEW MINUTES AGO... NEARBY...
OKAY. WE'VE WAITED LONG ENOUGH.
LET'S MAKE A START, SHALL WE?
PRESENT TODAY ARE MYSELF...
Liberty
Diva
glitter
MR MUSCLES
BUTCH
Prowler
ABSENT IS indigo
SALUTATIONS
SpandeX!

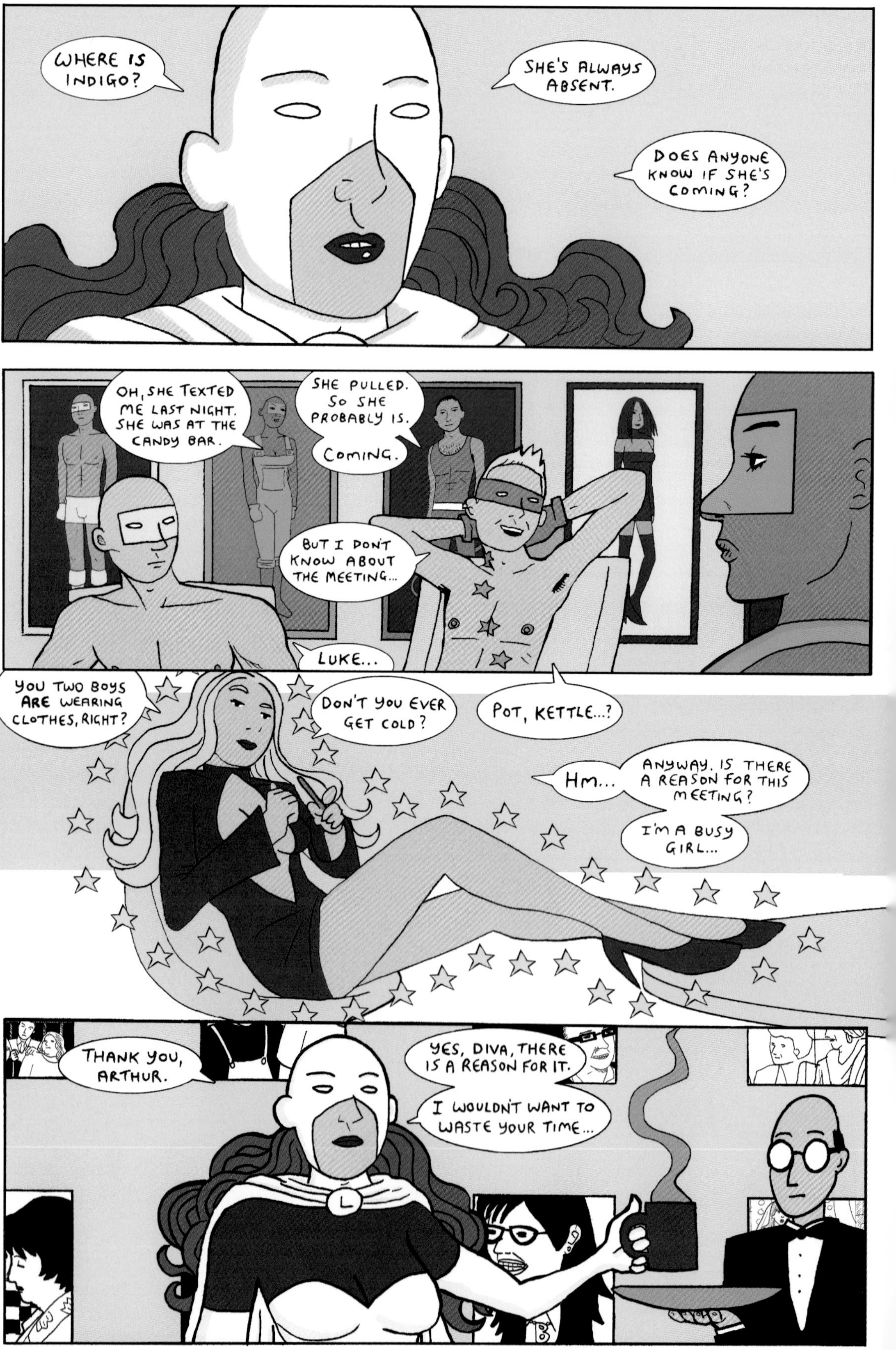
WHERE IS INDIGO?
SHE'S ALWAYS ABSENT.
DOES ANYONE KNOW IF SHE'S COMING?
OH, SHE TEXTED ME LAST NIGHT. SHE WAS AT THE CANDY BAR.
SHE PULLED. SO SHE PROBABLY IS.
COMING.
BUT I DON'T KNOW ABOUT THE MEETING...
LUKE...
YOU TWO BOYS ARE WEARING CLOTHES, RIGHT?
DON'T YOU EVER GET COLD?
POT, KETTLE...?
HM...
ANYWAY. IS THERE A REASON FOR THIS MEETING?
I'M A BUSY GIRL...
THANK YOU, ARTHUR.
YES, DIVA, THERE IS A REASON FOR IT.
I WOULDN'T WANT TO WASTE YOUR TIME...

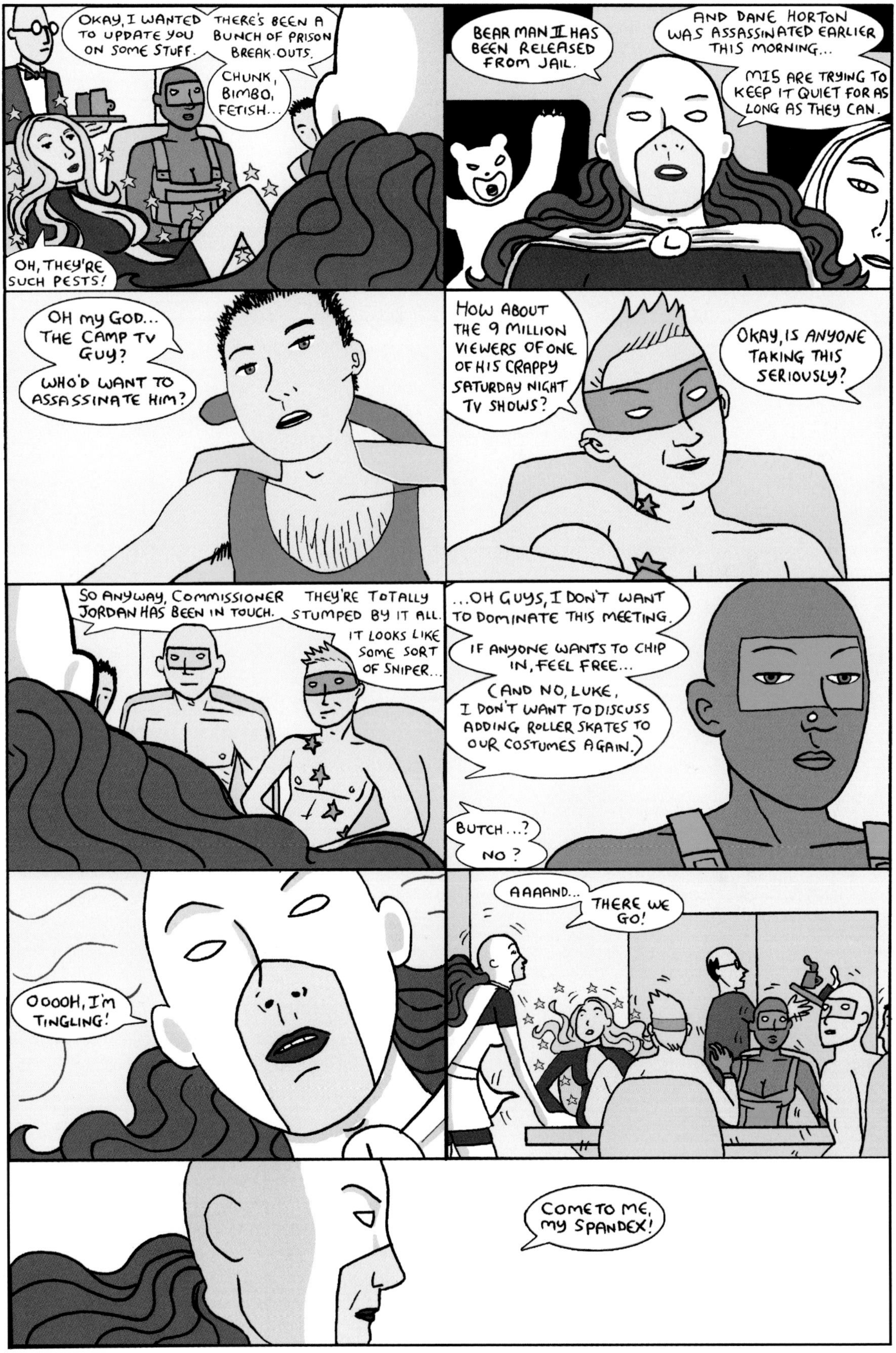
OKAY, I WANTED TO UPDATE YOU ON SOME STUFF.
THERE'S BEEN A BUNCH OF PRISON BREAK-OUTS.
CHUNK, BIMBO, FETISH...
OH, THEY'RE SUCH PESTS!
BEAR MAN II HAS BEEN RELEASED FROM JAIL.
AND DANE HORTON WAS ASSASSINATED EARLIER THIS MORNING...
MI5 ARE TRYING TO KEEP IT QUIET FOR AS LONG AS THEY CAN.
OH MY GOD... THE CAMP TV GUY?
WHO'D WANT TO ASSASSINATE HIM?
HOW ABOUT THE 9 MILLION VIEWERS OF ONE OF HIS CRAPPY SATURDAY NIGHT TV SHOWS?
OKAY, IS ANYONE TAKING THIS SERIOUSLY?
SO ANYWAY, COMMISSIONER JORDAN HAS BEEN IN TOUCH.
THEY'RE TOTALLY STUMPED BY IT ALL.
IT LOOKS LIKE SOME SORT OF SNIPER...
...OH GUYS, I DON'T WANT TO DOMINATE THIS MEETING.
IF ANYONE WANTS TO CHIP IN, FEEL FREE...
(AND NO, LUKE, I DON'T WANT TO DISCUSS ADDING ROLLER SKATES TO OUR COSTUMES AGAIN.)
BUTCH...?
NO?
OOOOH, I'M TINGLING!
AAAAND...
THERE WE GO!
COME TO ME, MY SPANDEX!

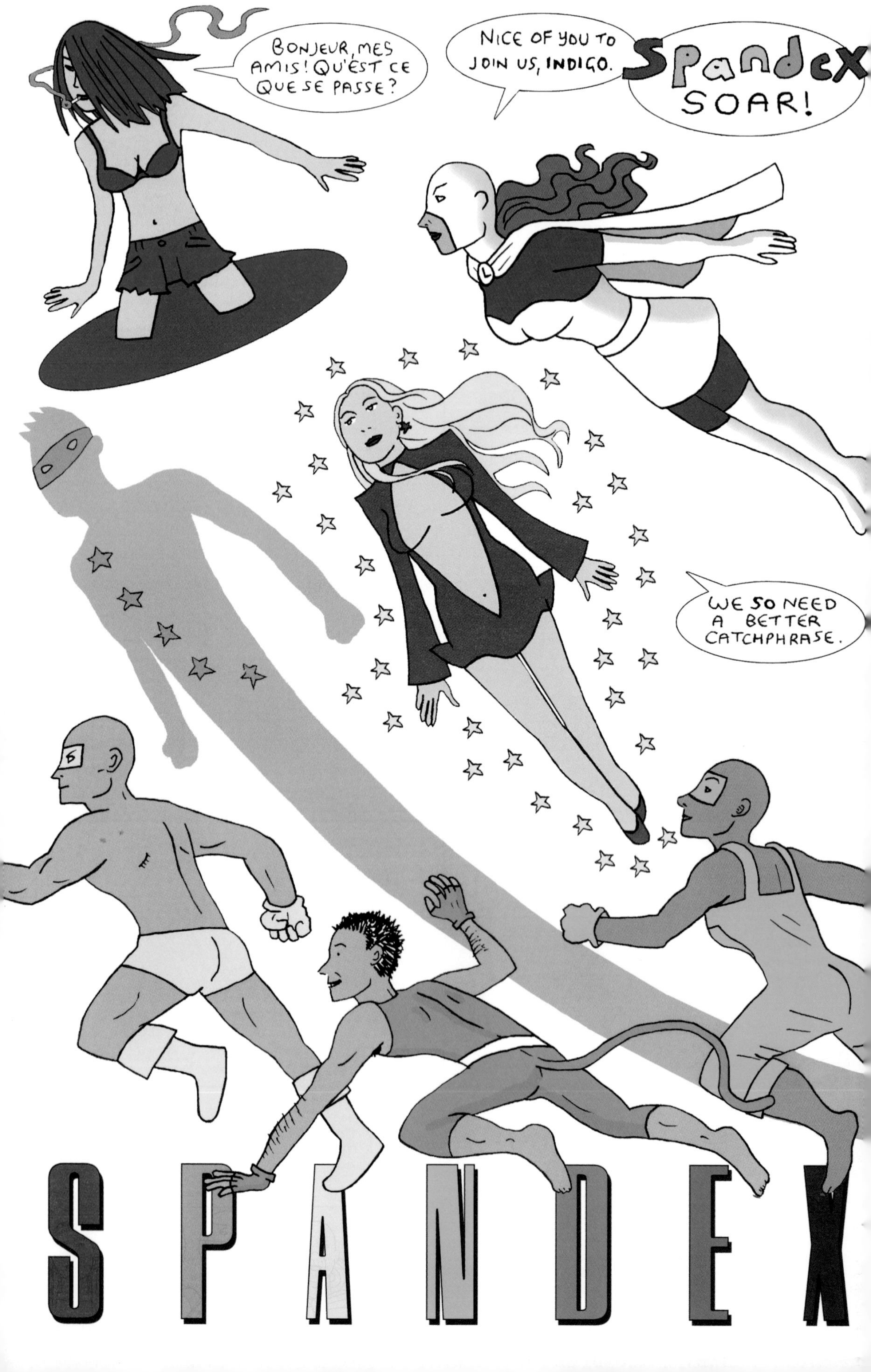
BONJEUR, MES AMIS! QU'EST CE QUE SE PASSE?
NICE OF YOU TO JOIN US, INDIGO.
Spandex SOAR!
WE SO NEED A BETTER CATCHPHRASE.
SPANDEX

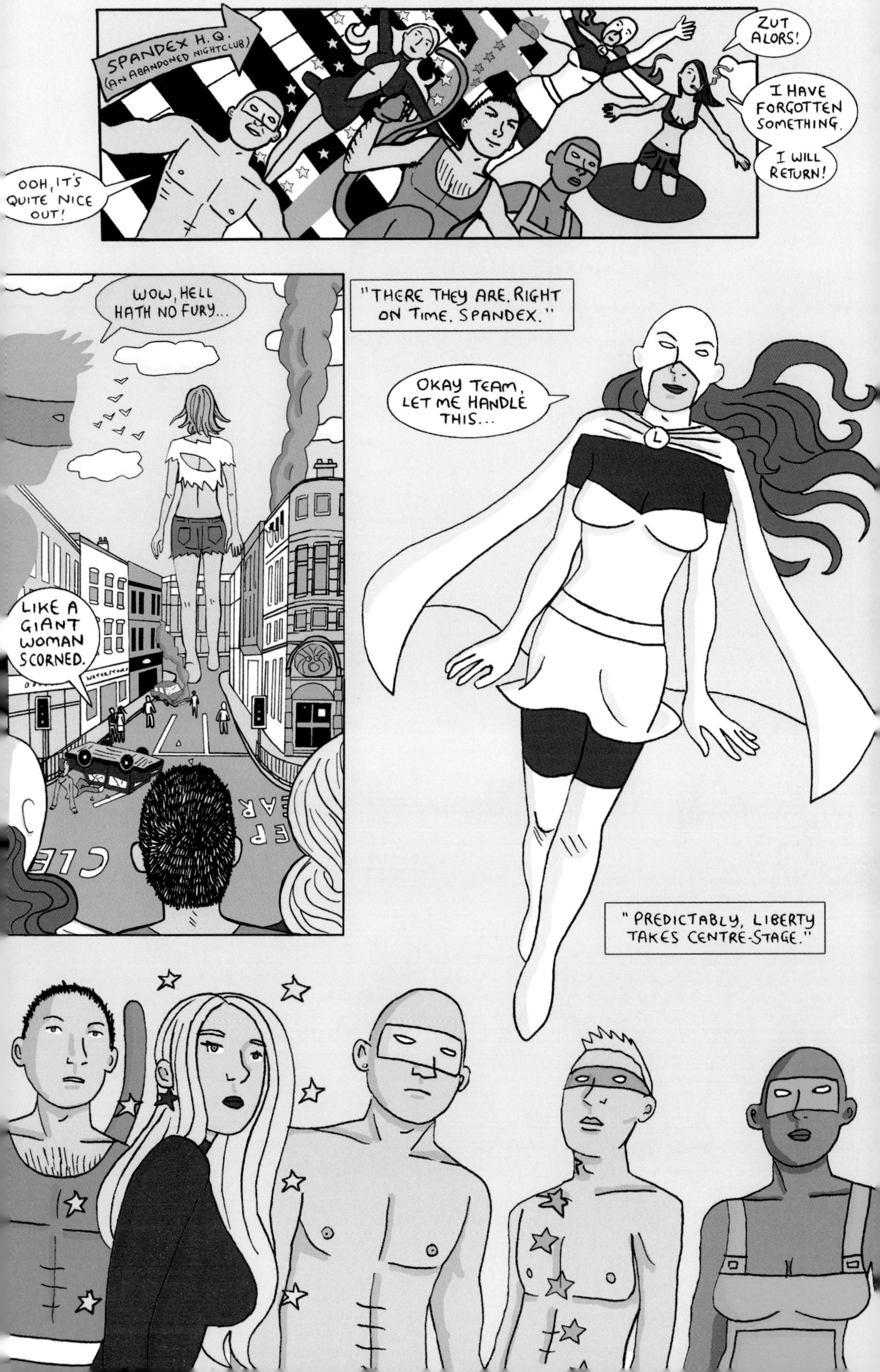
SPANDEX H.Q.
(AN ABANDONED NIGHTCLUB)
OOH, IT'S QUITE NICE OUT!
ZUT ALORS!
I HAVE FORGOTTEN SOMETHING.
I WILL RETURN!
WOW, HELL HATH NO FURY...
LIKE A GIANT WOMAN SCORNED.
"THERE THEY ARE. RIGHT ON TIME. SPANDEX."
OKAY TEAM, LET ME HANDLE THIS...
"PREDICTABLY, LIBERTY TAKES CENTRE-STAGE."

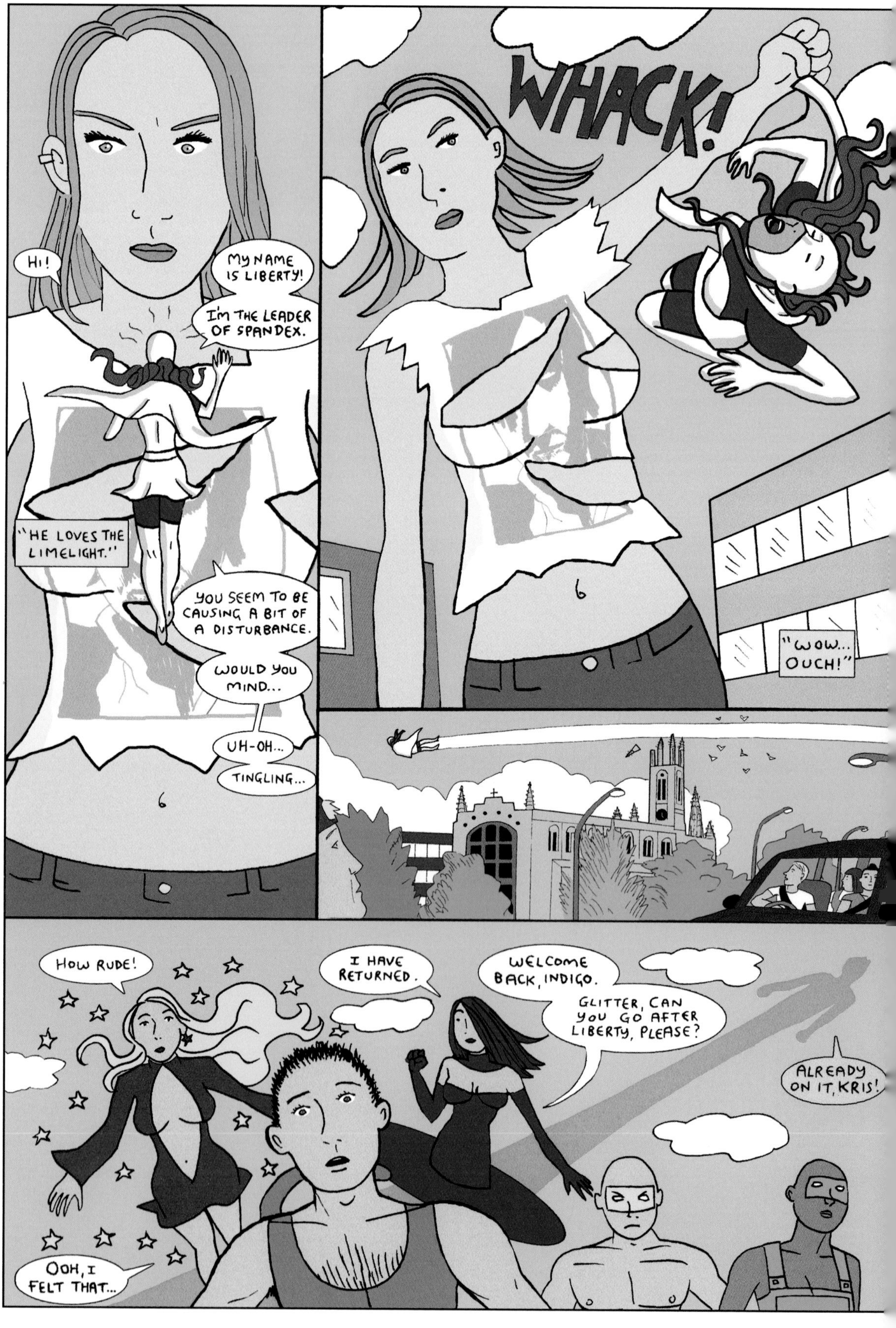
Hi!
My NAME IS LIBERTY!
I'M THE LEADER OF SPANDEX.
"HE LOVES THE LIMELIGHT."
YOU SEEM TO BE CAUSING A BIT OF A DISTURBANCE.
WOULD YOU MIND...
UH-OH...
TINGLING...
WHACK!
"WOW... OUCH!"
HOW RUDE!
I HAVE RETURNED.
WELCOME BACK, INDIGO.
GLITTER, CAN YOU GO AFTER LIBERTY, PLEASE?
ALREADY ON IT, KRIS!
OOH, I FELT THAT...

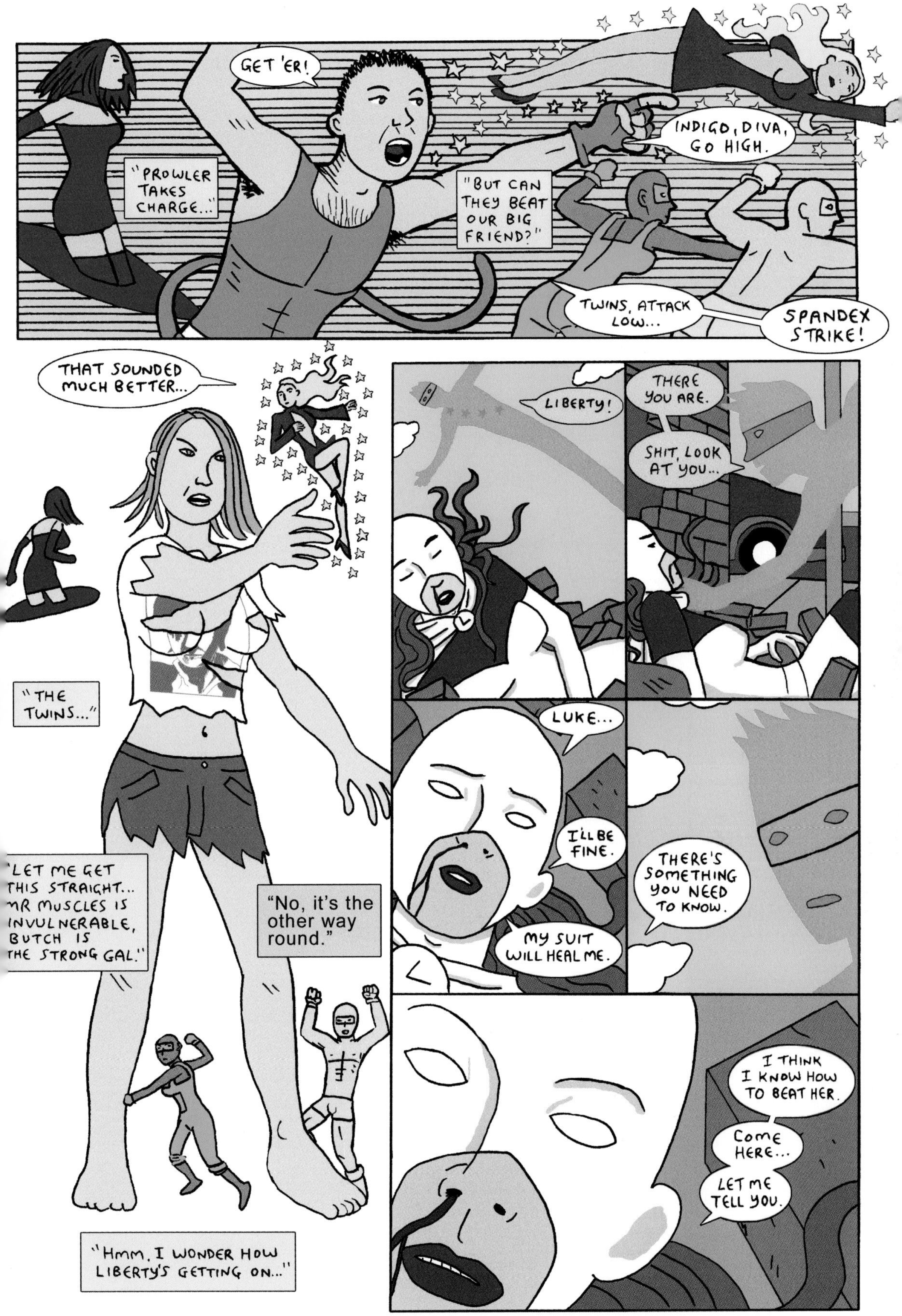
GET 'ER!
"PROWLER TAKES CHARGE..."
INDIGO, DIVA, GO HIGH.
"BUT CAN THEY BEAT OUR BIG FRIEND?"
TWINS, ATTACK LOW...
SPANDEX STRIKE!
THAT SOUNDED MUCH BETTER...
"THE TWINS..."
"LET ME GET THIS STRAIGHT... MR MUSCLES IS INVULNERABLE, BUTCH IS THE STRONG GAL."
"No, it's the other way round."
"Hmm, I WONDER HOW LIBERTY'S GETTING ON..."
LIBERTY!
THERE YOU ARE.
SHIT, LOOK AT YOU...
LUKE...
I'LL BE FINE.
MY SUIT WILL HEAL ME.
THERE'S SOMETHING YOU NEED TO KNOW.
I THINK I KNOW HOW TO BEAT HER.
COME HERE...
LET ME TELL YOU.

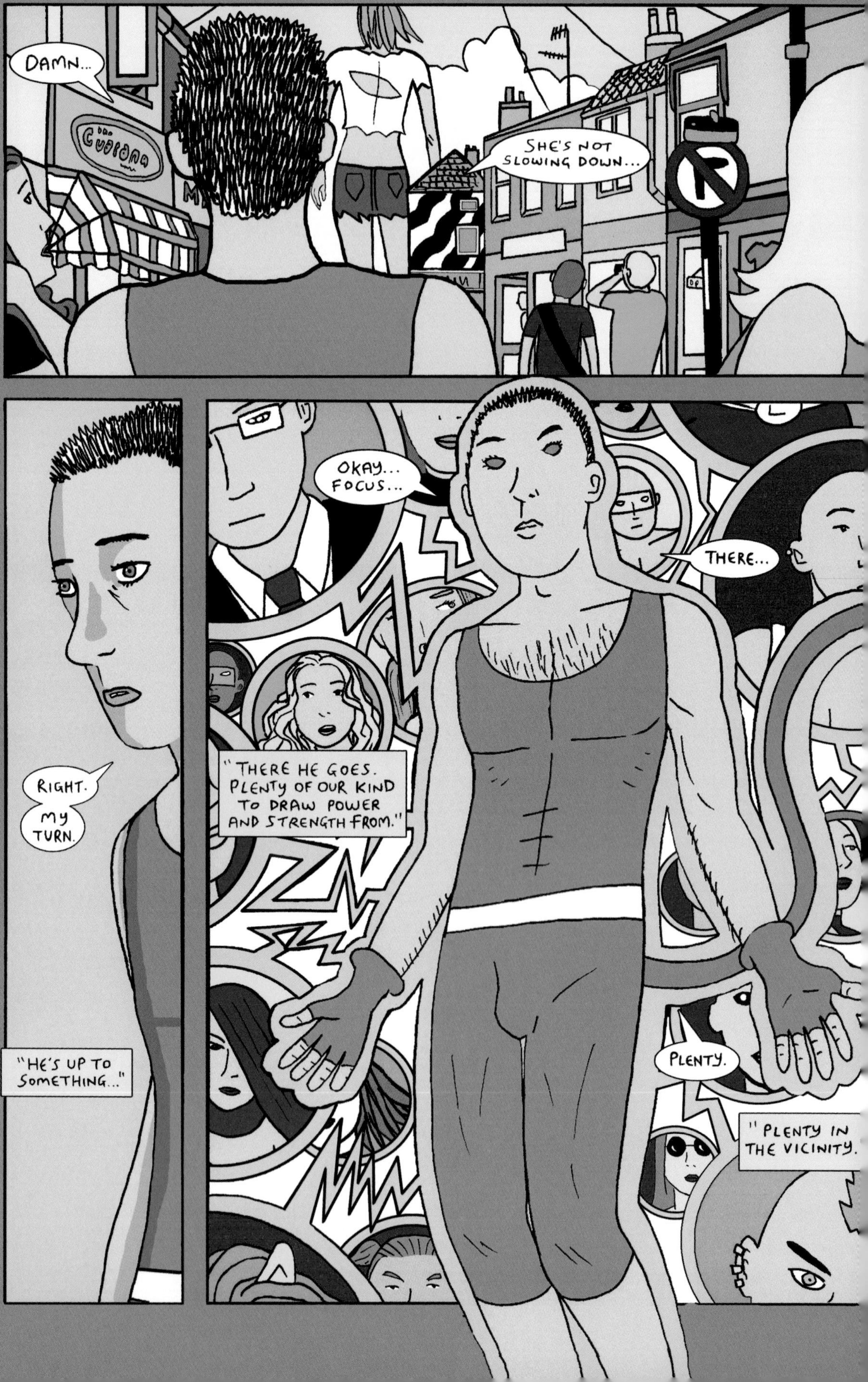
DAMN...
SHE'S NOT SLOWING DOWN...
RIGHT.
MY TURN.
"HE'S UP TO SOMETHING..."
OKAY... FOCUS...
THERE...
"THERE HE GOES. PLENTY OF OUR KIND TO DRAW POWER AND STRENGTH FROM."
PLENTY.
"PLENTY IN THE VICINITY.

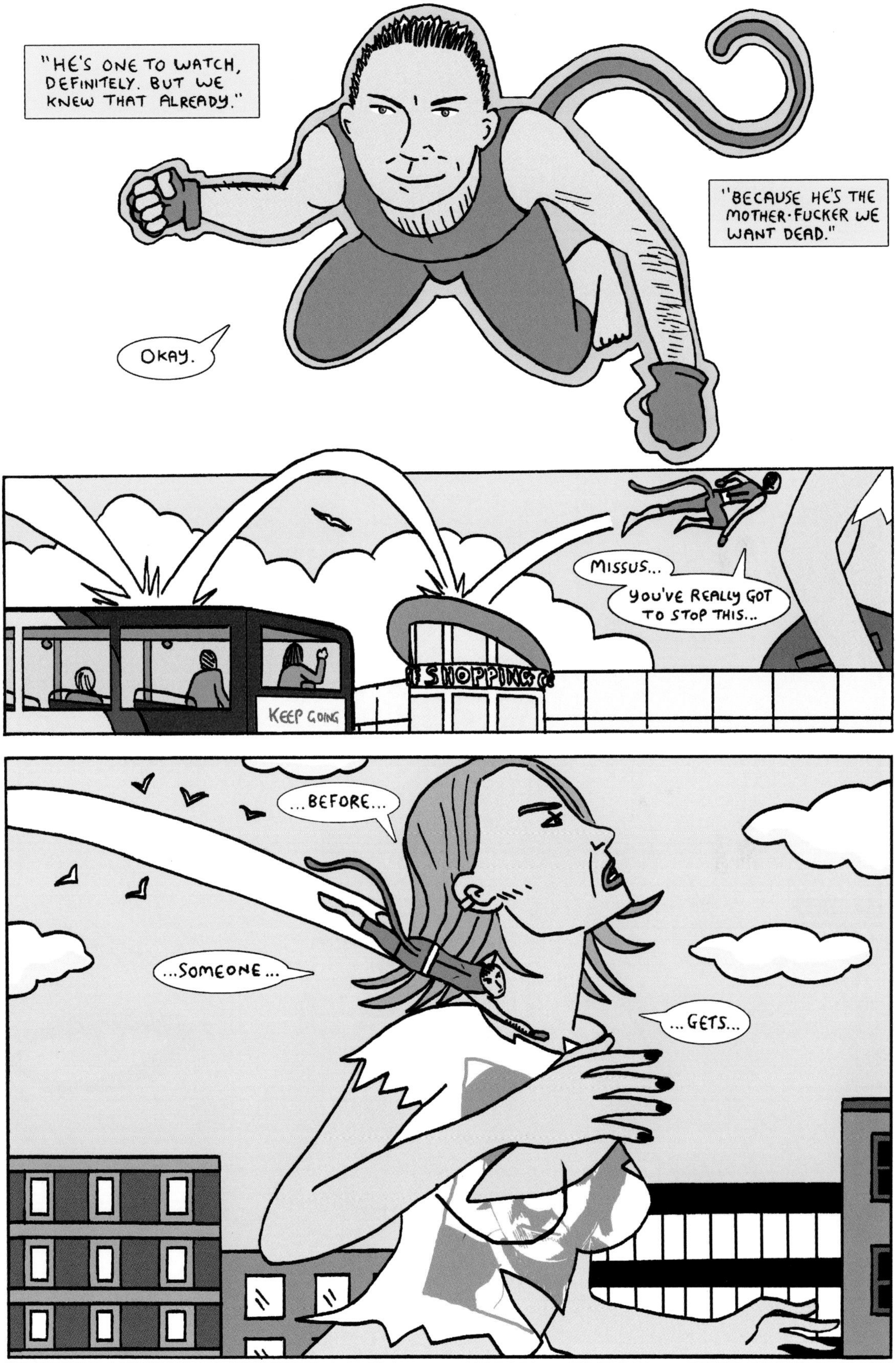
"HE'S ONE TO WATCH, DEFINITELY. BUT WE KNEW THAT ALREADY."
"BECAUSE HE'S THE MOTHER-FUCKER WE WANT DEAD."
OKAY.
MISSUS...
YOU'VE REALLY GOT TO STOP THIS...
KEEP GOING
SHOPPING
...BEFORE...
...SOMEONE...
...GETS...

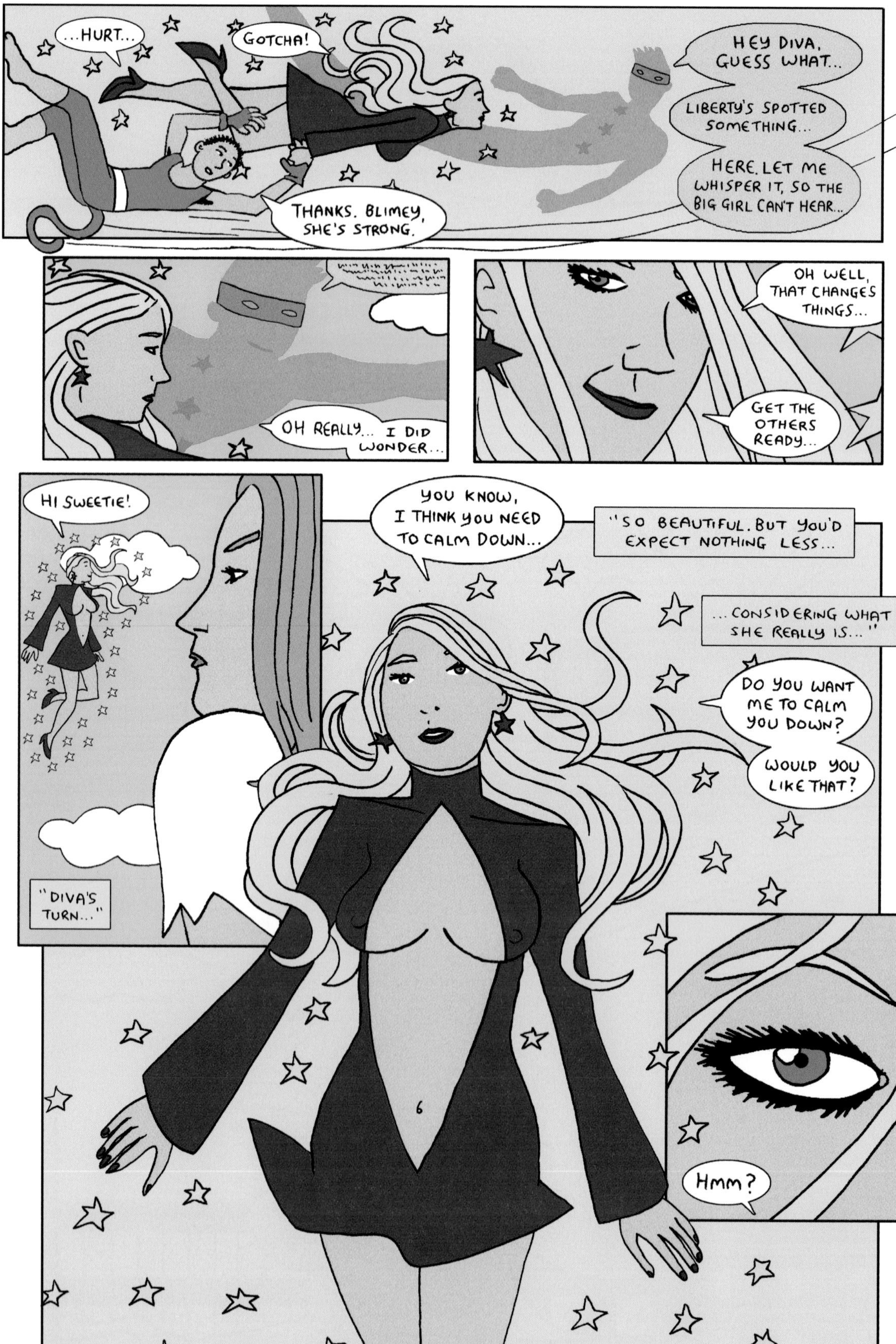
...HURT...
GOTCHA!
THANKS. BLIMEY, SHE'S STRONG.
HEY DIVA, GUESS WHAT...
LIBERTY'S SPOTTED SOMETHING...
HERE. LET ME WHISPER IT, SO THE BIG GIRL CAN'T HEAR...
OH REALLY... I DID WONDER...
OH WELL, THAT CHANGES THINGS...
GET THE OTHERS READY...
HI SWEETIE!
"DIVA'S TURN..."
YOU KNOW, I THINK YOU NEED TO CALM DOWN...
"SO BEAUTIFUL. BUT YOU'D EXPECT NOTHING LESS...
...CONSIDERING WHAT SHE REALLY IS..."
DO YOU WANT ME TO CALM YOU DOWN?
WOULD YOU LIKE THAT?
Hmm?

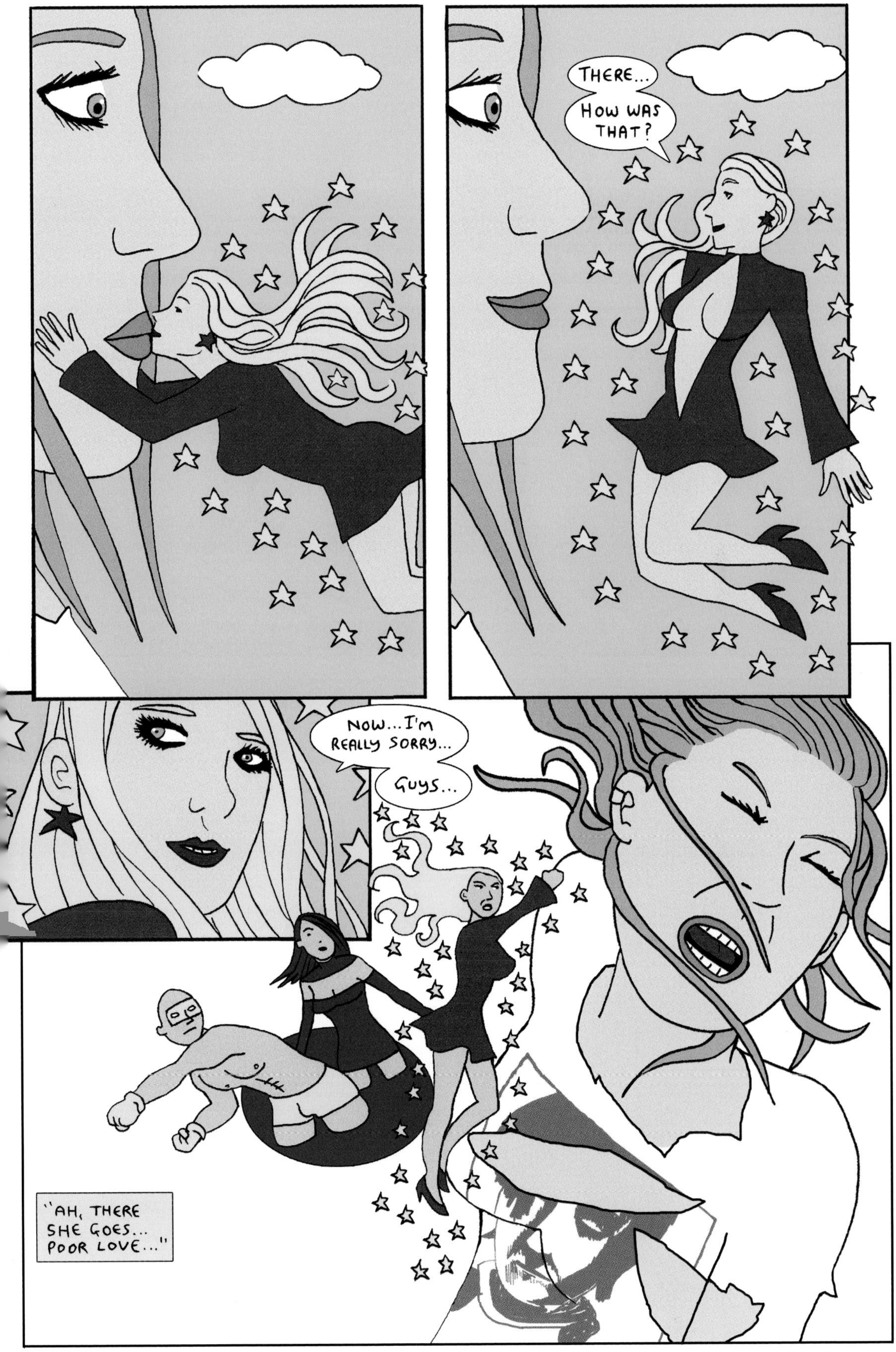
THERE...
HOW WAS THAT?
NOW... I'M REALLY SORRY...
GUYS...
"AH, THERE SHE GOES... POOR LOVE..."

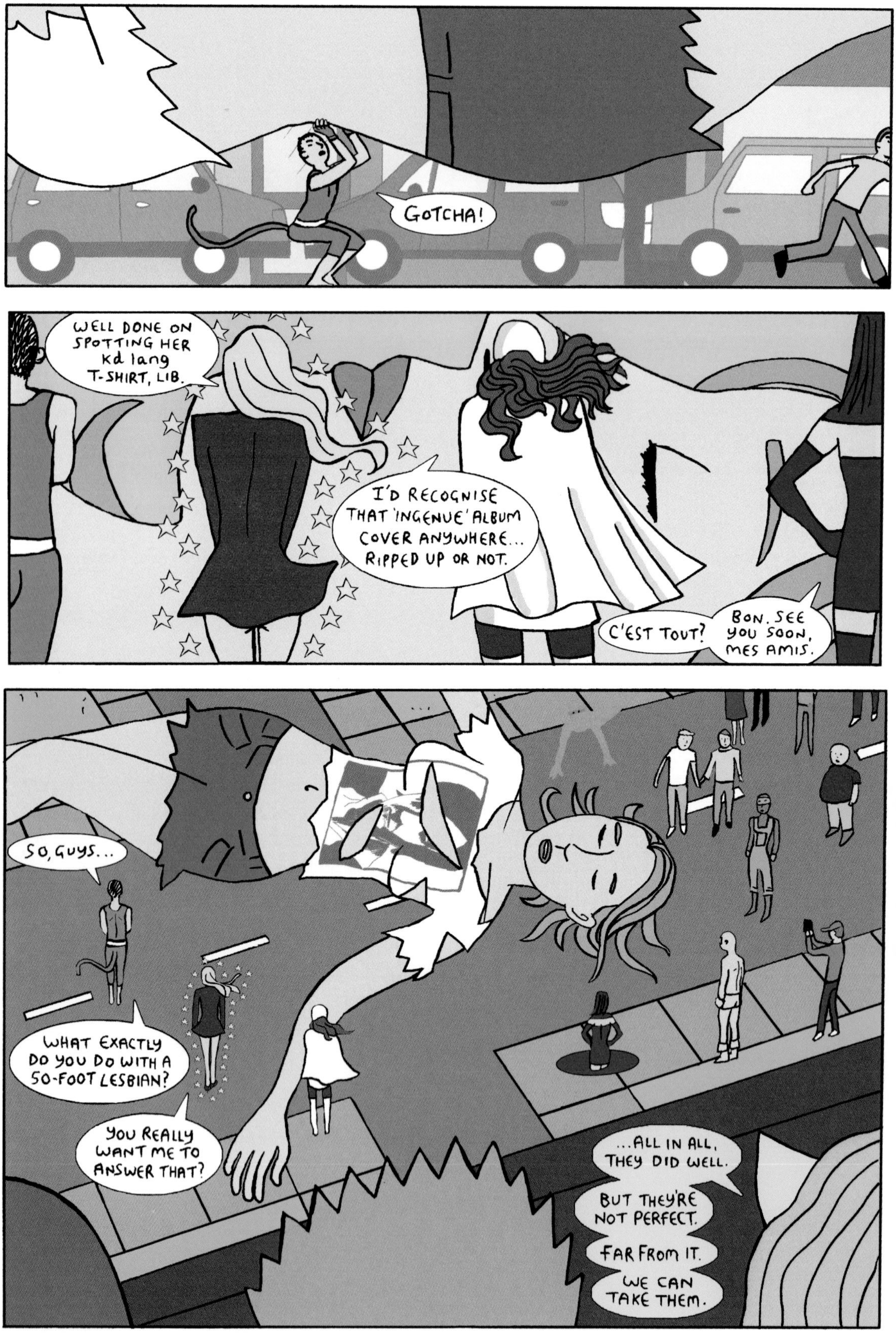
GOTCHA!
WELL DONE ON SPOTTING HER kd lang T-SHIRT, LIB.
I'D RECOGNISE THAT 'INGENUE' ALBUM COVER ANYWHERE... RIPPED UP OR NOT.
C'EST TOUT?
BON. SEE YOU SOON, MES AMIS.
SO, GUYS...
WHAT EXACTLY DO YOU DO WITH A 50-FOOT LESBIAN?
YOU REALLY WANT ME TO ANSWER THAT?
...ALL IN ALL, THEY DID WELL.
BUT THEY'RE NOT PERFECT.
FAR FROM IT.
WE CAN TAKE THEM.

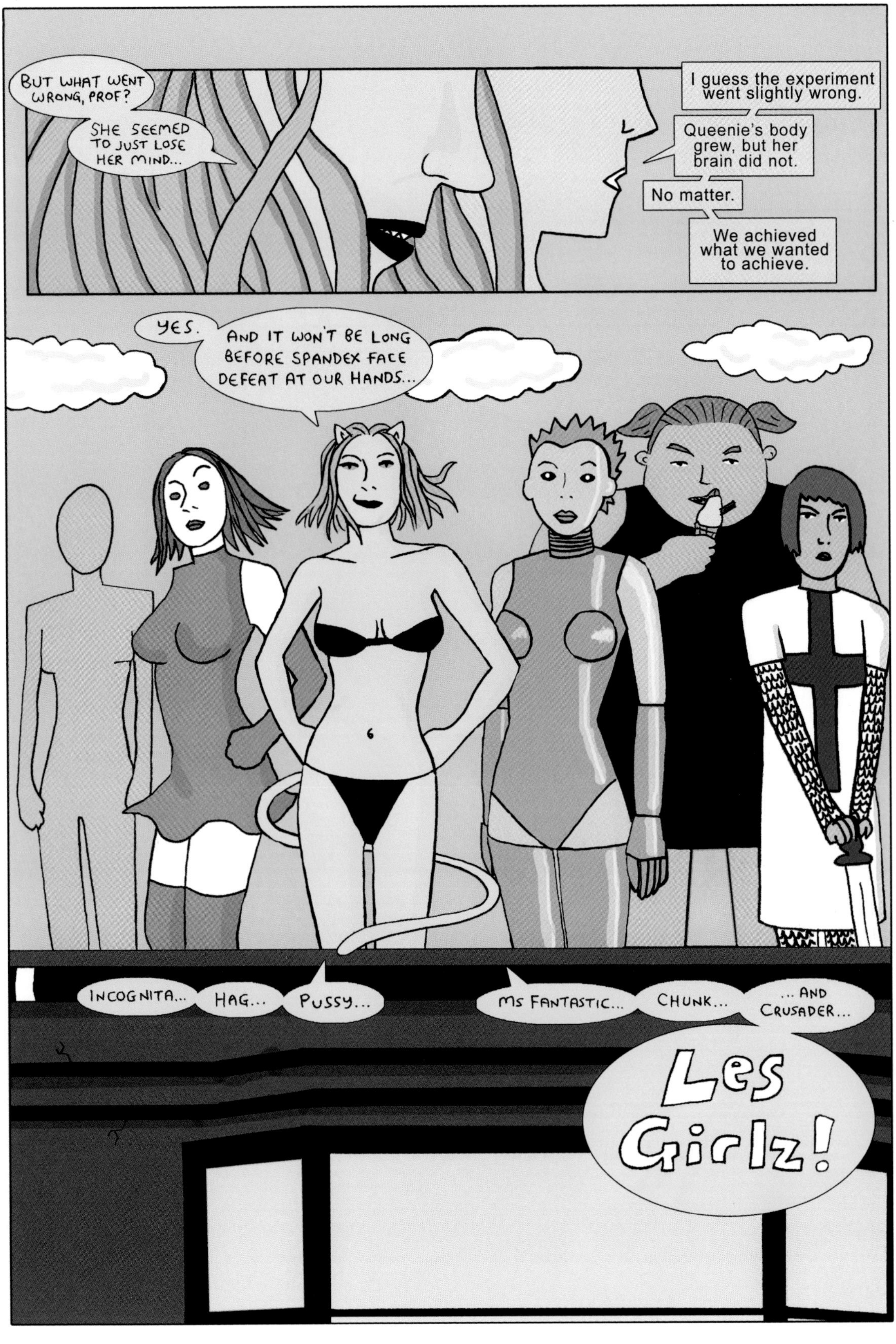
BUT WHAT WENT WRONG, PROF?
SHE SEEMED TO JUST LOSE HER MIND...
I guess the experiment went slightly wrong.
Queenie's body grew, but her brain did not.
No matter.
We achieved what we wanted to achieve.
YES.
AND IT WON'T BE LONG BEFORE SPANDEX FACE DEFEAT AT OUR HANDS...
INCOGNITA...
HAG...
PUSSY...
MS FANTASTIC...
CHUNK...
... AND CRUSADER...
Les Girlz!

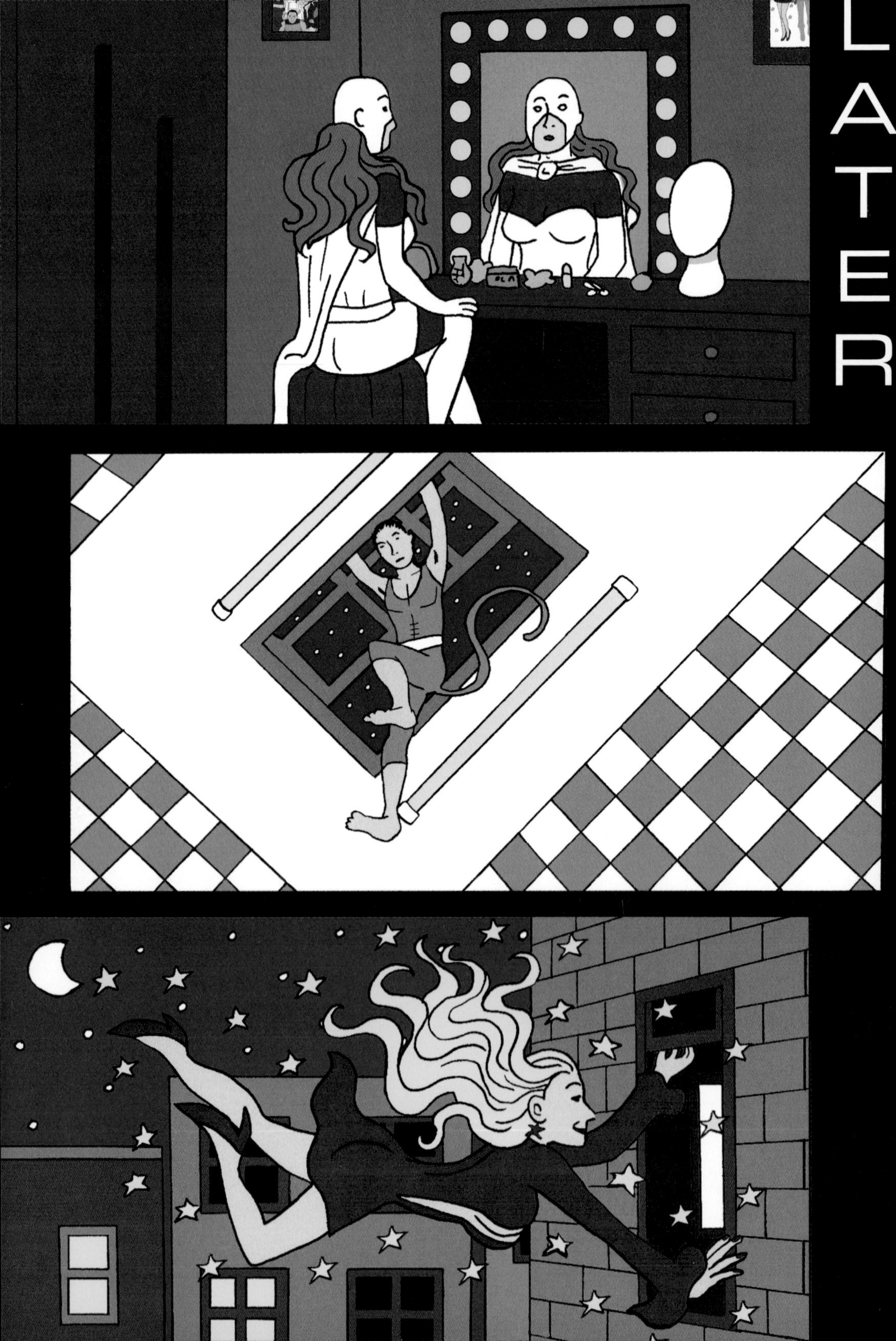
LATER

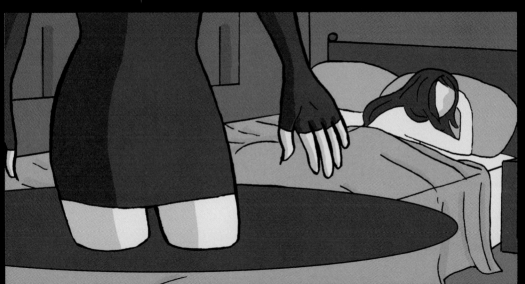

Mmmmm...

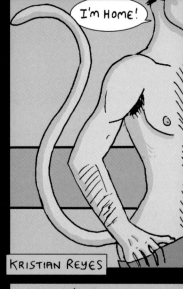

KRISTIAN REYES

I'M HOME!

ALLO...

HI.

JOANIE JONES

AH...

ISABELLE SHAW

INDIGO LORMAIN

DID YOU MISS ME...?

MM-HMM.

EXCITING DAY, TODAY...

JASON FORD

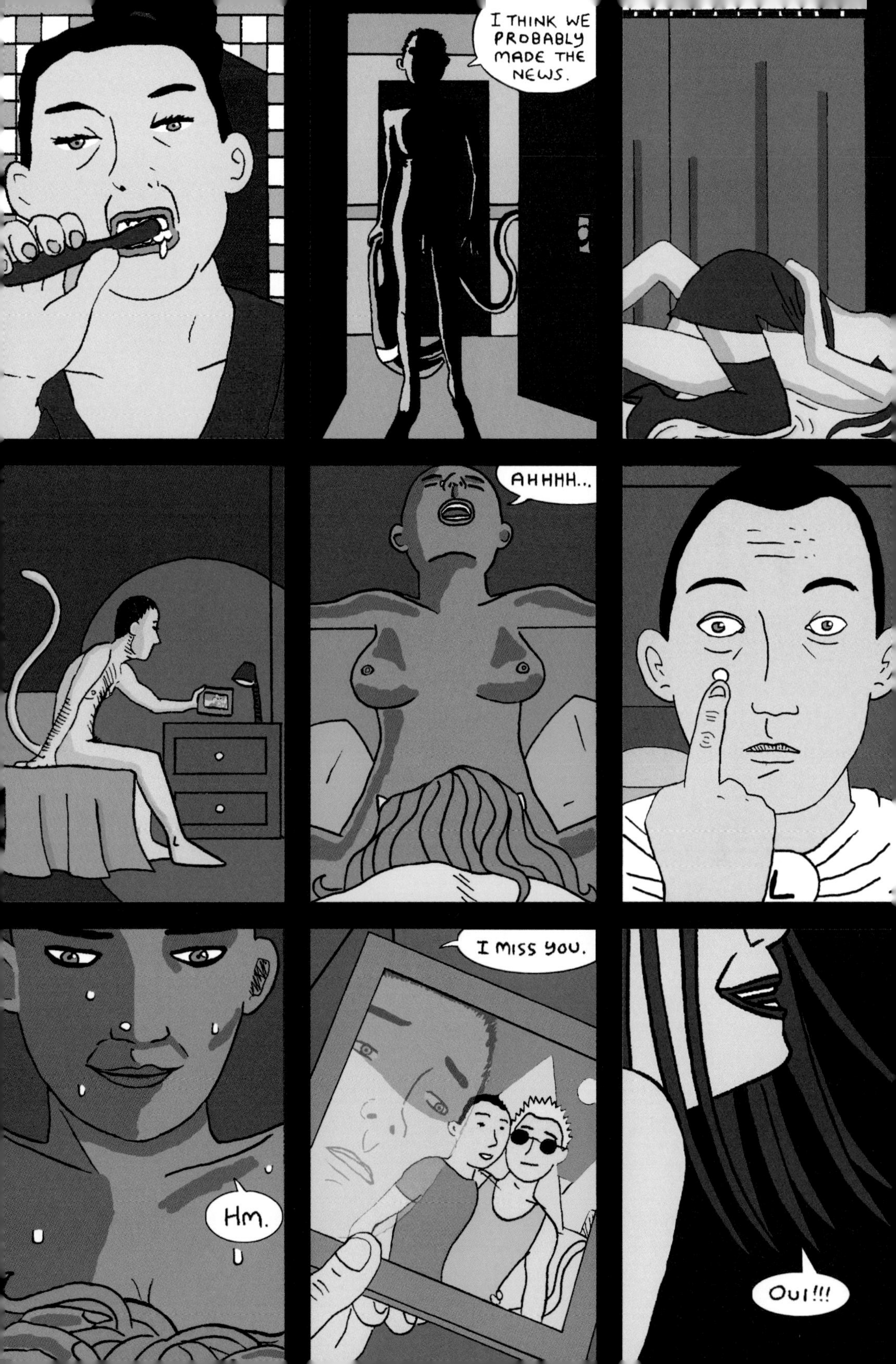
I THINK WE PROBABLY MADE THE NEWS.
AHHHH...
Hm.
I MISS YOU.
OUI!!!

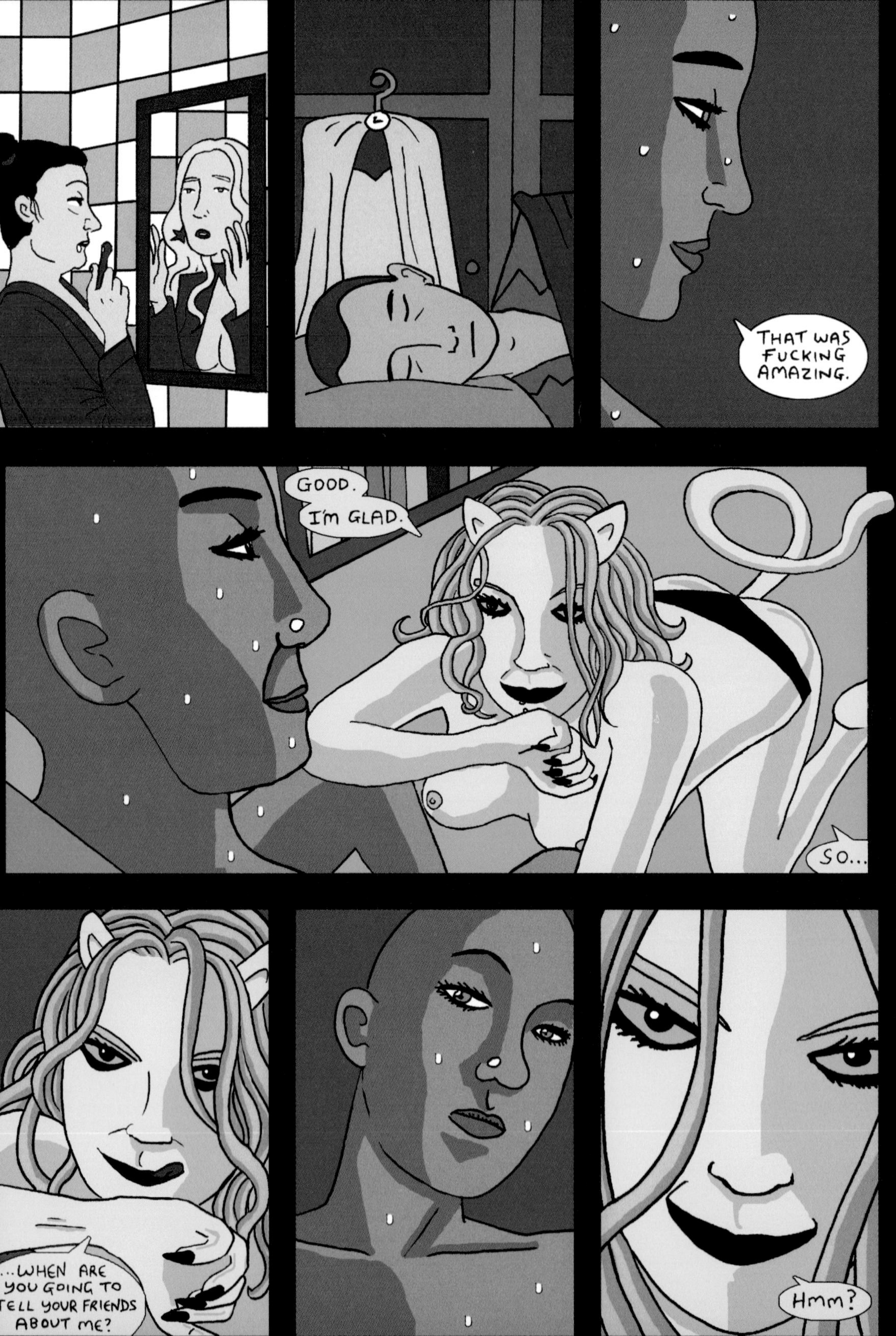
THAT WAS FUCKING AMAZING.
GOOD. I'M GLAD.
SO...
...WHEN ARE YOU GOING TO TELL YOUR FRIENDS ABOUT ME?
Hmm?

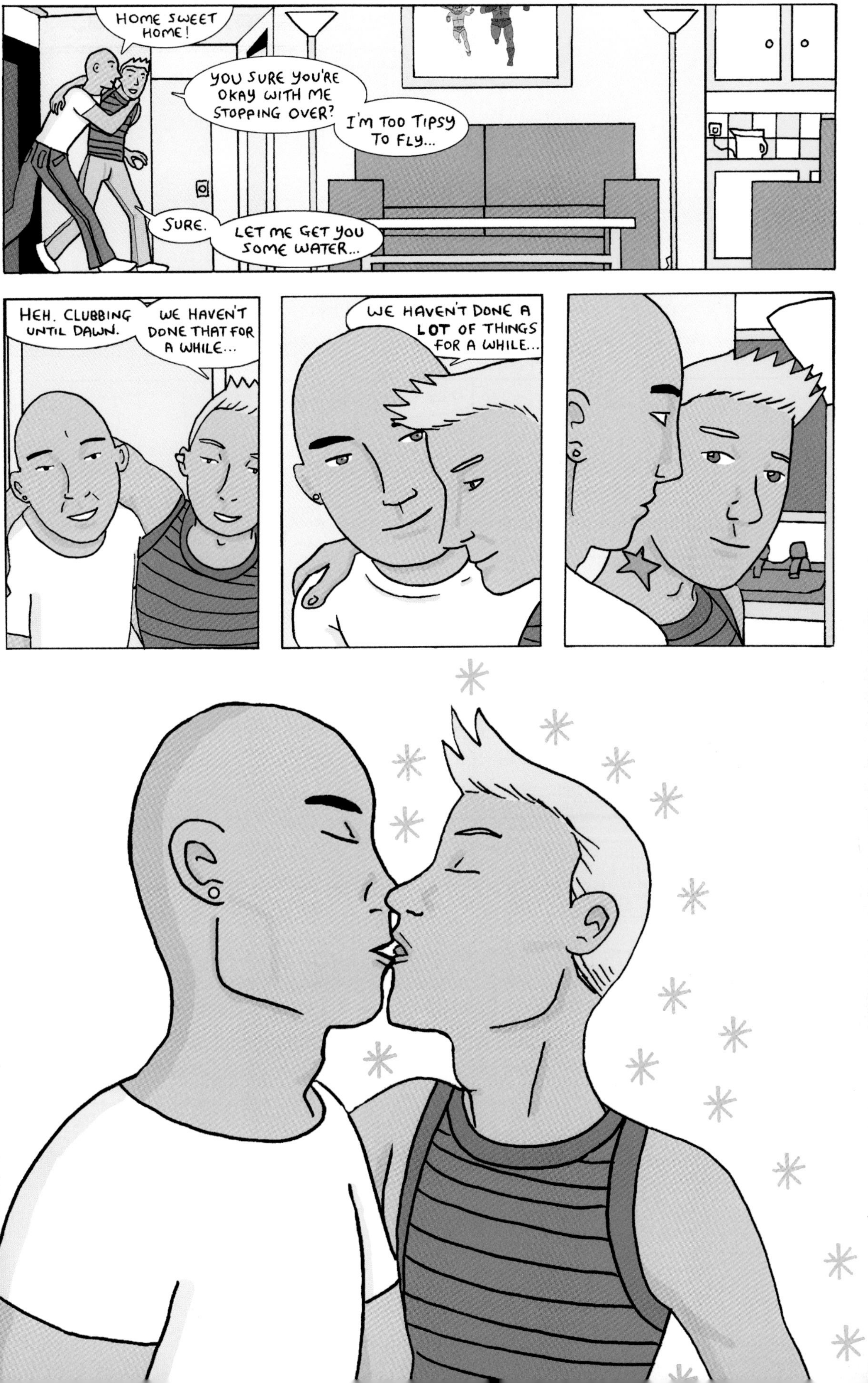
HOME SWEET HOME!
YOU SURE YOU'RE OKAY WITH ME STOPPING OVER?
I'M TOO TIPSY TO FLY...
SURE.
LET ME GET YOU SOME WATER...
HEH. CLUBBING UNTIL DAWN.
WE HAVEN'T DONE THAT FOR A WHILE...
WE HAVEN'T DONE A LOT OF THINGS FOR A WHILE...

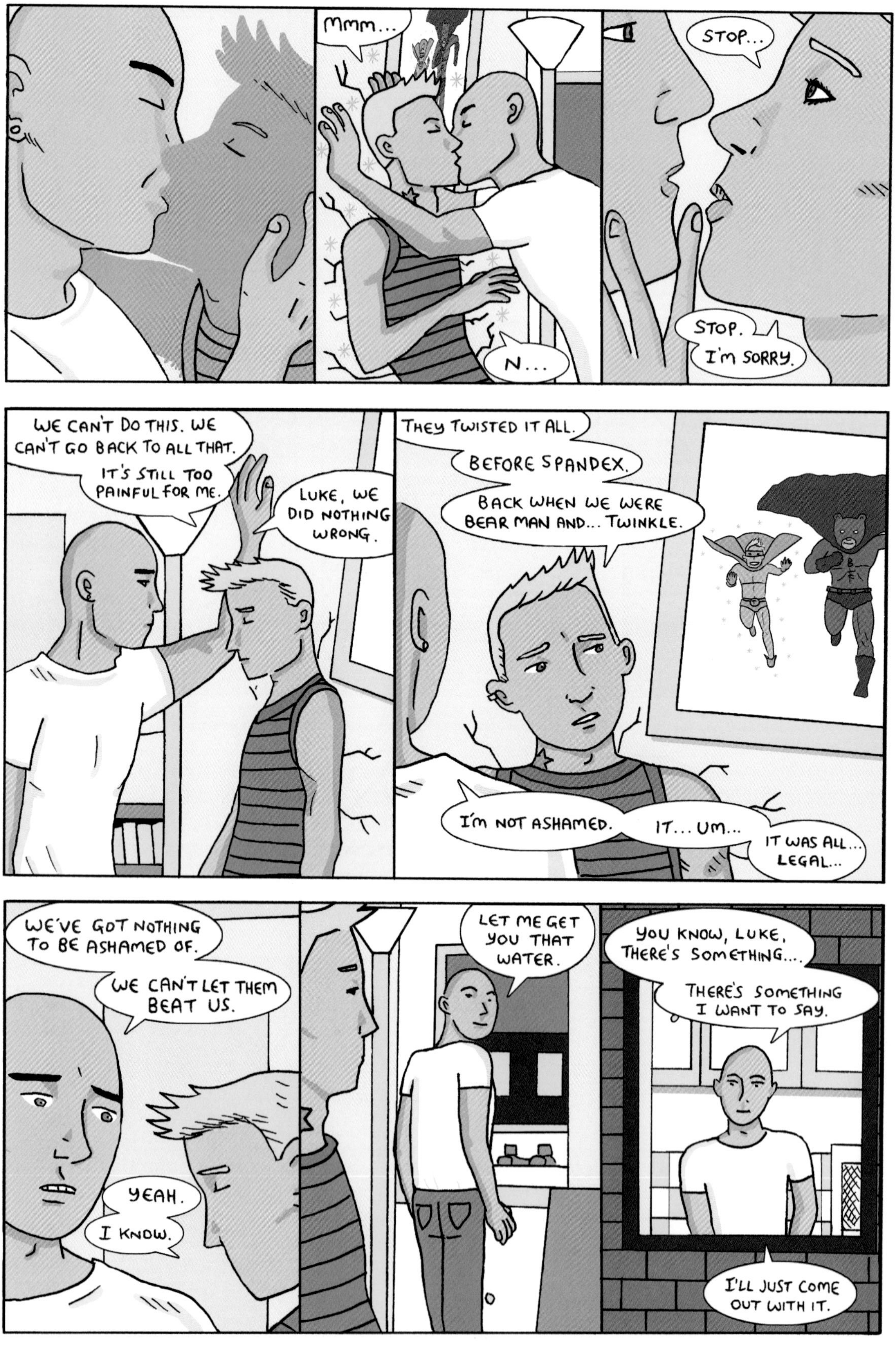
MMM...
N...
STOP...
STOP.
I'M SORRY.
WE CAN'T DO THIS. WE CAN'T GO BACK TO ALL THAT.
IT'S STILL TOO PAINFUL FOR ME.
LUKE, WE DID NOTHING WRONG.
THEY TWISTED IT ALL.
BEFORE SPANDEX.
BACK WHEN WE WERE BEAR MAN AND... TWINKLE.
I'M NOT ASHAMED.
IT... UM...
IT WAS ALL... LEGAL...
WE'VE GOT NOTHING TO BE ASHAMED OF.
WE CAN'T LET THEM BEAT US.
YEAH.
I KNOW.
LET ME GET YOU THAT WATER.
YOU KNOW, LUKE, THERE'S SOMETHING....
THERE'S SOMETHING I WANT TO SAY.
I'LL JUST COME OUT WITH IT.

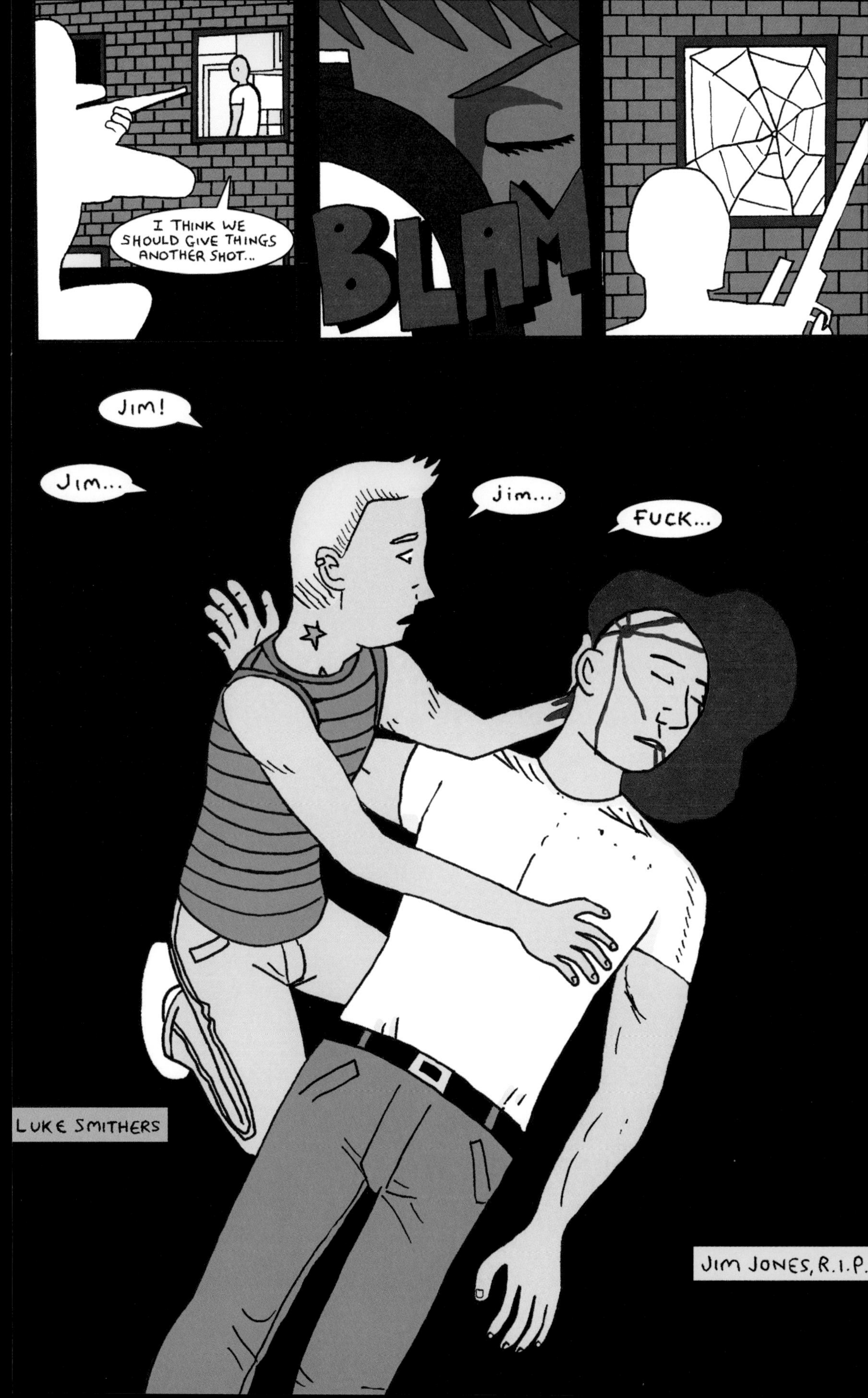
I THINK WE SHOULD GIVE THINGS ANOTHER SHOT...
BLAM
JIM!
JIM...
jim...
FUCK...
LUKE SMITHERS
JIM JONES, R.I.P.

CHAPTER TWO

"PINK NINJAS"

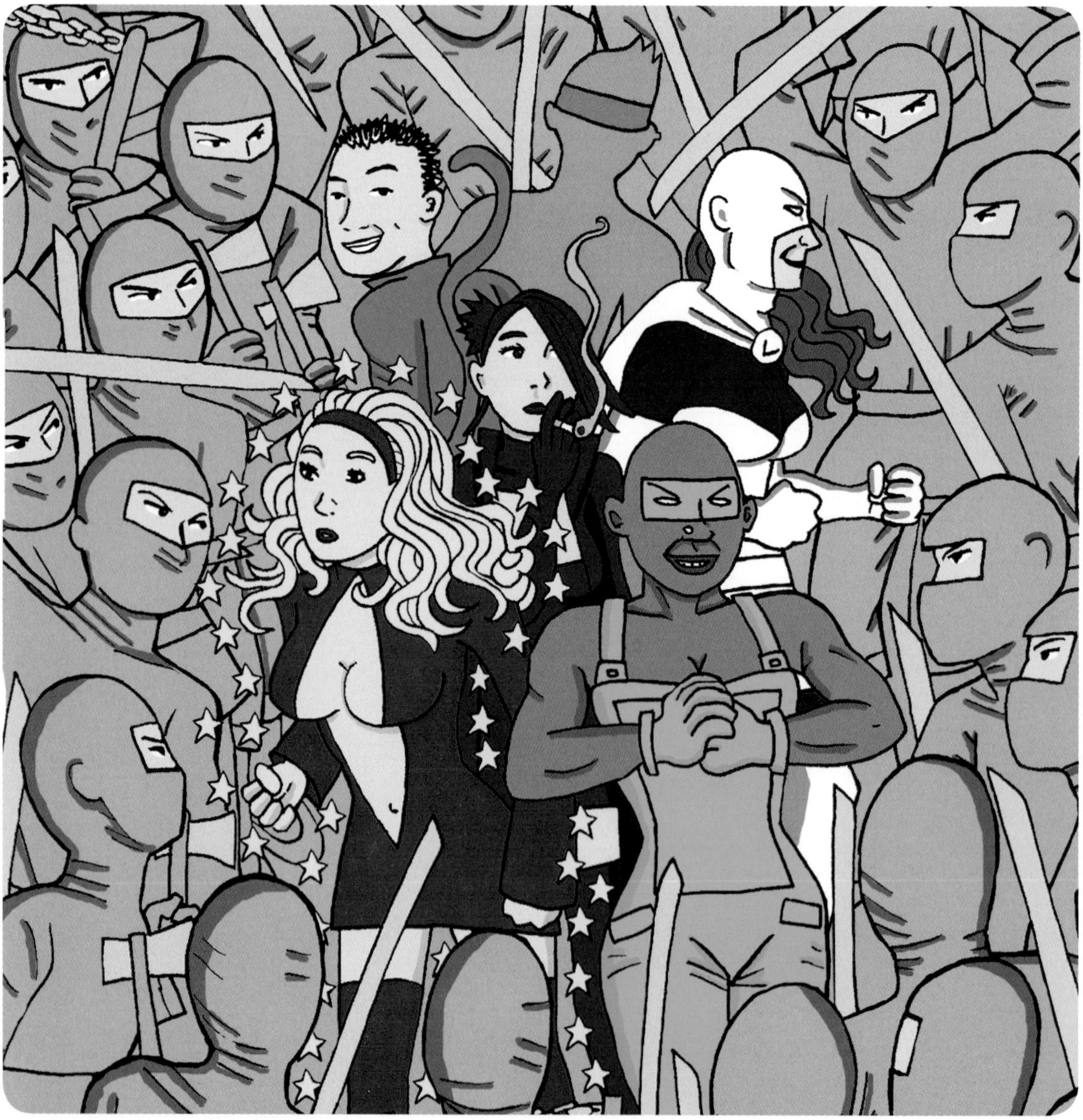

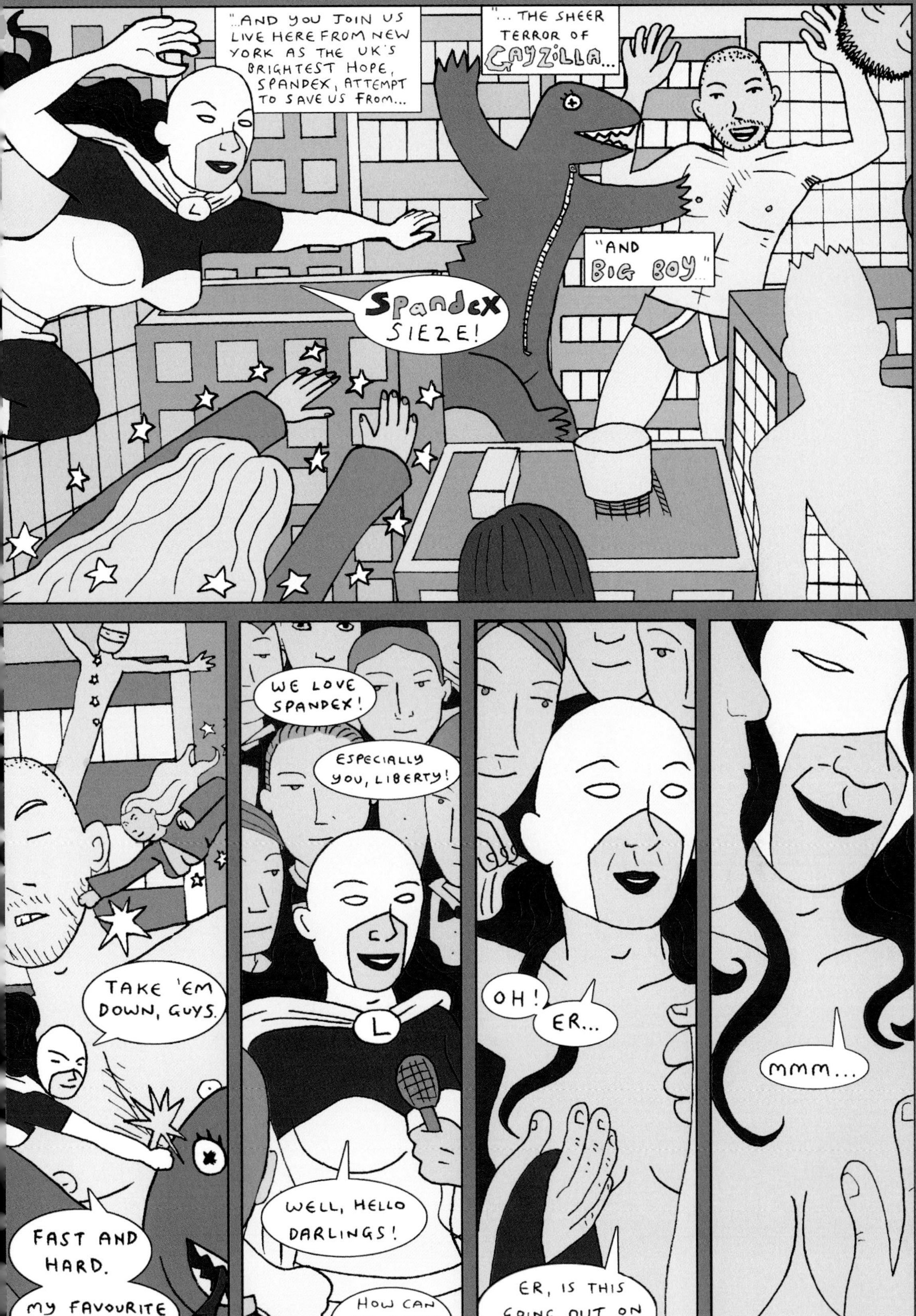
"...AND YOU JOIN US LIVE HERE FROM NEW YORK AS THE UK'S BRIGHTEST HOPE, SPANDEX, ATTEMPT TO SAVE US FROM...
"... THE SHEER TERROR OF GAYZILLA...
"AND BIG BOY"...
SPANDEX SIEZE!
TAKE 'EM DOWN, GUYS.
FAST AND HARD.
MY FAVOURITE STYLE!
WE LOVE SPANDEX!
ESPECIALLY YOU, LIBERTY!
WELL, HELLO DARLINGS!
HOW CAN WE REPAY YOU?!
OH!
ER...
ER, IS THIS GOING OUT ON LIVE TV...?
MMM...

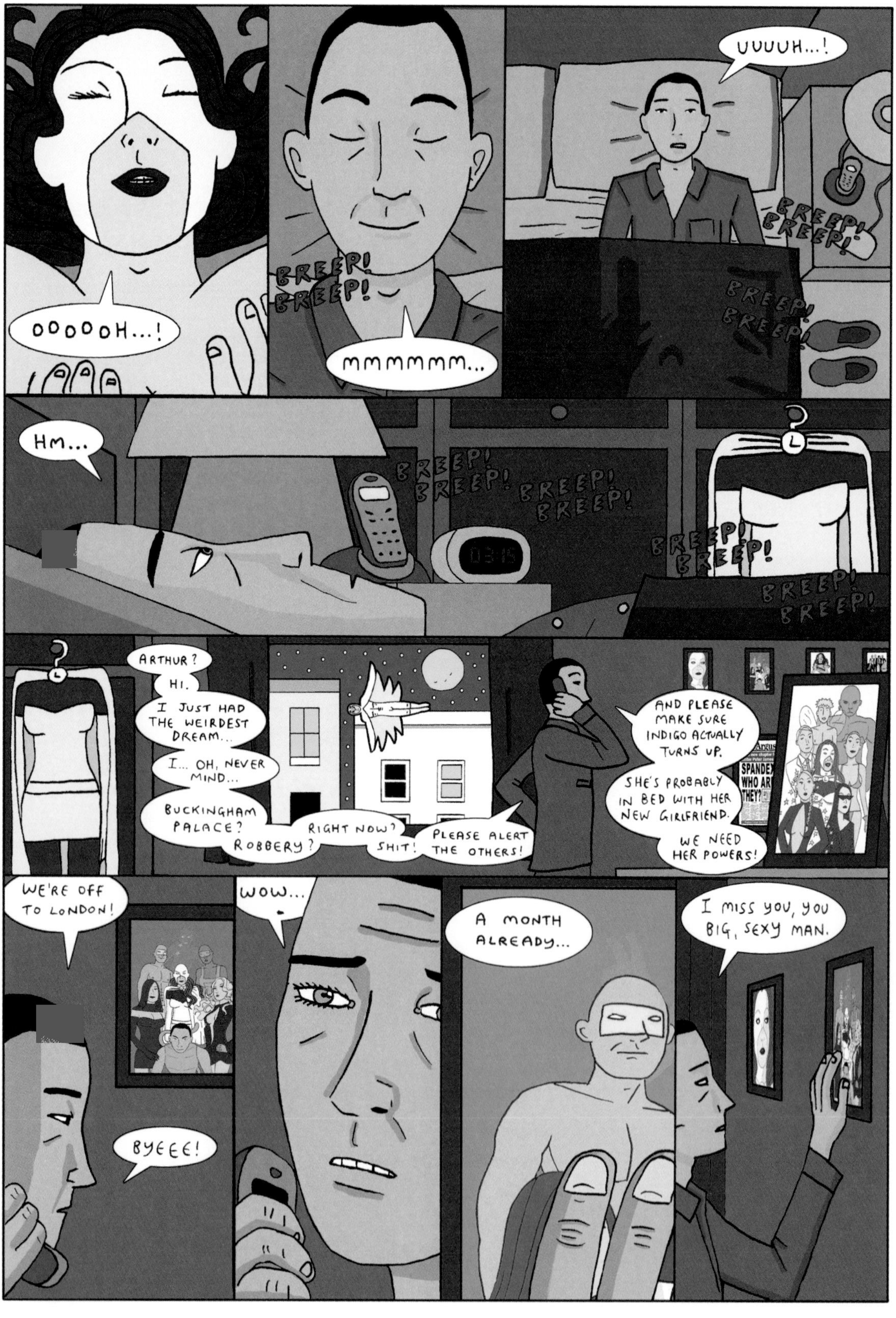
OOOOOH...!
BREEP! BREEP!
MMMMMM...
UUUUH...!
BREEP! BREEP!
BREEP! BREEP!
HM...
BREEP! BREEP!
BREEP! BREEP!
BREEP! BREEP!
BREEP! BREEP!
03:15
ARTHUR?
HI.
I JUST HAD THE WEIRDEST DREAM...
I... OH, NEVER MIND...
BUCKINGHAM PALACE?
ROBBERY?
RIGHT NOW?
SHIT!
PLEASE ALERT THE OTHERS!
AND PLEASE MAKE SURE INDIGO ACTUALLY TURNS UP.
SHE'S PROBABLY IN BED WITH HER NEW GIRLFRIEND.
WE NEED HER POWERS!
Argus
SPANDEX
WE'RE OFF TO LONDON!
BYEEE!
WOW...
A MONTH ALREADY...
I MISS YOU, YOU BIG, SEXY MAN.

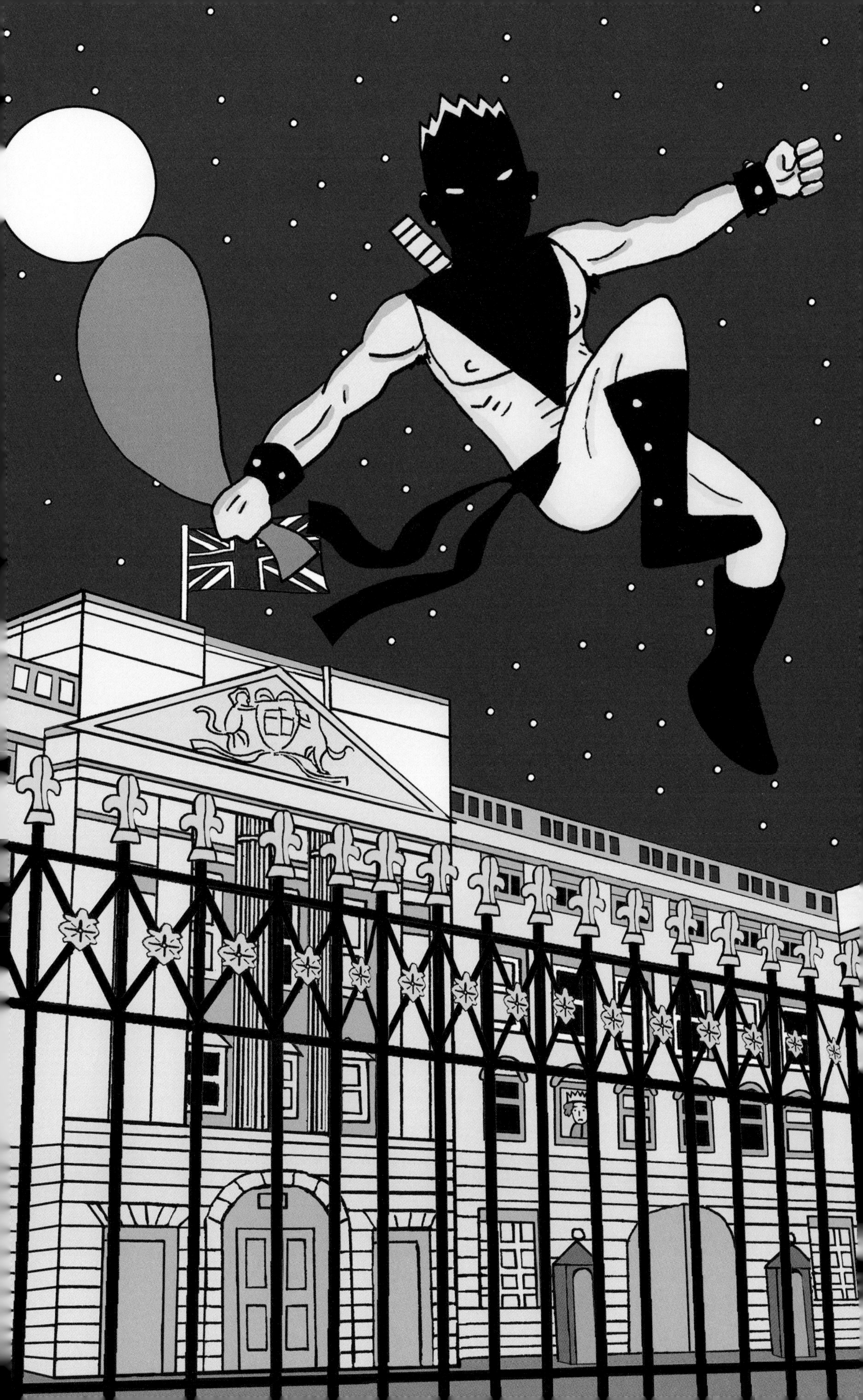

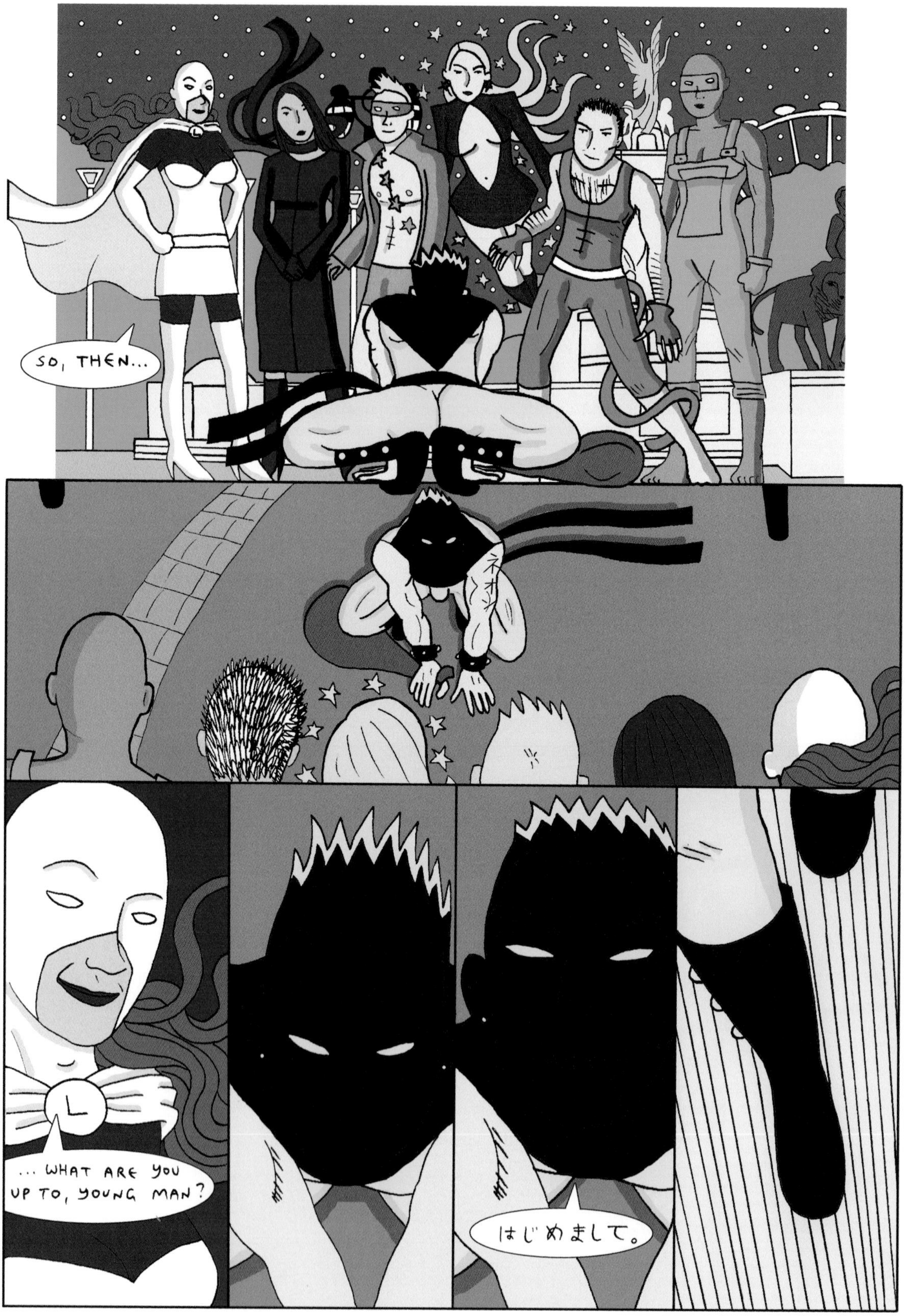
SO, THEN...
... WHAT ARE YOU UP TO, YOUNG MAN?
はじめまして。

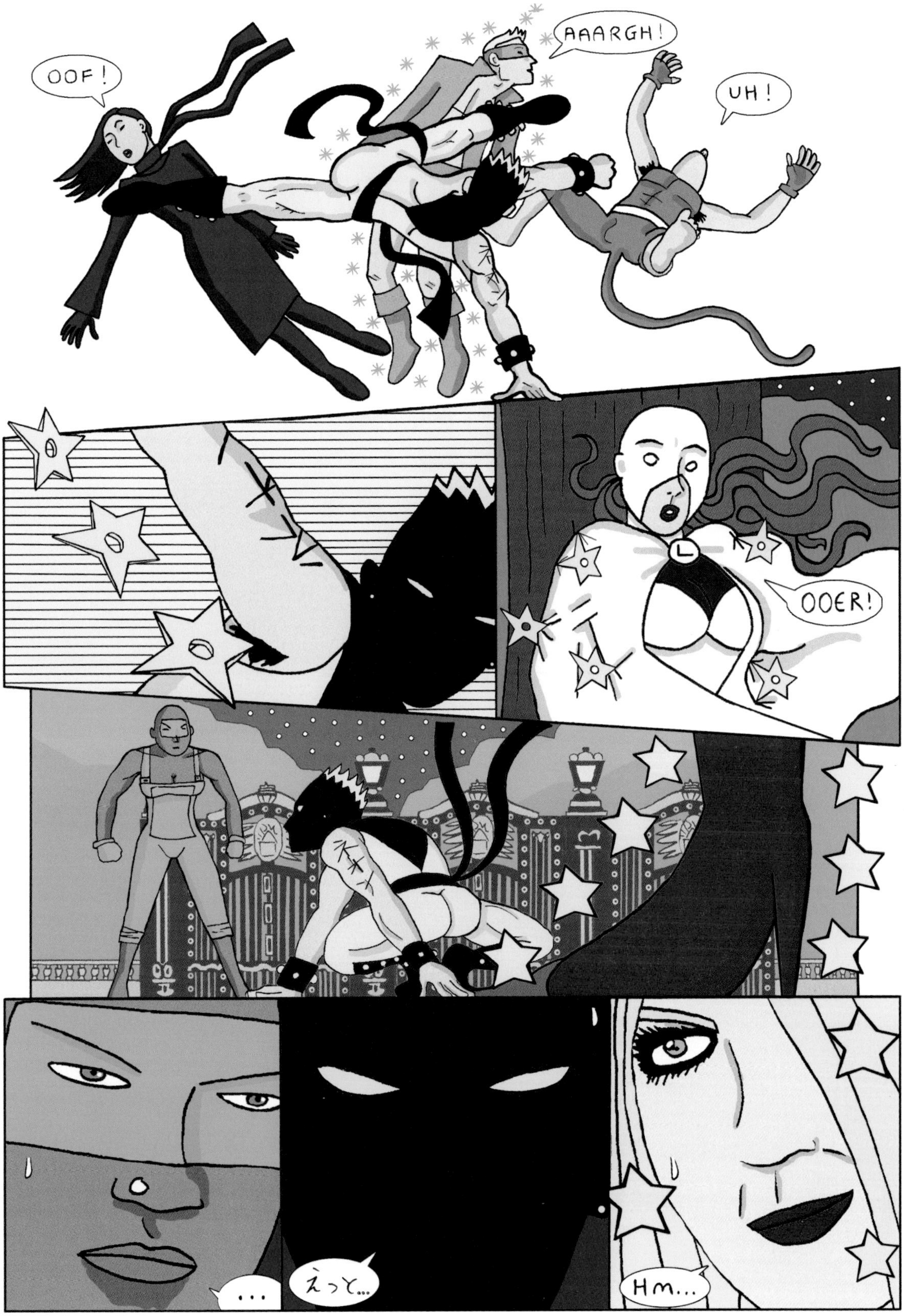
OOF!
AAARGH!
UH!
OOER!
...
えっと...
Hm...

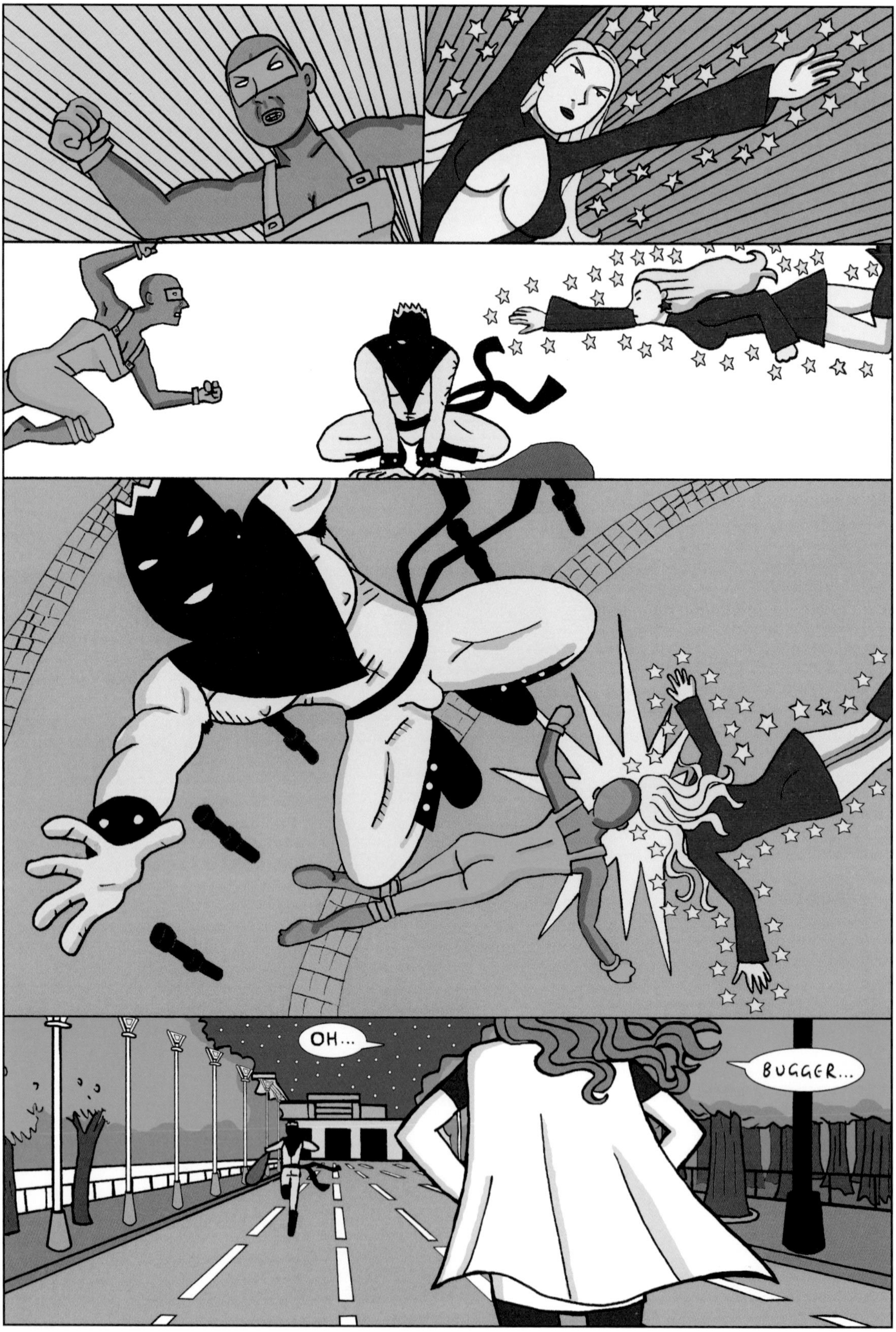
OH...
BUGGER...

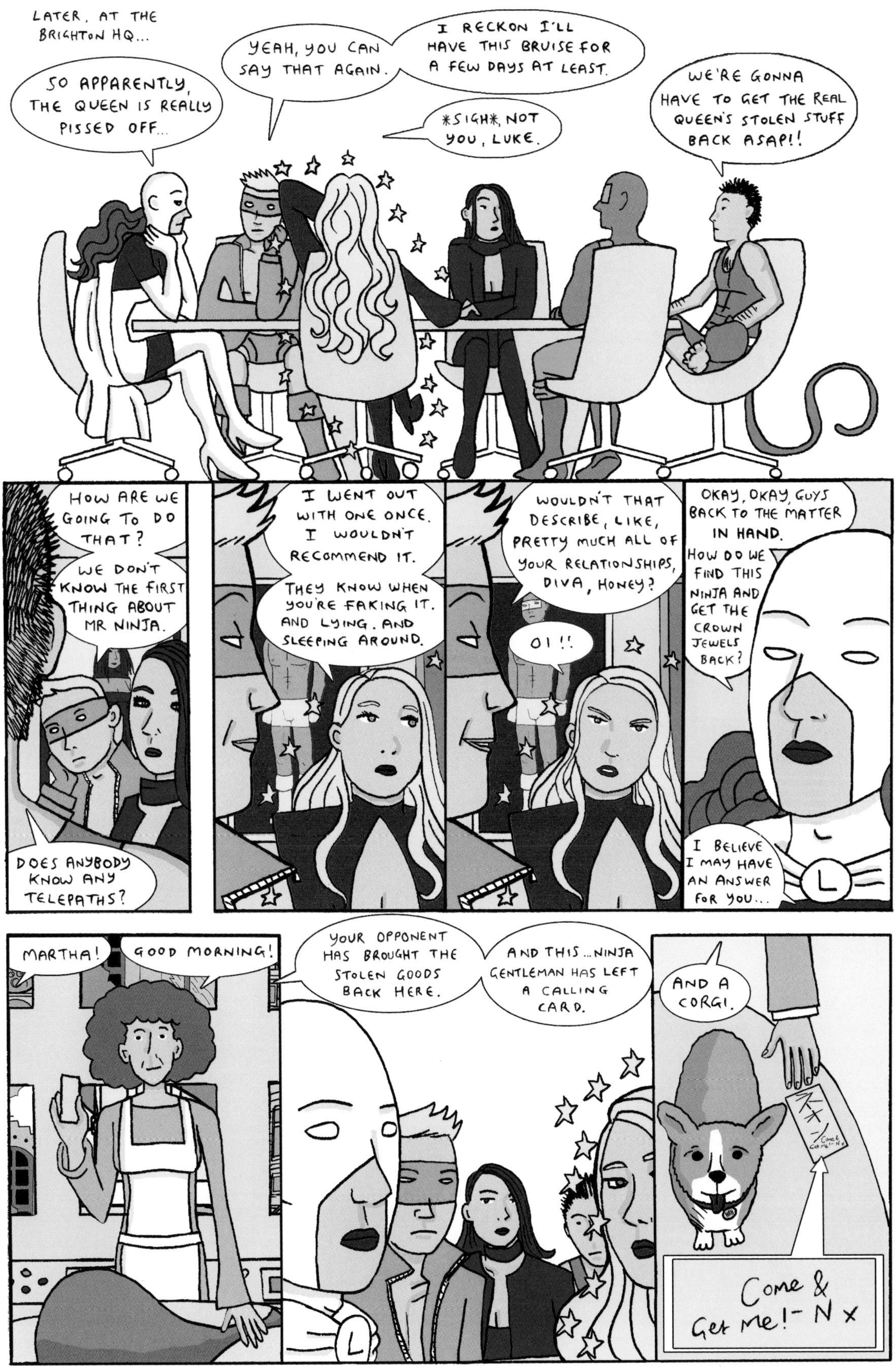
LATER, AT THE BRIGHTON HQ...
SO APPARENTLY, THE QUEEN IS REALLY PISSED OFF...
YEAH, YOU CAN SAY THAT AGAIN.
I RECKON I'LL HAVE THIS BRUISE FOR A FEW DAYS AT LEAST.
SIGH, NOT YOU, LUKE.
WE'RE GONNA HAVE TO GET THE REAL QUEEN'S STOLEN STUFF BACK ASAP!!
HOW ARE WE GOING TO DO THAT?
WE DON'T KNOW THE FIRST THING ABOUT MR NINJA.
DOES ANYBODY KNOW ANY TELEPATHS?
I WENT OUT WITH ONE ONCE. I WOULDN'T RECOMMEND IT.
THEY KNOW WHEN YOU'RE FAKING IT. AND LYING. AND SLEEPING AROUND.
WOULDN'T THAT DESCRIBE, LIKE, PRETTY MUCH ALL OF YOUR RELATIONSHIPS, DIVA, HONEY?
OI!!
OKAY, OKAY, GUYS BACK TO THE MATTER IN HAND.
HOW DO WE FIND THIS NINJA AND GET THE CROWN JEWELS BACK?
I BELIEVE I MAY HAVE AN ANSWER FOR YOU...
MARTHA!
GOOD MORNING!
YOUR OPPONENT HAS BROUGHT THE STOLEN GOODS BACK HERE.
AND THIS... NINJA GENTLEMAN HAS LEFT A CALLING CARD.
AND A CORGI.
Come & Get Me! - N x

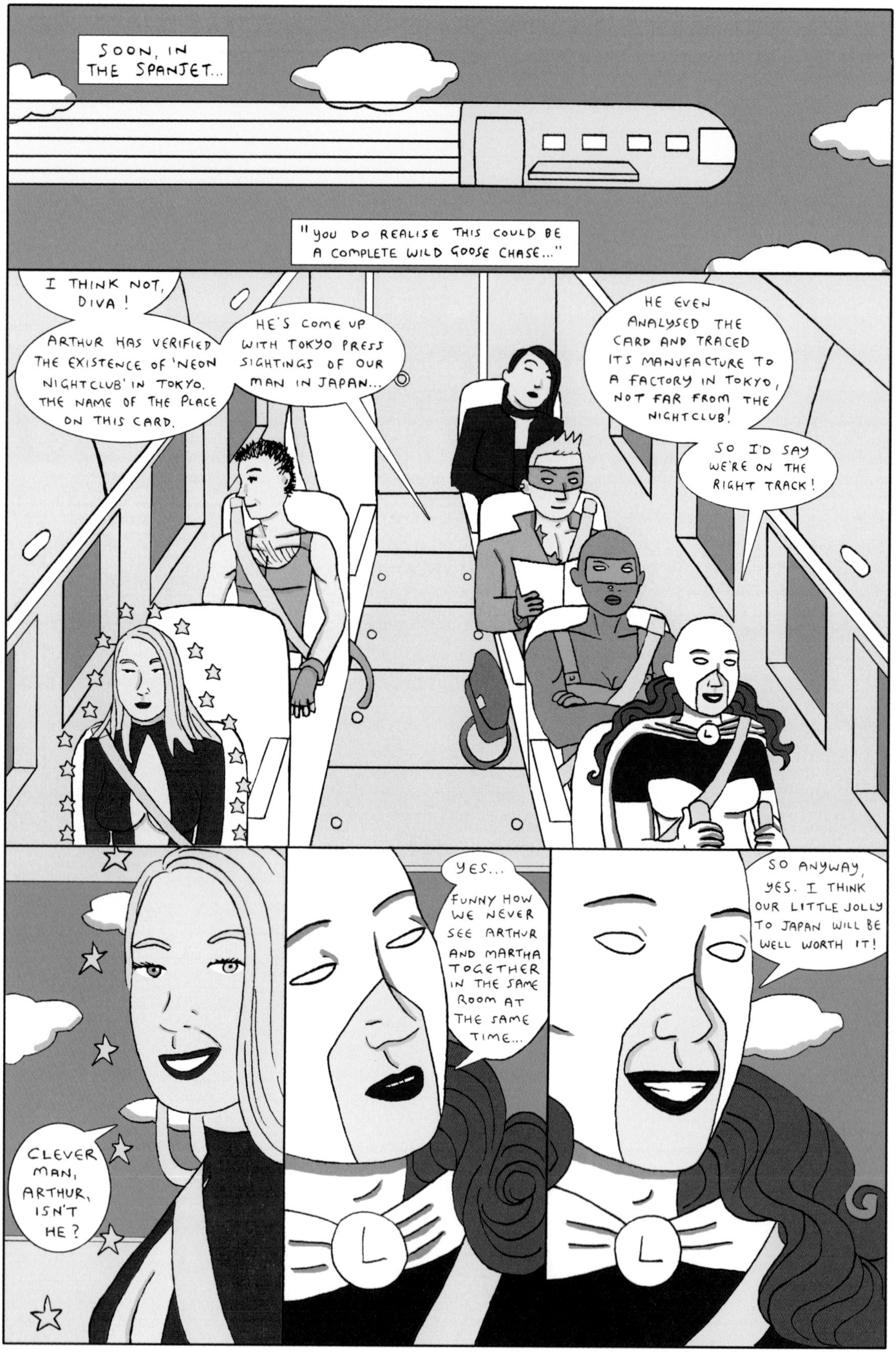
SOON, IN THE SPANJET...
"YOU DO REALISE THIS COULD BE A COMPLETE WILD GOOSE CHASE..."
I THINK NOT, DIVA!
ARTHUR HAS VERIFIED THE EXISTENCE OF 'NEON NIGHTCLUB' IN TOKYO. THE NAME OF THE PLACE ON THIS CARD.
HE'S COME UP WITH TOKYO PRESS SIGHTINGS OF OUR MAN IN JAPAN...
HE EVEN ANALYSED THE CARD AND TRACED ITS MANUFACTURE TO A FACTORY IN TOKYO, NOT FAR FROM THE NIGHTCLUB!
SO I'D SAY WE'RE ON THE RIGHT TRACK!
CLEVER MAN, ARTHUR, ISN'T HE?
YES...
FUNNY HOW WE NEVER SEE ARTHUR AND MARTHA TOGETHER IN THE SAME ROOM AT THE SAME TIME...
SO ANYWAY, YES. I THINK OUR LITTLE JOLLY TO JAPAN WILL BE WELL WORTH IT!

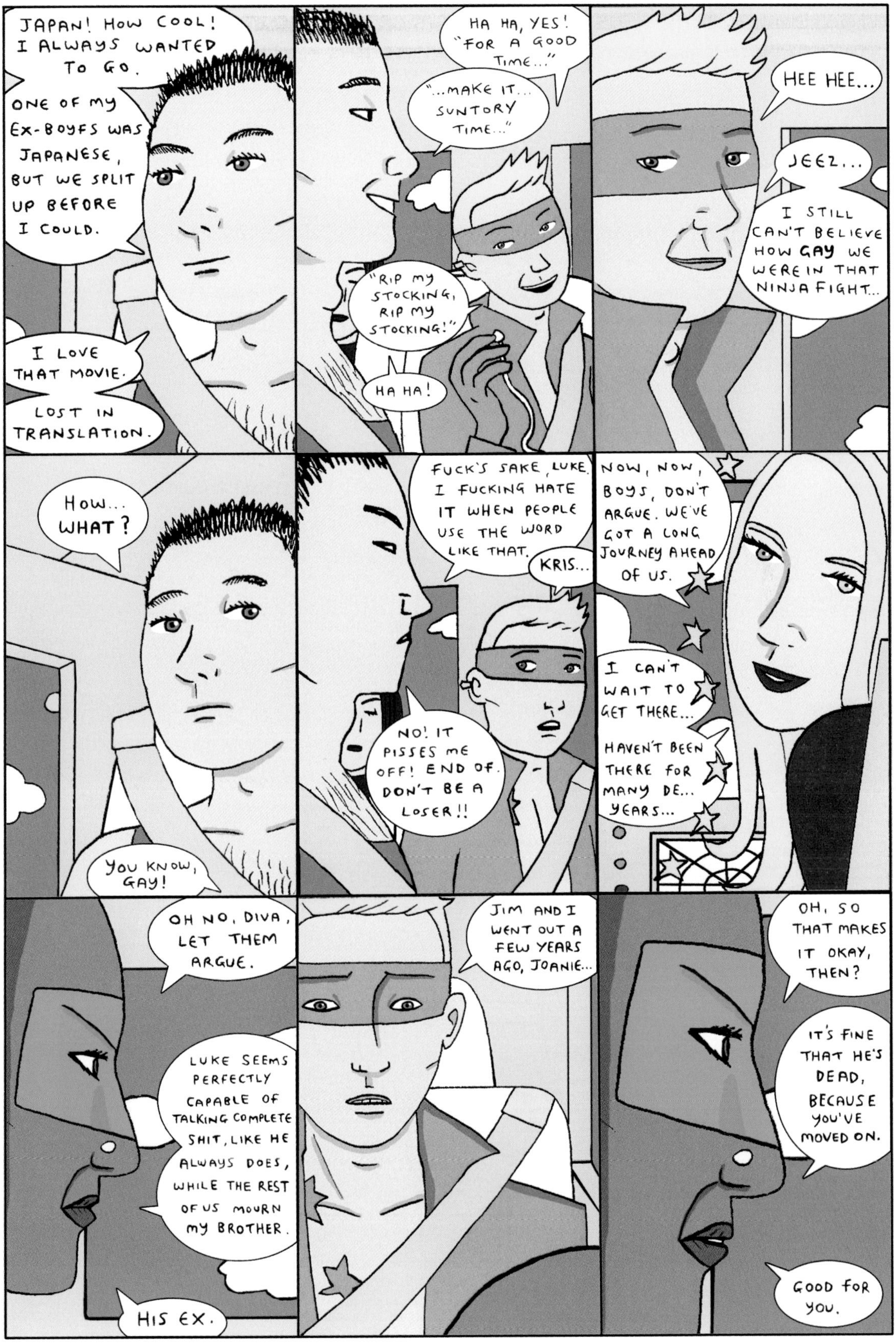
JAPAN! HOW COOL! I ALWAYS WANTED TO GO.
ONE OF MY EX-BOYFS WAS JAPANESE, BUT WE SPLIT UP BEFORE I COULD.
I LOVE THAT MOVIE.
LOST IN TRANSLATION.
HA HA, YES! "FOR A GOOD TIME..."
"...MAKE IT... SUNTORY TIME..."
"RIP MY STOCKING, RIP MY STOCKING!"
HA HA!
HEE HEE...
JEEZ...
I STILL CAN'T BELIEVE HOW GAY WE WERE IN THAT NINJA FIGHT...
HOW... WHAT?
YOU KNOW, GAY!
FUCK'S SAKE, LUKE. I FUCKING HATE IT WHEN PEOPLE USE THE WORD LIKE THAT.
KRIS...
NO! IT PISSES ME OFF! END OF. DON'T BE A LOSER!!
NOW, NOW, BOYS, DON'T ARGUE. WE'VE GOT A LONG JOURNEY AHEAD OF US.
I CAN'T WAIT TO GET THERE...
HAVEN'T BEEN THERE FOR MANY DE... YEARS...
OH NO, DIVA, LET THEM ARGUE.
LUKE SEEMS PERFECTLY CAPABLE OF TALKING COMPLETE SHIT, LIKE HE ALWAYS DOES, WHILE THE REST OF US MOURN MY BROTHER.
HIS EX.
JIM AND I WENT OUT A FEW YEARS AGO, JOANIE...
OH, SO THAT MAKES IT OKAY, THEN?
IT'S FINE THAT HE'S DEAD, BECAUSE YOU'VE MOVED ON.
GOOD FOR YOU.

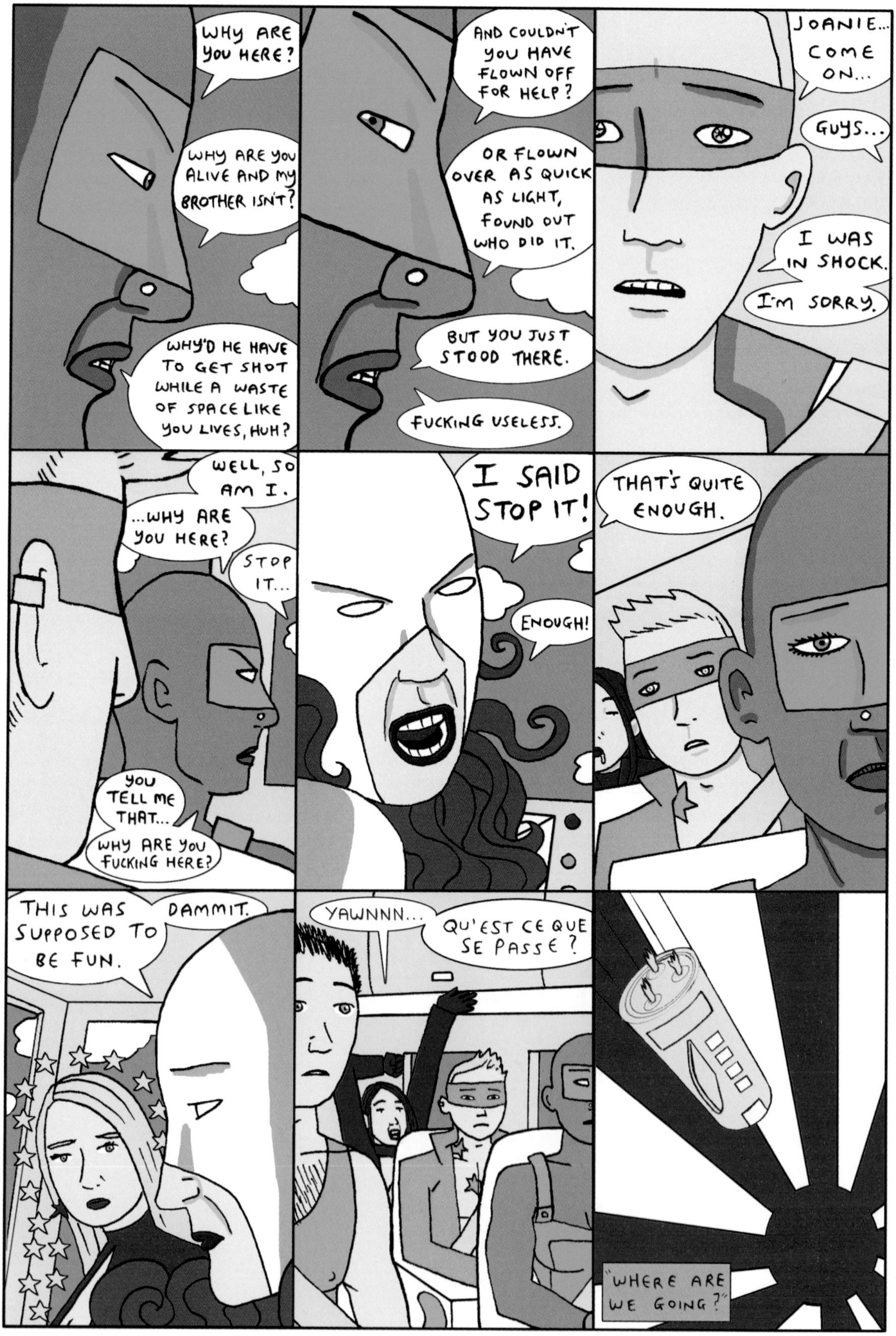
WHY ARE YOU HERE?
WHY ARE YOU ALIVE AND MY BROTHER ISN'T?
WHY'D HE HAVE TO GET SHOT WHILE A WASTE OF SPACE LIKE YOU LIVES, HUH?
AND COULDN'T YOU HAVE FLOWN OFF FOR HELP?
OR FLOWN OVER AS QUICK AS LIGHT, FOUND OUT WHO DID IT.
BUT YOU JUST STOOD THERE.
FUCKING USELESS.
JOANIE... COME ON...
GUYS...
I WAS IN SHOCK.
I'M SORRY.
WELL, SO AM I.
...WHY ARE YOU HERE?
STOP IT...
YOU TELL ME THAT...
WHY ARE YOU FUCKING HERE?
I SAID STOP IT!
ENOUGH!
THAT'S QUITE ENOUGH.
THIS WAS SUPPOSED TO BE FUN.
DAMMIT.
YAWNNN...
QU'EST CE QUE SE PASSE?
"WHERE ARE WE GOING?"

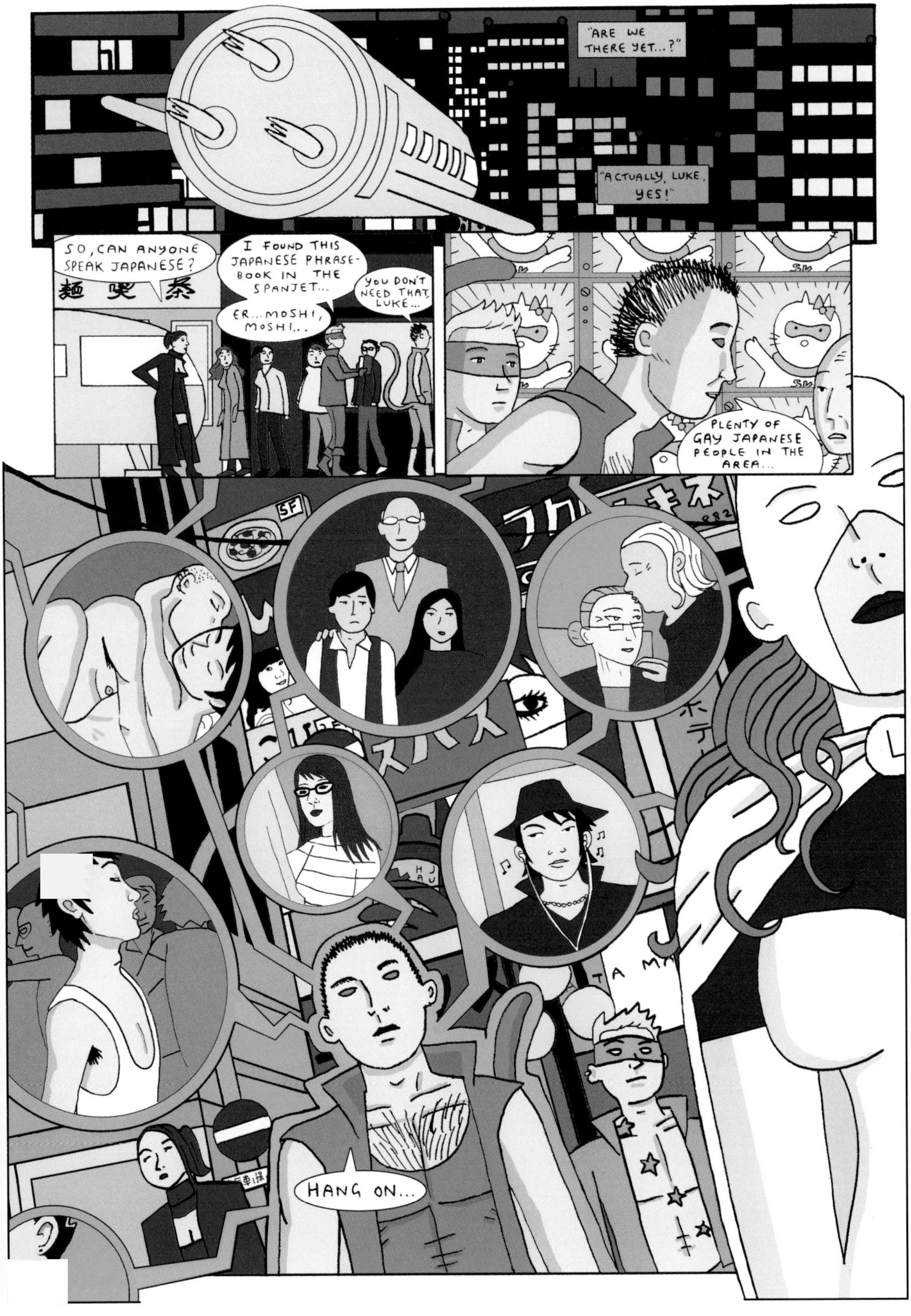
"ARE WE THERE YET...?"
"ACTUALLY, LUKE, YES!"
SO, CAN ANYONE SPEAK JAPANESE?
I FOUND THIS JAPANESE PHRASE-BOOK IN THE SPANJET...
ER... MOSHI, MOSHI!...
YOU DON'T NEED THAT, LUKE...
PLENTY OF GAY JAPANESE PEOPLE IN THE AREA...
HANG ON...

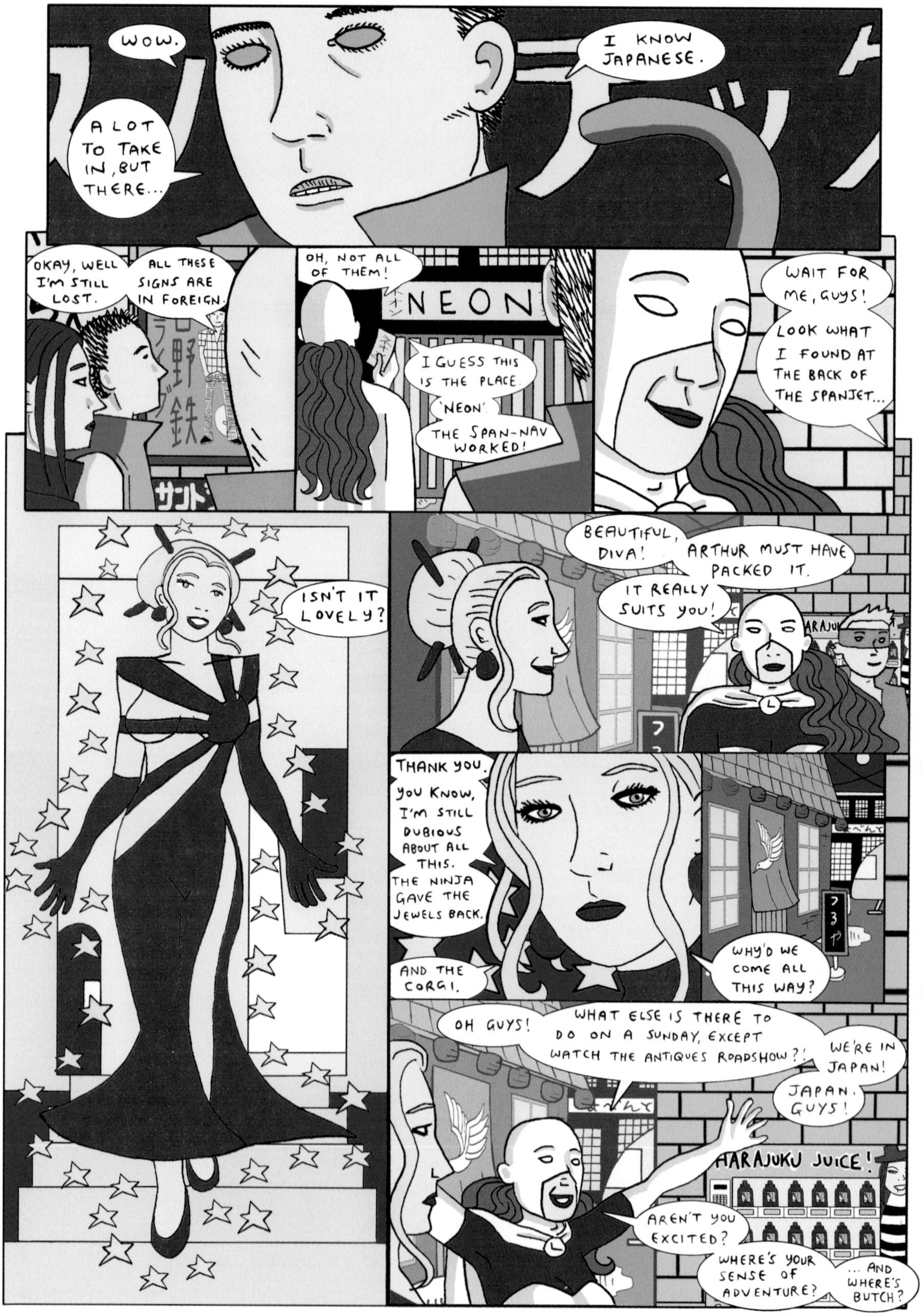
WOW.
A LOT TO TAKE IN, BUT THERE...
I KNOW JAPANESE.
OKAY, WELL I'M STILL LOST.
ALL THESE SIGNS ARE IN FOREIGN.
OH, NOT ALL OF THEM!
NEON
I GUESS THIS IS THE PLACE.
'NEON'.
THE SPAN-NAV WORKED!
WAIT FOR ME, GUYS!
LOOK WHAT I FOUND AT THE BACK OF THE SPANJET...
ISN'T IT LOVELY?
BEAUTIFUL, DIVA!
ARTHUR MUST HAVE PACKED IT.
IT REALLY SUITS YOU!
THANK YOU.
YOU KNOW, I'M STILL DUBIOUS ABOUT ALL THIS.
THE NINJA GAVE THE JEWELS BACK.
AND THE CORGI.
WHY'D WE COME ALL THIS WAY?
OH GUYS!
WHAT ELSE IS THERE TO DO ON A SUNDAY, EXCEPT WATCH THE ANTIQUES ROADSHOW?!
WE'RE IN JAPAN!
JAPAN, GUYS!
HARAJUKU JUICE!
AREN'T YOU EXCITED?
WHERE'S YOUR SENSE OF ADVENTURE?
... AND WHERE'S BUTCH?

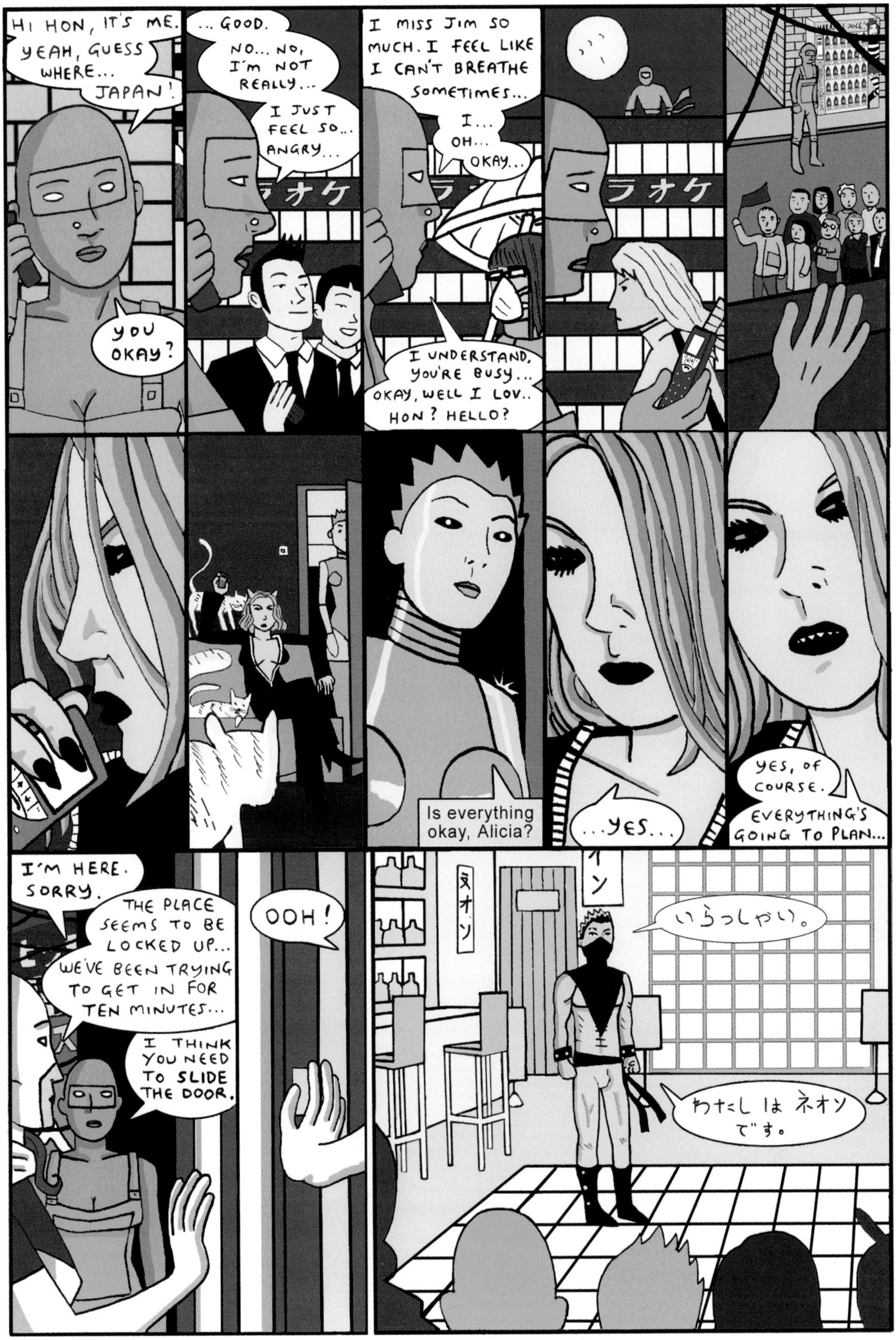
HI HON, IT'S ME.
YEAH, GUESS WHERE... JAPAN!
YOU OKAY?
... GOOD.
NO... NO, I'M NOT REALLY...
I JUST FEEL SO... ANGRY...
ラオケ
I MISS JIM SO MUCH. I FEEL LIKE I CAN'T BREATHE SOMETIMES...
I... OH... OKAY...
I UNDERSTAND, YOU'RE BUSY... OKAY, WELL I LOV.. HON? HELLO?
ラオケ
Is everything okay, Alicia?
...YES...
YES, OF COURSE.
EVERYTHING'S GOING TO PLAN...
I'M HERE. SORRY.
THE PLACE SEEMS TO BE LOCKED UP...
WE'VE BEEN TRYING TO GET IN FOR TEN MINUTES...
I THINK YOU NEED TO **SLIDE** THE DOOR.
OOH!
いらっしゃい。
わたしは ネオン です。

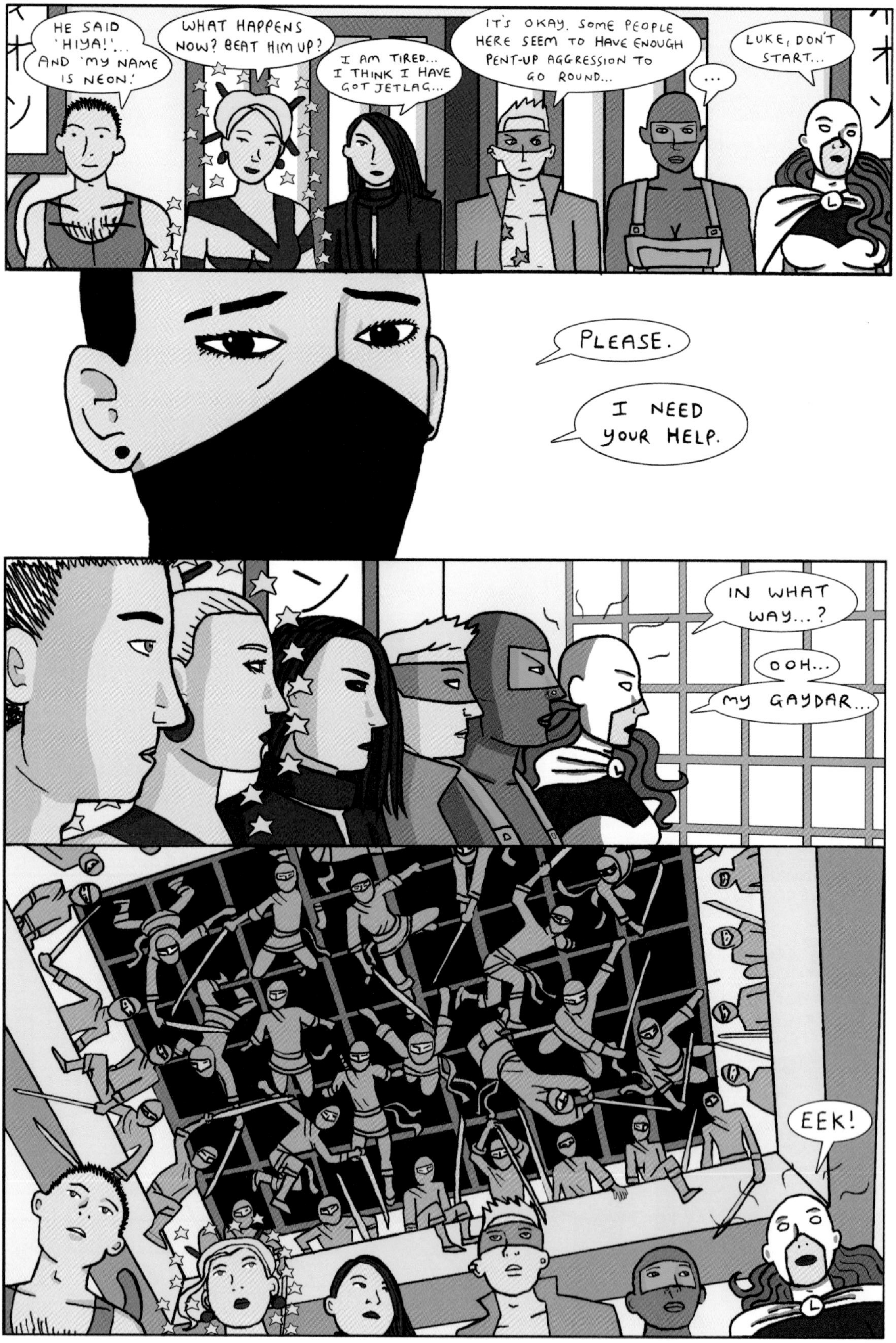
HE SAID 'HIYA!'... AND 'MY NAME IS NEON.'
WHAT HAPPENS NOW? BEAT HIM UP?
I AM TIRED... I THINK I HAVE GOT JETLAG...
IT'S OKAY. SOME PEOPLE HERE SEEM TO HAVE ENOUGH PENT-UP AGGRESSION TO GO ROUND...
...
LUKE, DON'T START...
PLEASE.
I NEED YOUR HELP.
IN WHAT WAY...?
OOH...
MY GAYDAR...
EEK!

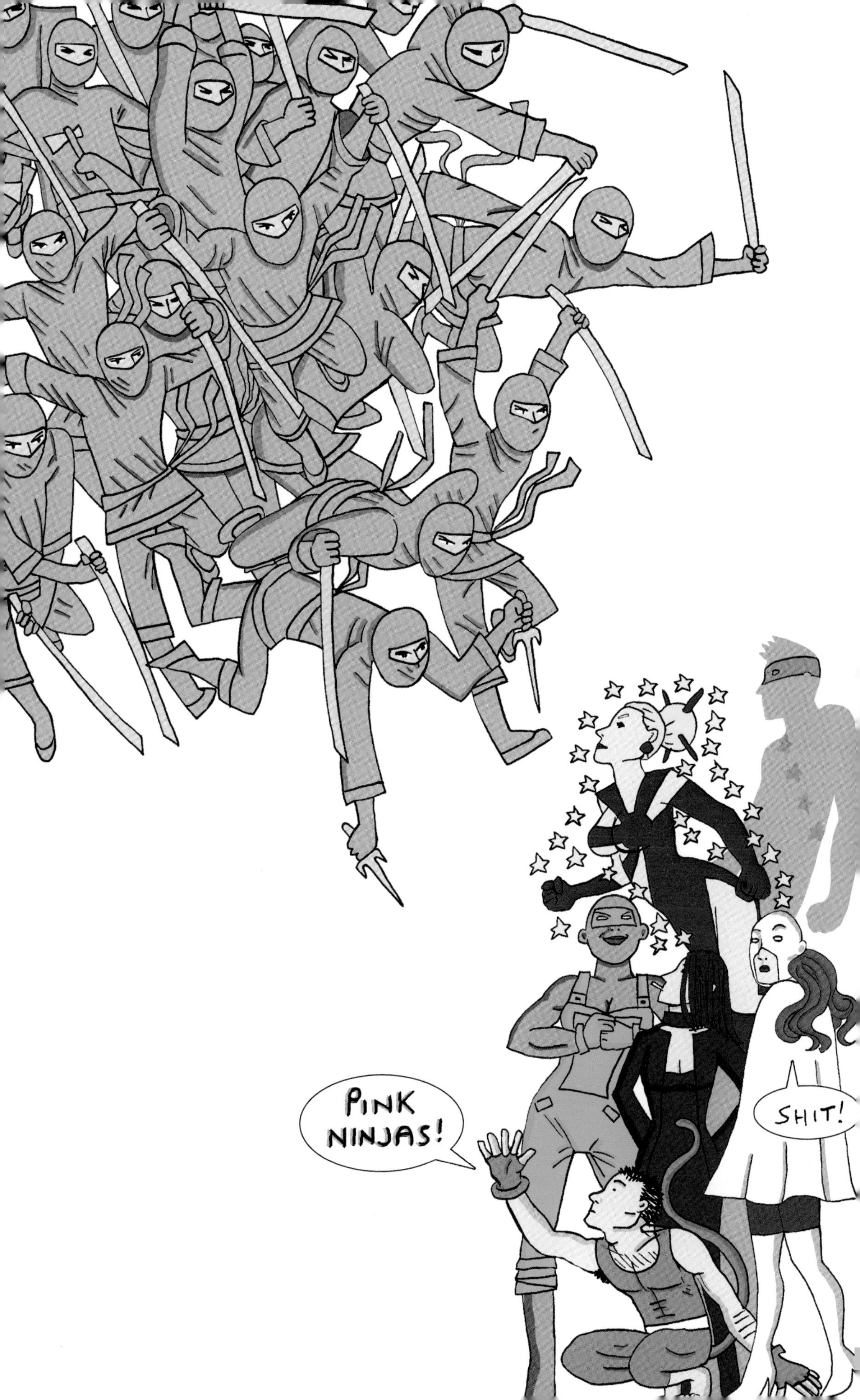
PINK NINJAS!
SHIT!

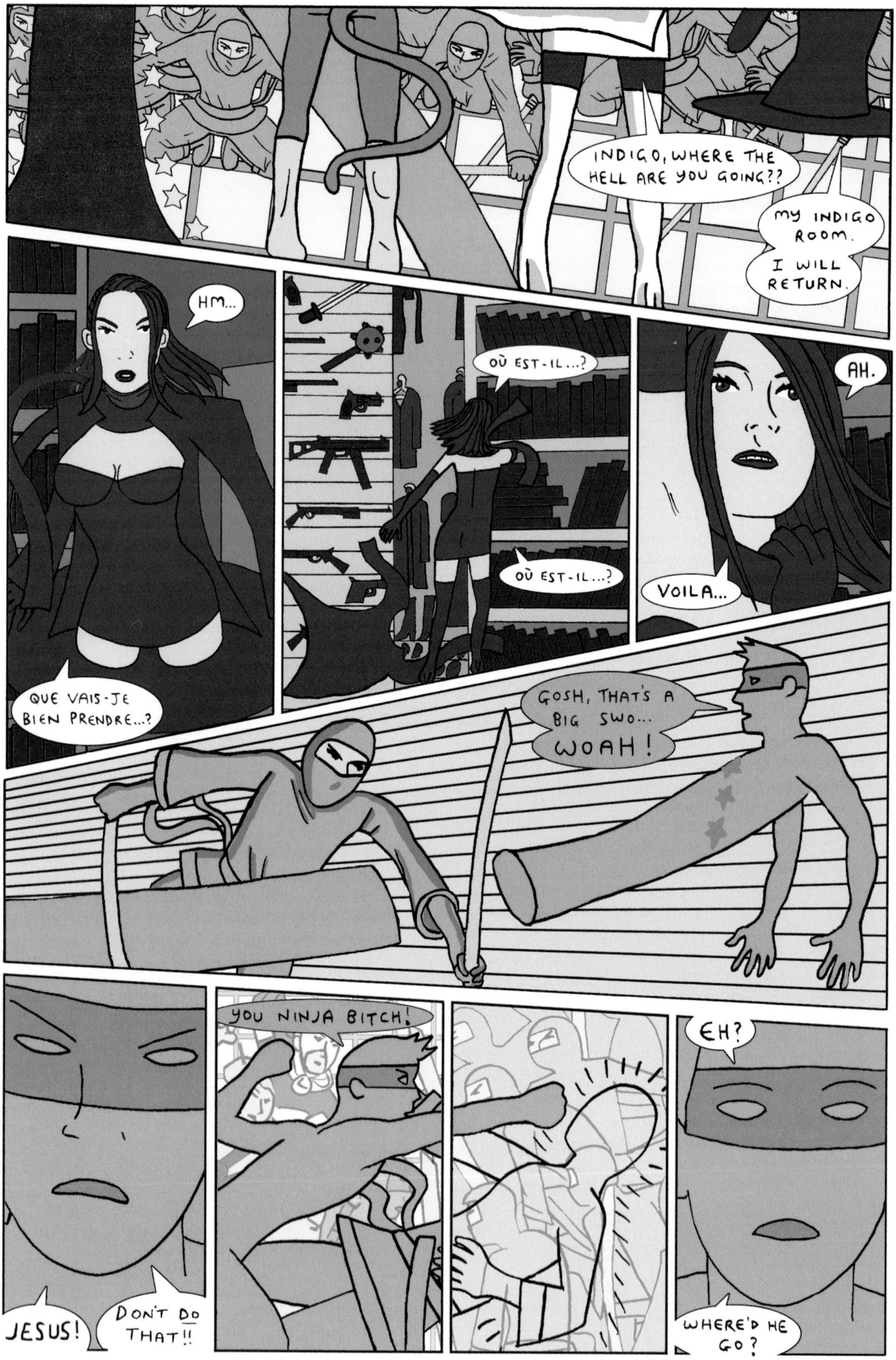
INDIGO, WHERE THE HELL ARE YOU GOING??
MY INDIGO ROOM.
I WILL RETURN.
HM...
QUE VAIS-JE BIEN PRENDRE...?
OÙ EST-IL...?
OÙ EST-IL...?
AH.
VOILA...
GOSH, THAT'S A BIG SWO... WOAH!
JESUS!
DON'T DO THAT!!
YOU NINJA BITCH!
EH?
WHERE'D HE GO?

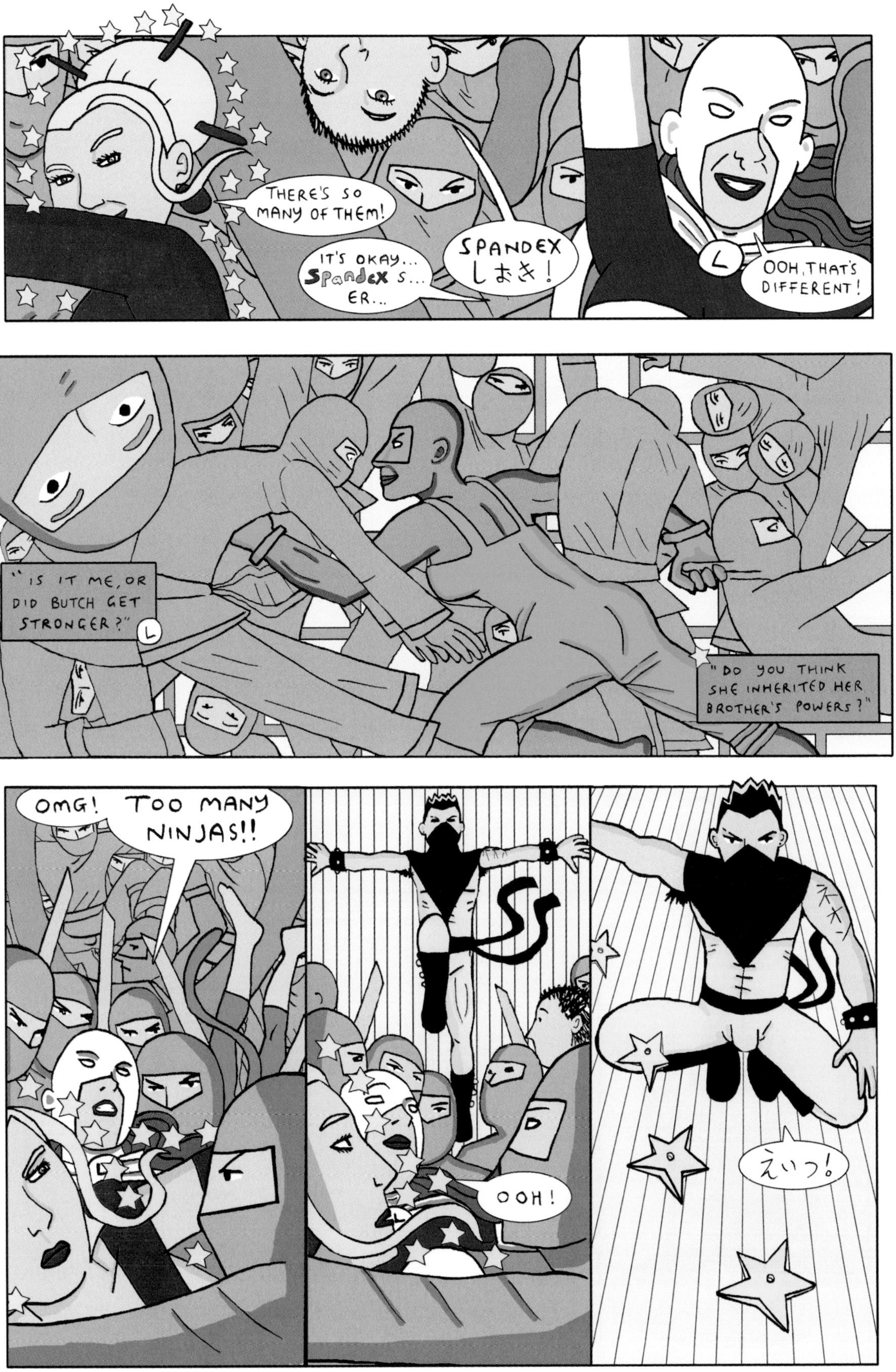
THERE'S SO MANY OF THEM!
IT'S OKAY... SPANDEX S... ER...
SPANDEX しおき!
OOH, THAT'S DIFFERENT!
"IS IT ME, OR DID BUTCH GET STRONGER?"
"DO YOU THINK SHE INHERITED HER BROTHER'S POWERS?"
OMG!
TOO MANY NINJAS!!
OOH!
えいっ!

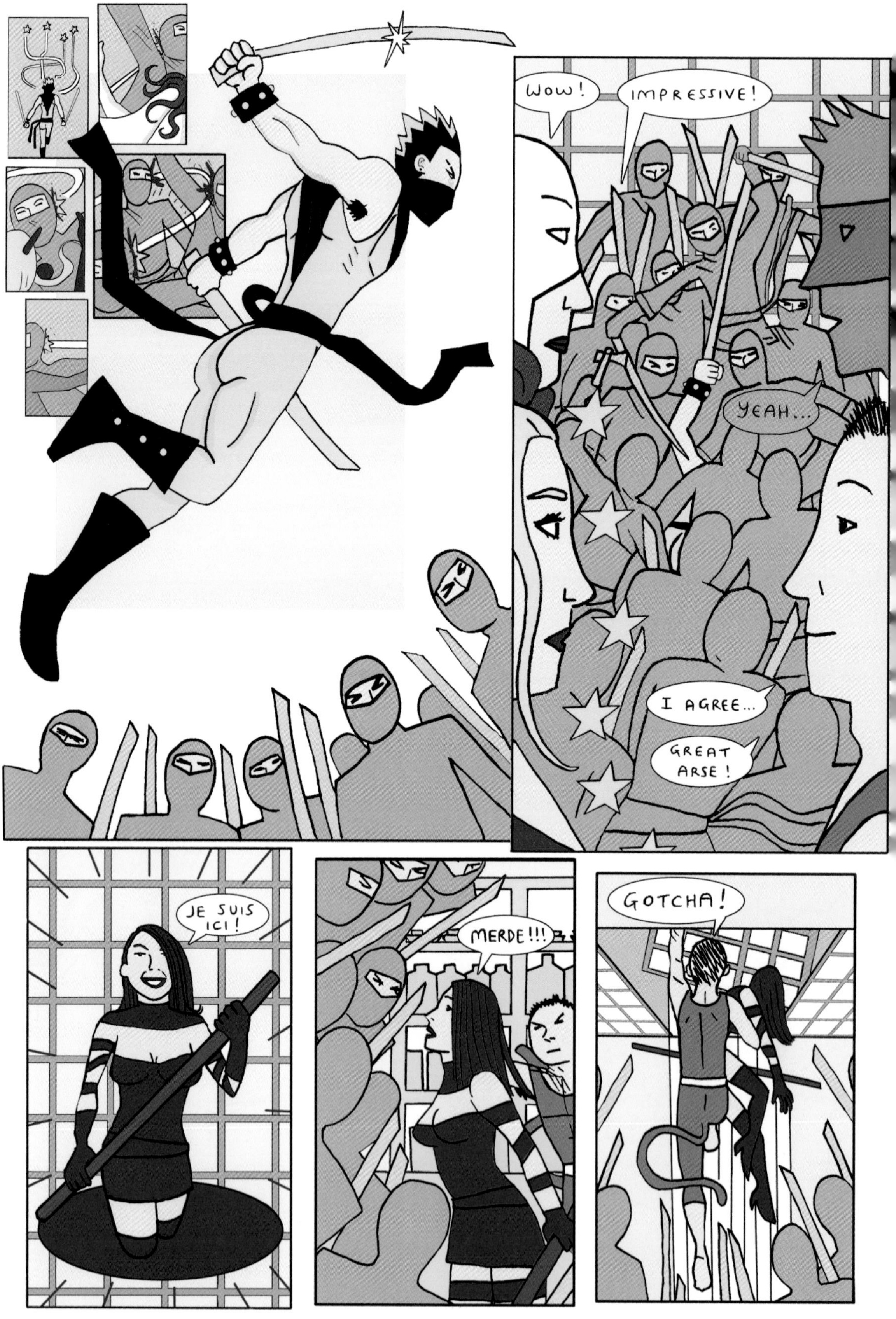
WOW!
IMPRESSIVE!
YEAH...
I AGREE...
GREAT ARSE!
JE SUIS ICI!
MERDE!!!
GOTCHA!

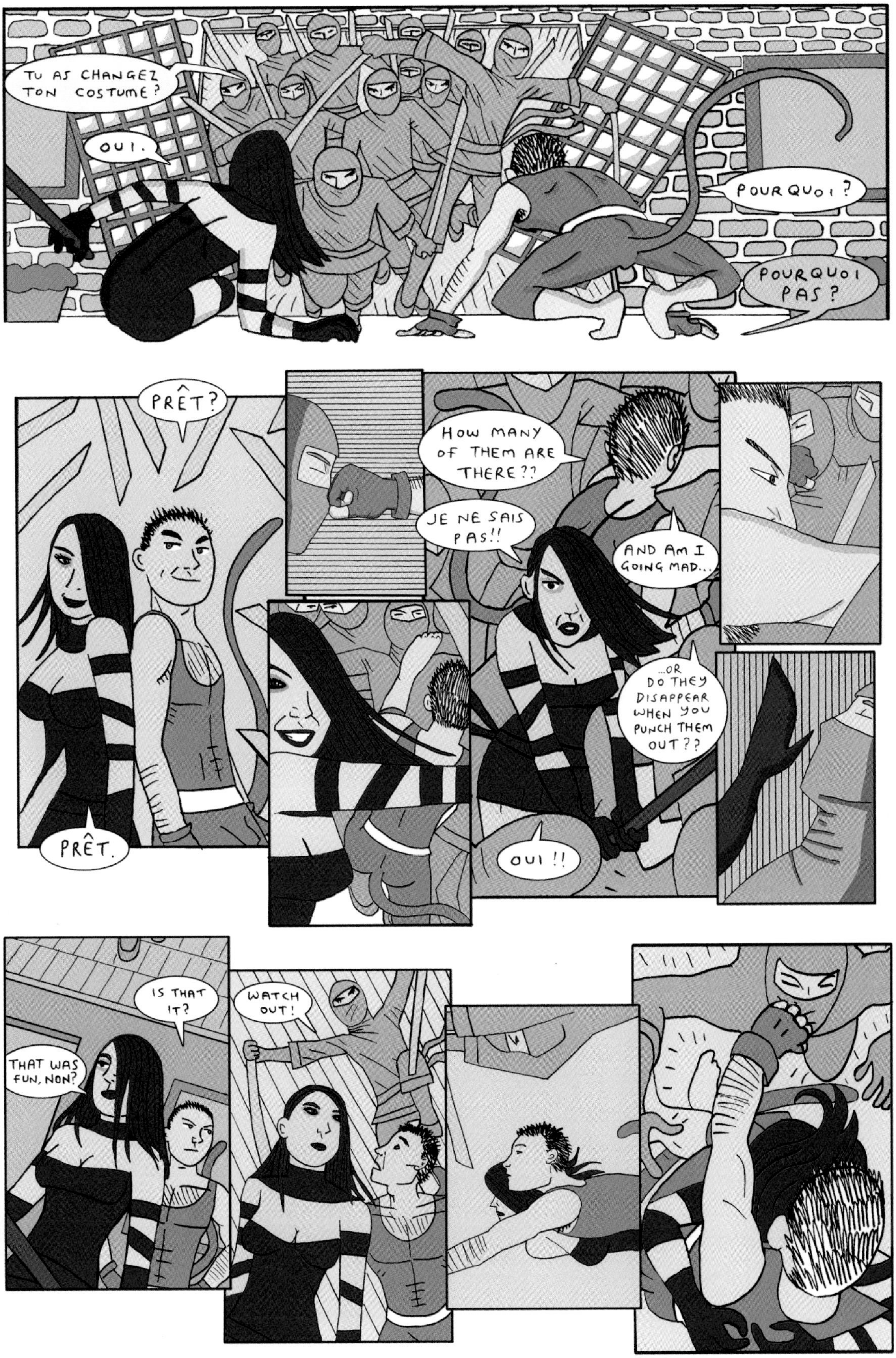
TU AS CHANGEZ TON COSTUME?
OUI.
POURQUOI?
POURQUOI PAS?
PRÊT?
PRÊT.
HOW MANY OF THEM ARE THERE??
JE NE SAIS PAS!!
AND AM I GOING MAD...
...OR DO THEY DISAPPEAR WHEN YOU PUNCH THEM OUT??
OUI!!
THAT WAS FUN, NON?
IS THAT IT?
WATCH OUT!

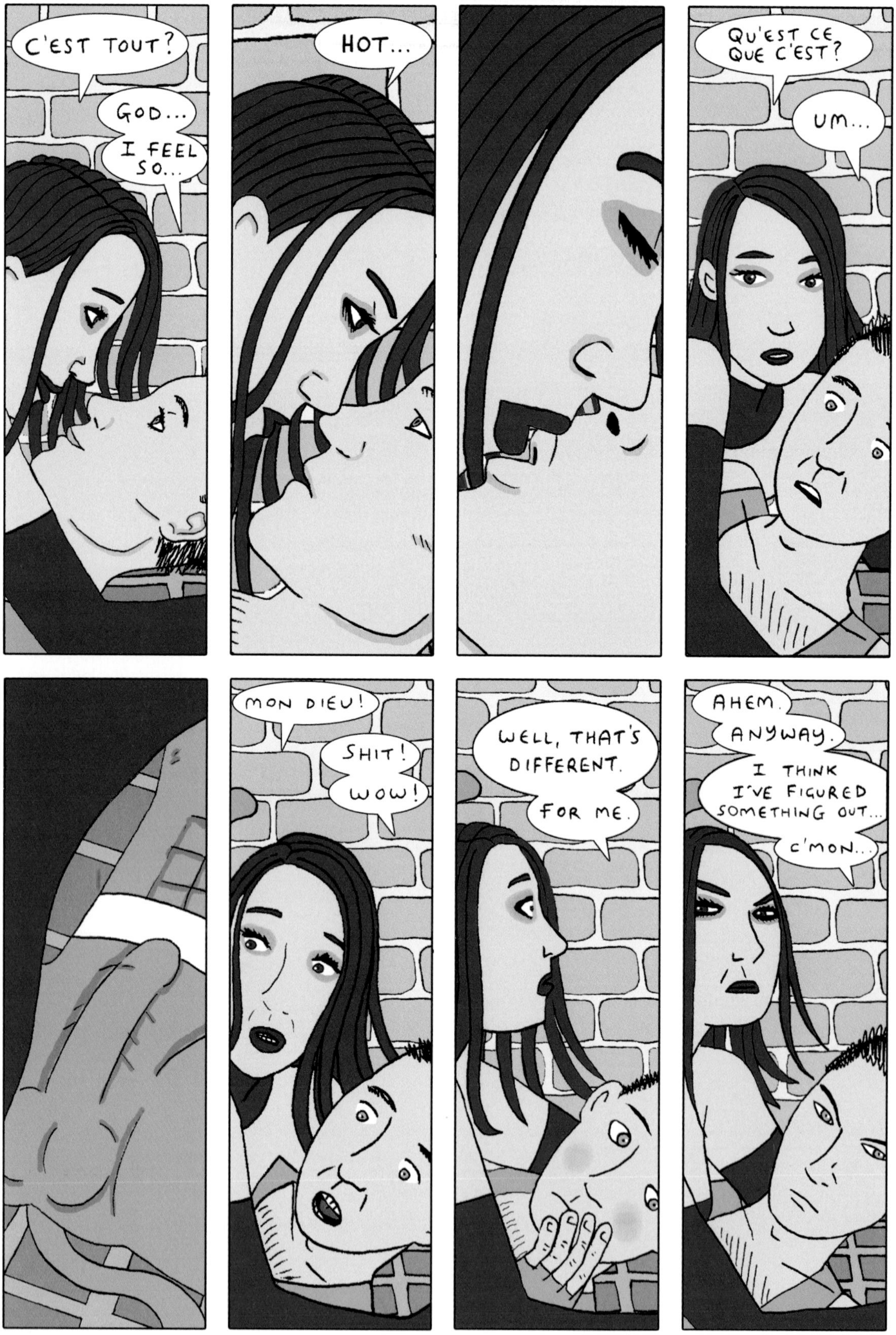
C'EST TOUT?
GOD...
I FEEL SO...
HOT...
QU'EST CE QUE C'EST?
UM...
MON DIEU!
SHIT!
WOW!
WELL, THAT'S DIFFERENT.
FOR ME.
AHEM.
ANYWAY.
I THINK I'VE FIGURED SOMETHING OUT...
C'MON...

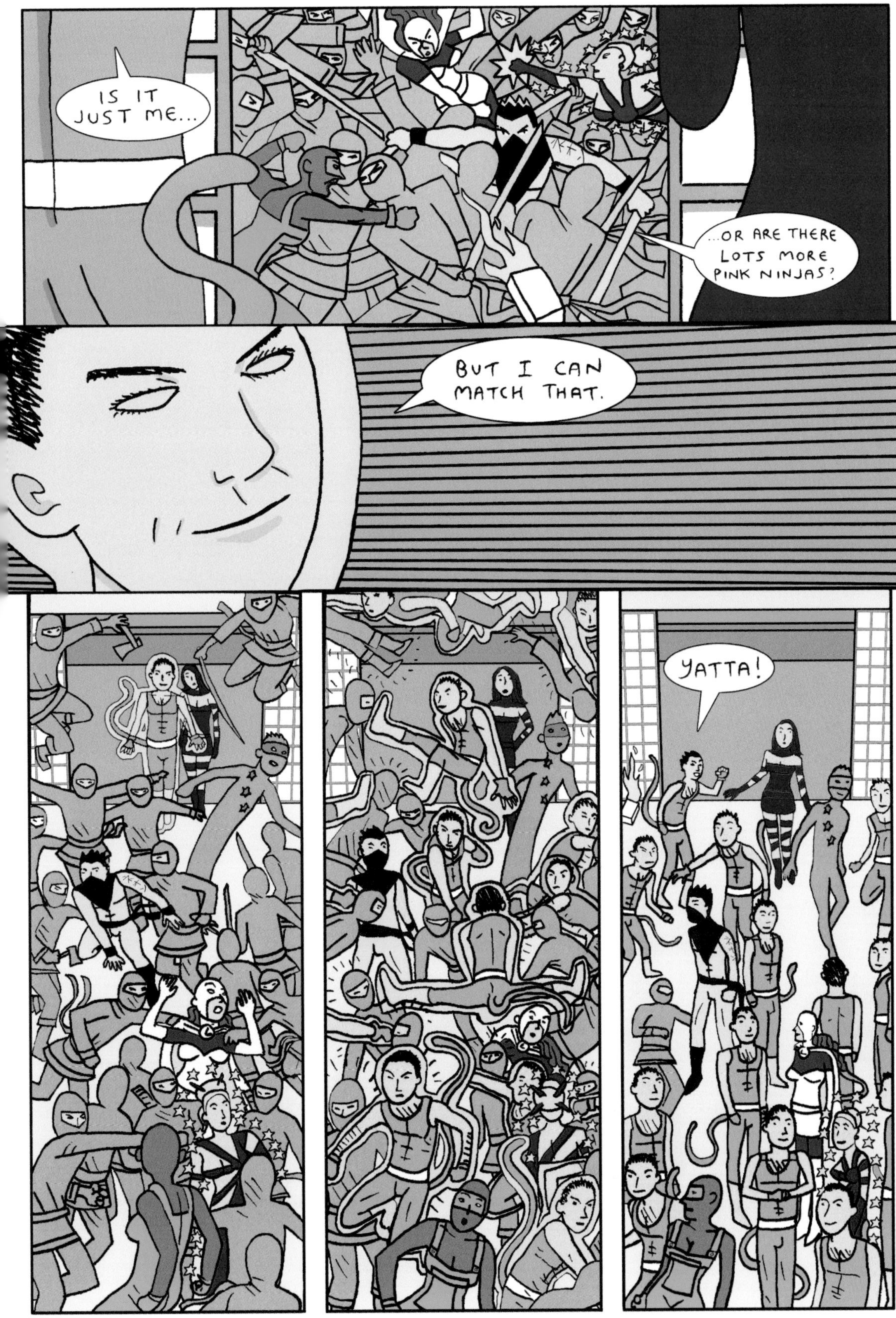
IS IT JUST ME...
...OR ARE THERE LOTS MORE PINK NINJAS?
BUT I CAN MATCH THAT.
YATTA!

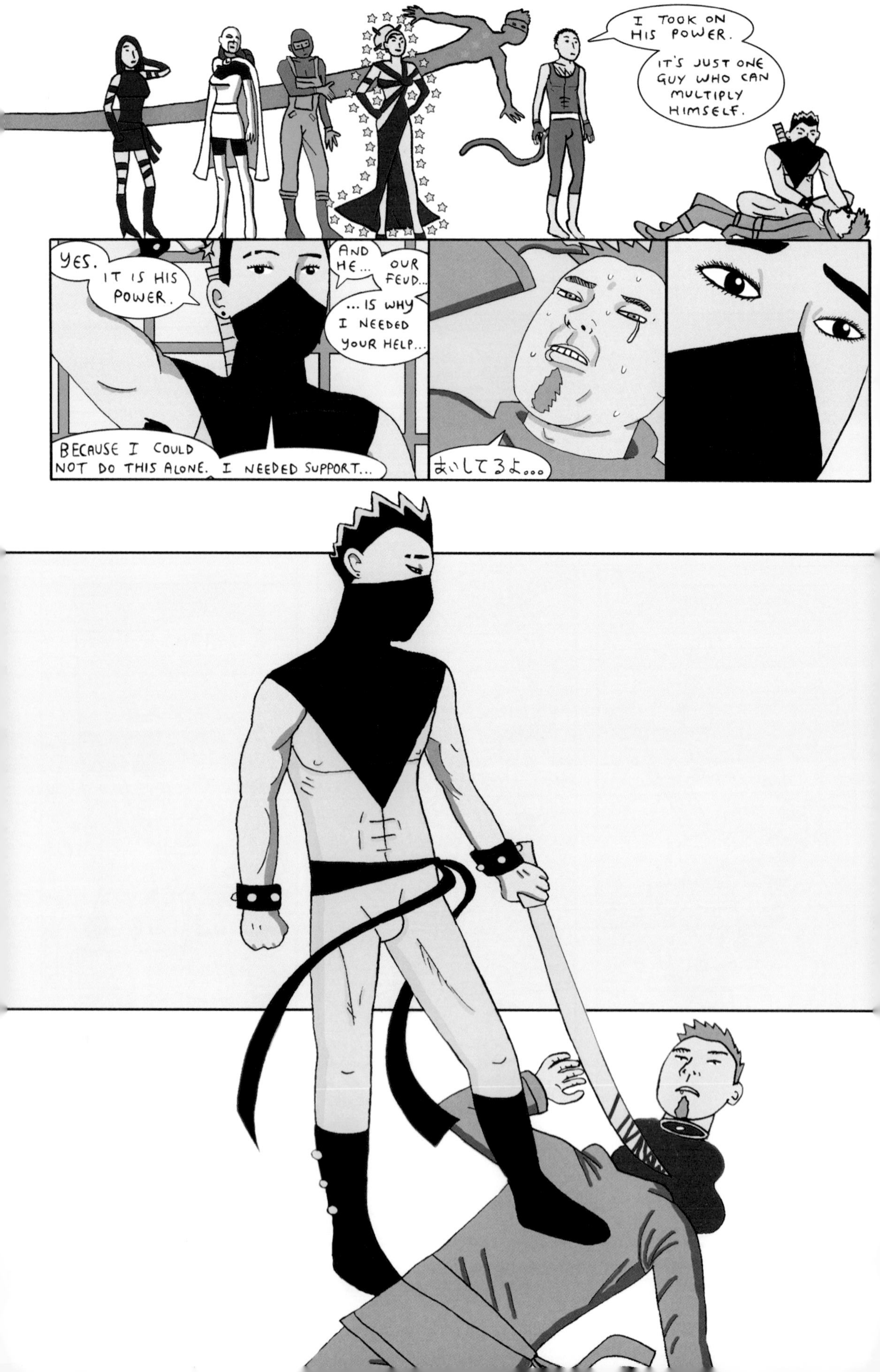
I TOOK ON HIS POWER.
IT'S JUST ONE GUY WHO CAN MULTIPLY HIMSELF.
YES.
IT IS HIS POWER.
AND HE...
OUR FEUD...
... IS WHY I NEEDED YOUR HELP...
BECAUSE I COULD NOT DO THIS ALONE. I NEEDED SUPPORT...
あいしてるよ。。。

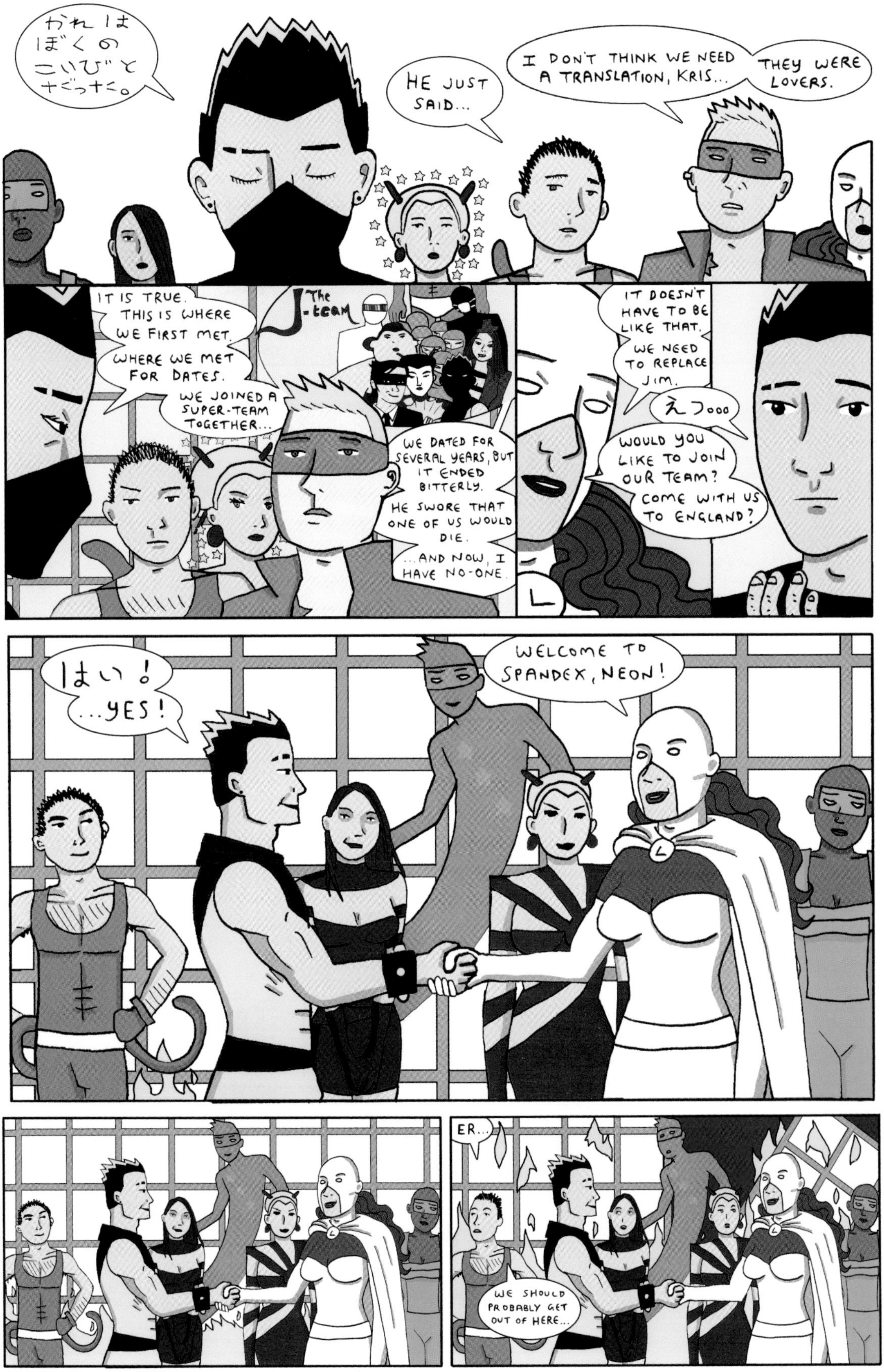
かれはぼくのこいびとだった。
HE JUST SAID...
I DON'T THINK WE NEED A TRANSLATION, KRIS...
THEY WERE LOVERS.
IT IS TRUE. THIS IS WHERE WE FIRST MET.
WHERE WE MET FOR DATES.
WE JOINED A SUPER-TEAM TOGETHER...
The J-team
WE DATED FOR SEVERAL YEARS, BUT IT ENDED BITTERLY.
HE SWORE THAT ONE OF US WOULD DIE.
...AND NOW, I HAVE NO-ONE.
IT DOESN'T HAVE TO BE LIKE THAT.
WE NEED TO REPLACE JIM.
えっ。。。
WOULD YOU LIKE TO JOIN OUR TEAM?
COME WITH US TO ENGLAND?
はい！
...YES!
WELCOME TO SPANDEX, NEON!
ER...
WE SHOULD PROBABLY GET OUT OF HERE...

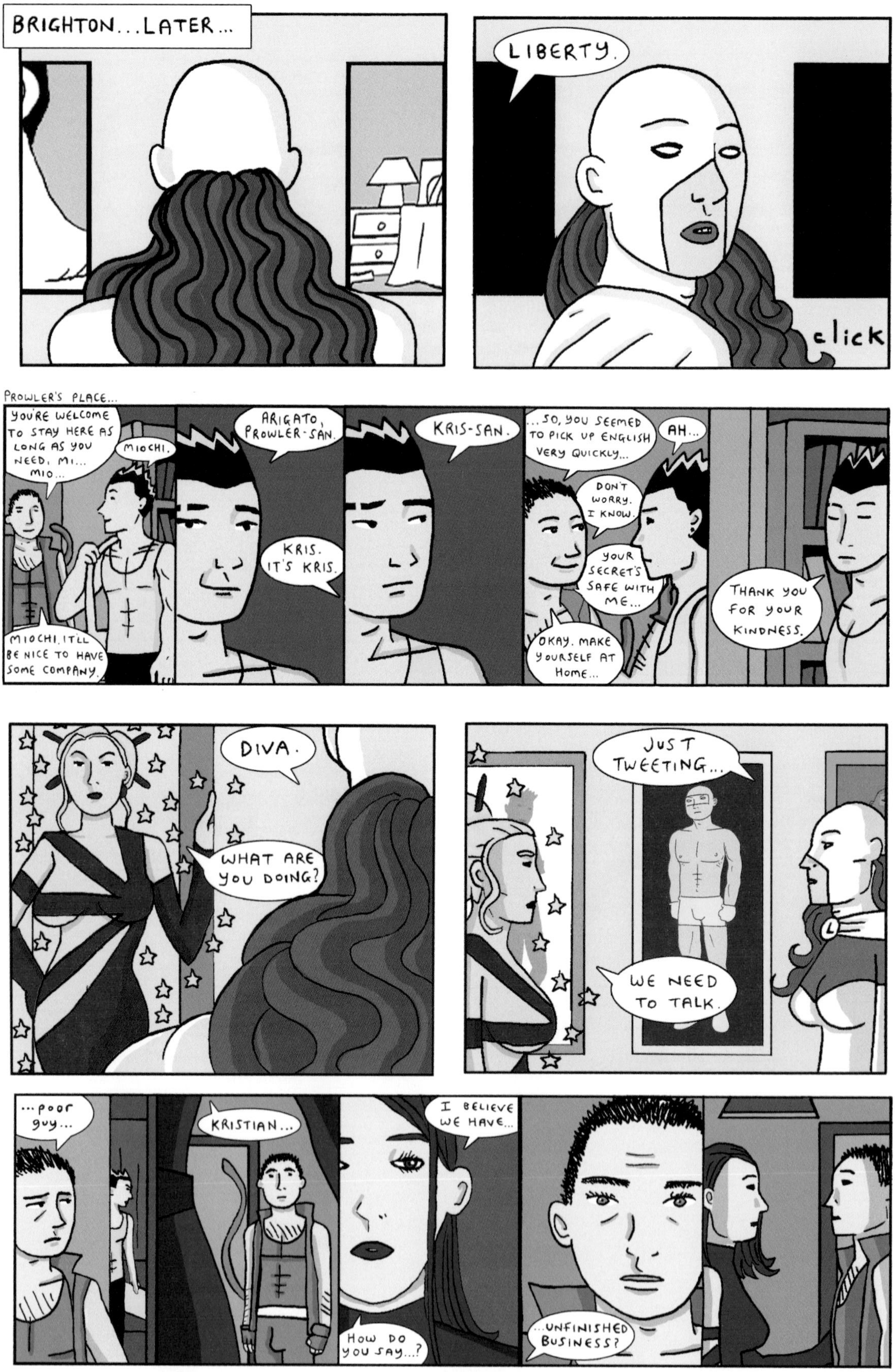
BRIGHTON...LATER...
LIBERTY.
click
PROWLER'S PLACE...
YOU'RE WELCOME TO STAY HERE AS LONG AS YOU NEED, MI... MIO...
MIOCHI.
MIOCHI, IT'LL BE NICE TO HAVE SOME COMPANY.
ARIGATO, PROWLER-SAN.
KRIS. IT'S KRIS.
KRIS-SAN.
...SO, YOU SEEMED TO PICK UP ENGLISH VERY QUICKLY...
AH...
DON'T WORRY. I KNOW.
YOUR SECRET'S SAFE WITH ME...
OKAY. MAKE YOURSELF AT HOME...
THANK YOU FOR YOUR KINDNESS.
DIVA.
WHAT ARE YOU DOING?
JUST TWEETING...
WE NEED TO TALK.
...poor guy...
KRISTIAN...
I BELIEVE WE HAVE...
HOW DO YOU SAY...?
...UNFINISHED BUSINESS?

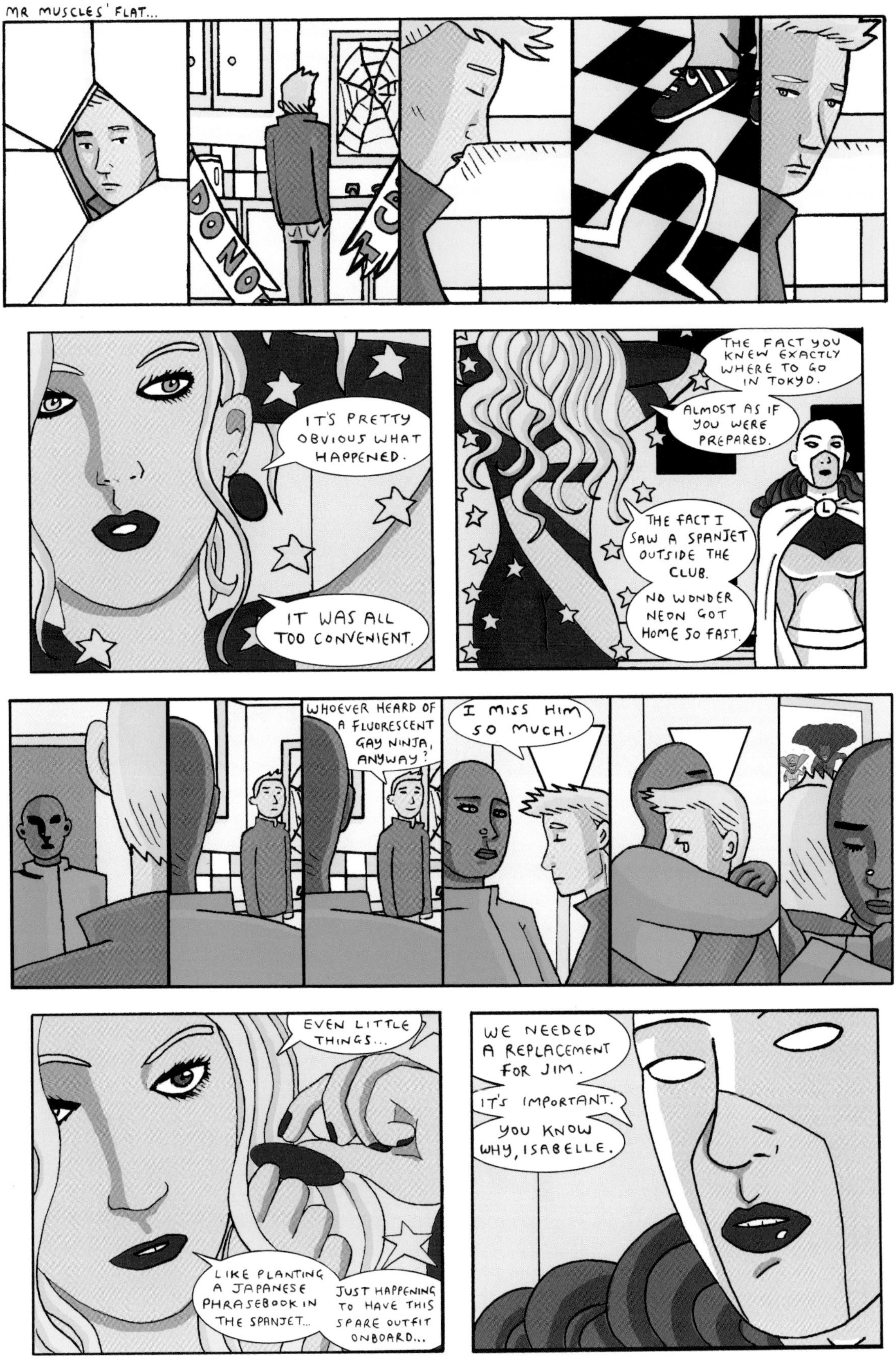
MR MUSCLES' FLAT...
IT'S PRETTY OBVIOUS WHAT HAPPENED.
IT WAS ALL TOO CONVENIENT.
THE FACT YOU KNEW EXACTLY WHERE TO GO IN TOKYO.
ALMOST AS IF YOU WERE PREPARED.
THE FACT I SAW A SPANJET OUTSIDE THE CLUB.
NO WONDER NEON GOT HOME SO FAST.
WHOEVER HEARD OF A FLUORESCENT GAY NINJA, ANYWAY?
I MISS HIM SO MUCH.
EVEN LITTLE THINGS...
LIKE PLANTING A JAPANESE PHRASEBOOK IN THE SPANJET...
JUST HAPPENING TO HAVE THIS SPARE OUTFIT ONBOARD...
WE NEEDED A REPLACEMENT FOR JIM.
IT'S IMPORTANT.
YOU KNOW WHY, ISABELLE.

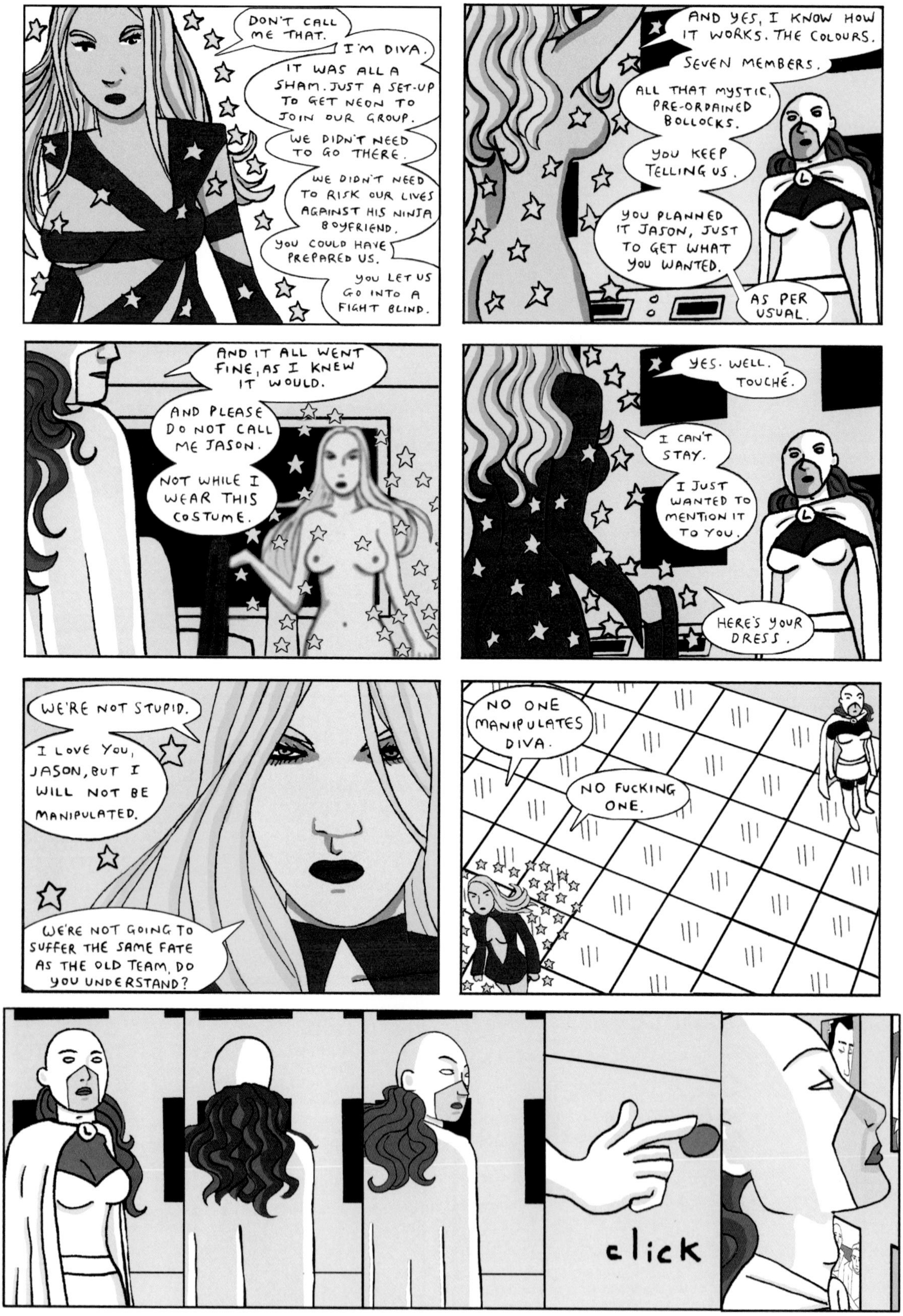
DON'T CALL ME THAT.
I'M DIVA.
IT WAS ALL A SHAM. JUST A SET-UP TO GET NEON TO JOIN OUR GROUP.
WE DIDN'T NEED TO GO THERE.
WE DIDN'T NEED TO RISK OUR LIVES AGAINST HIS NINJA BOYFRIEND.
YOU COULD HAVE PREPARED US.
YOU LET US GO INTO A FIGHT BLIND.
AND YES, I KNOW HOW IT WORKS. THE COLOURS.
SEVEN MEMBERS.
ALL THAT MYSTIC, PRE-ORDAINED BOLLOCKS.
YOU KEEP TELLING US.
YOU PLANNED IT JASON, JUST TO GET WHAT YOU WANTED.
AS PER USUAL.
AND IT ALL WENT FINE, AS I KNEW IT WOULD.
AND PLEASE DO NOT CALL ME JASON.
NOT WHILE I WEAR THIS COSTUME.
YES. WELL. TOUCHÉ.
I CAN'T STAY.
I JUST WANTED TO MENTION IT TO YOU.
HERE'S YOUR DRESS.
WE'RE NOT STUPID.
I LOVE YOU, JASON, BUT I WILL NOT BE MANIPULATED.
WE'RE NOT GOING TO SUFFER THE SAME FATE AS THE OLD TEAM, DO YOU UNDERSTAND?
NO ONE MANIPULATES DIVA.
NO FUCKING ONE.
click

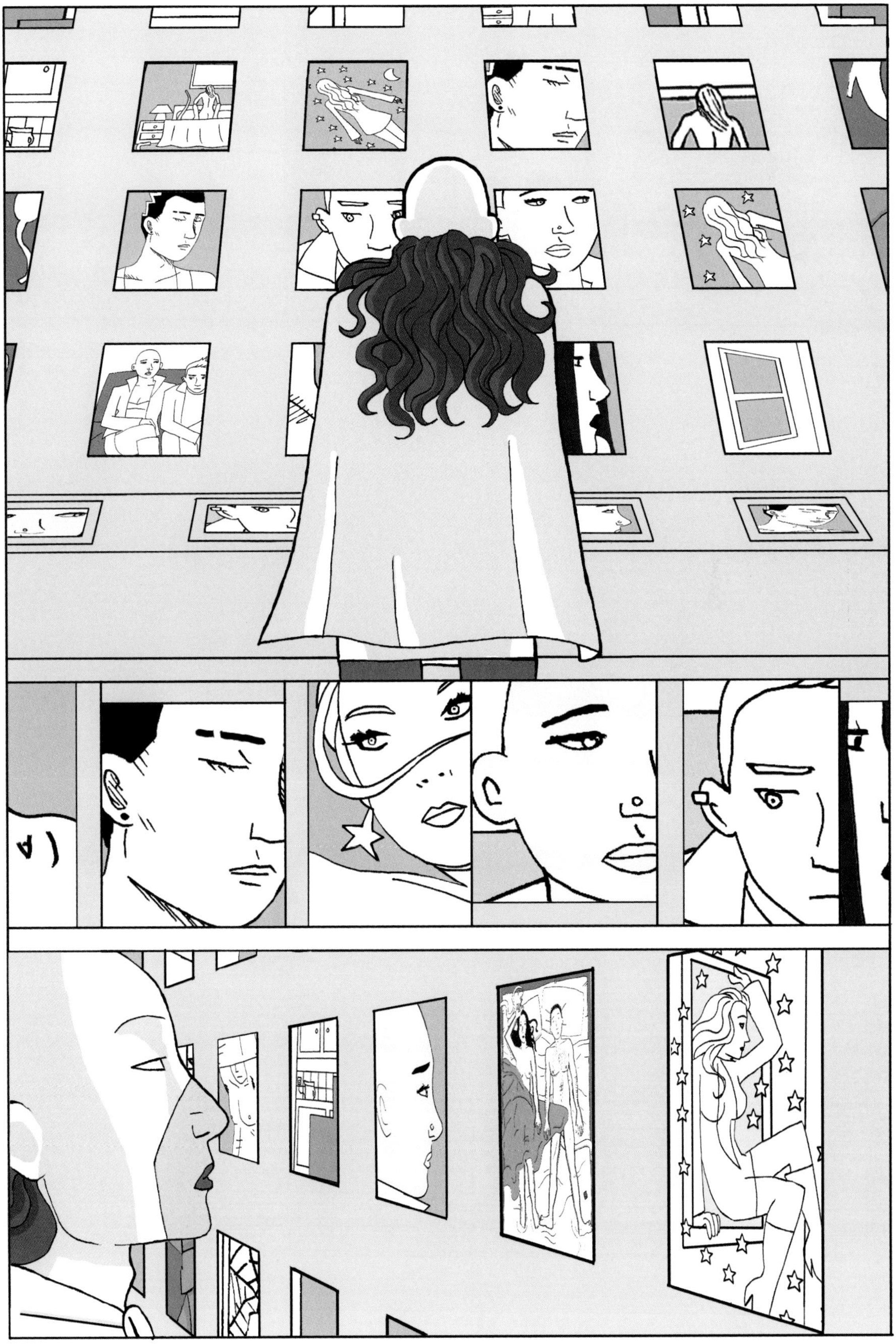

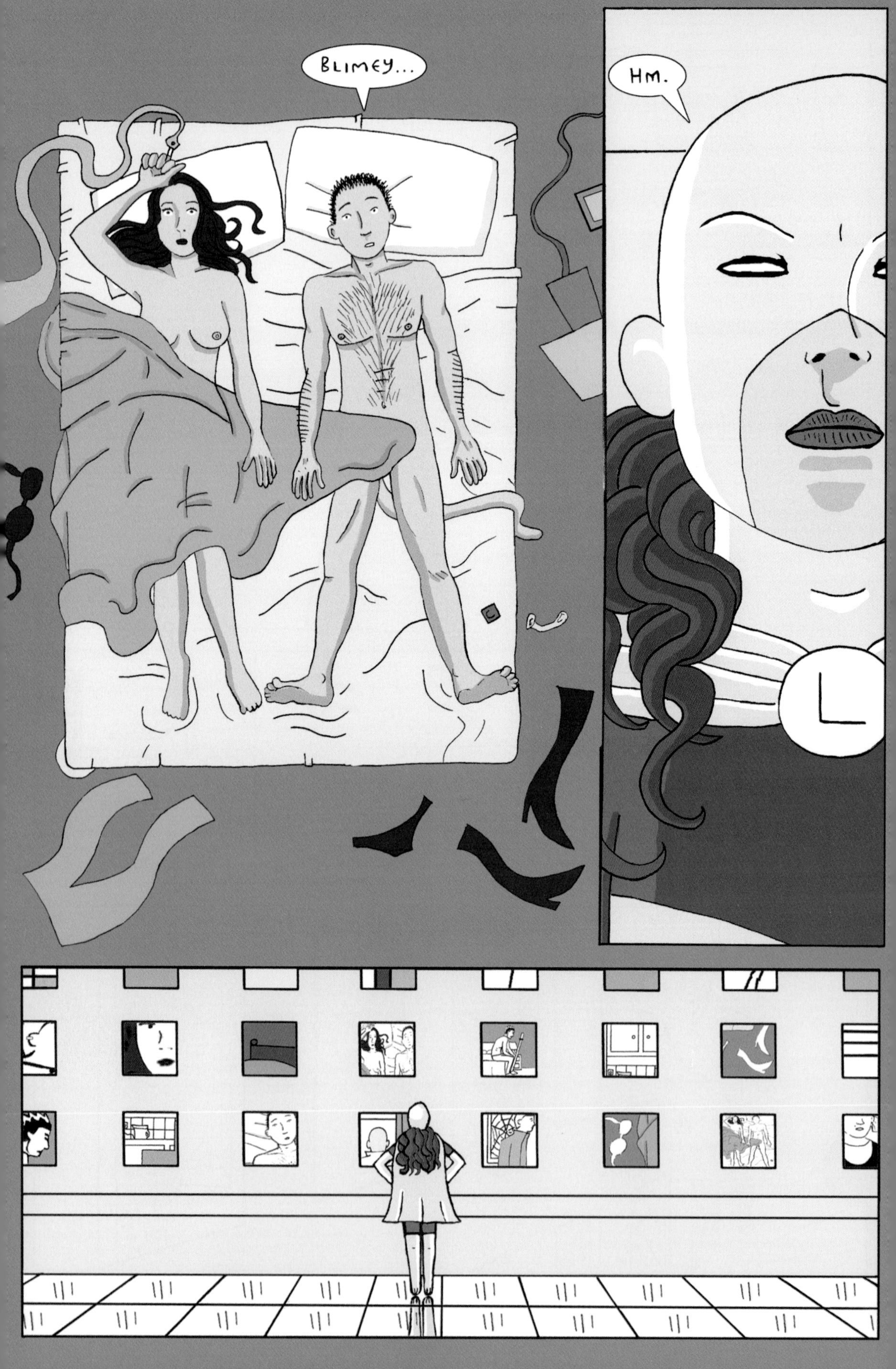
BLIMEY...
HM.

CHAPTER THREE

"...IF YOU WERE THE LAST PERSON ON EARTH"

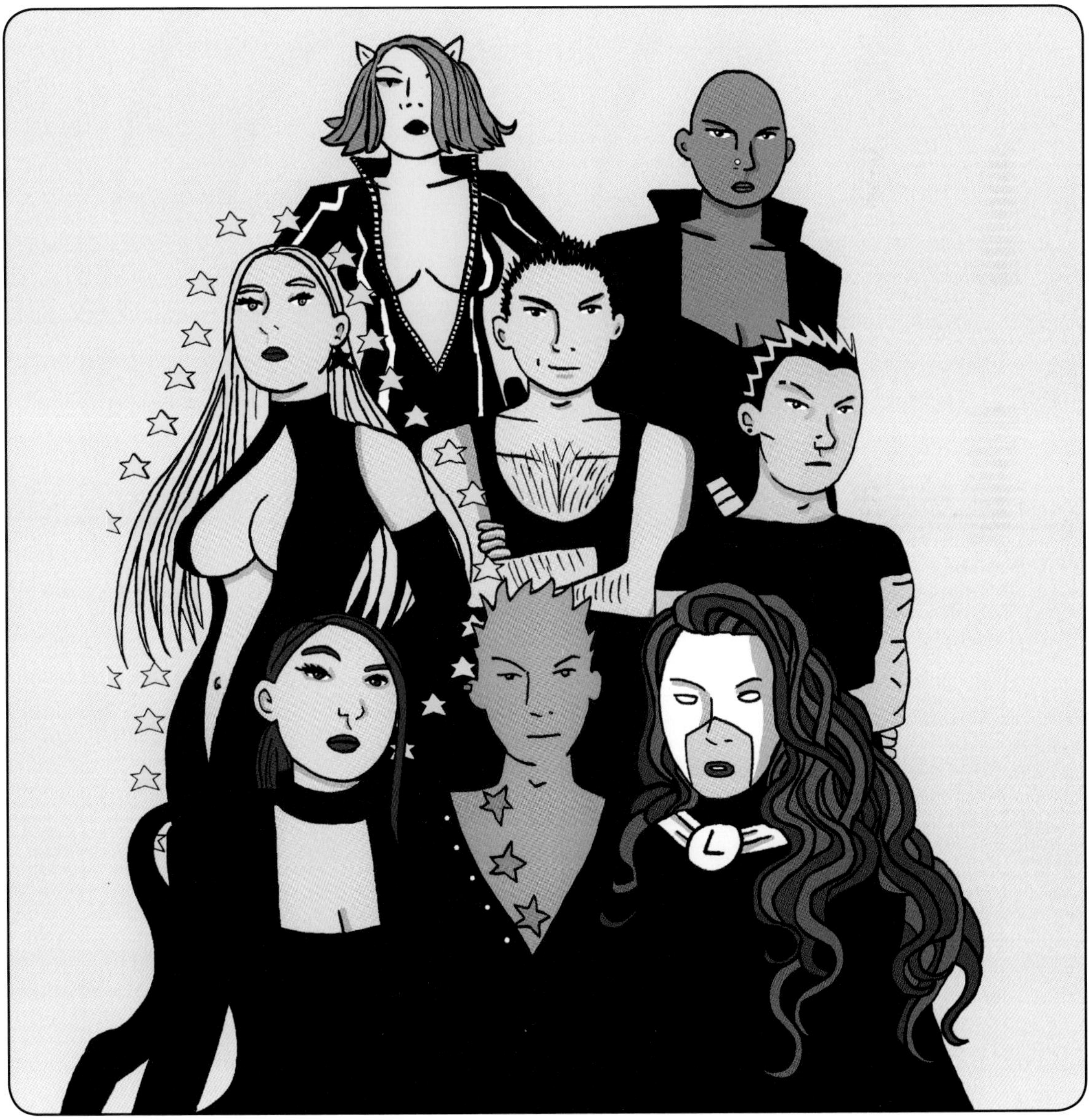

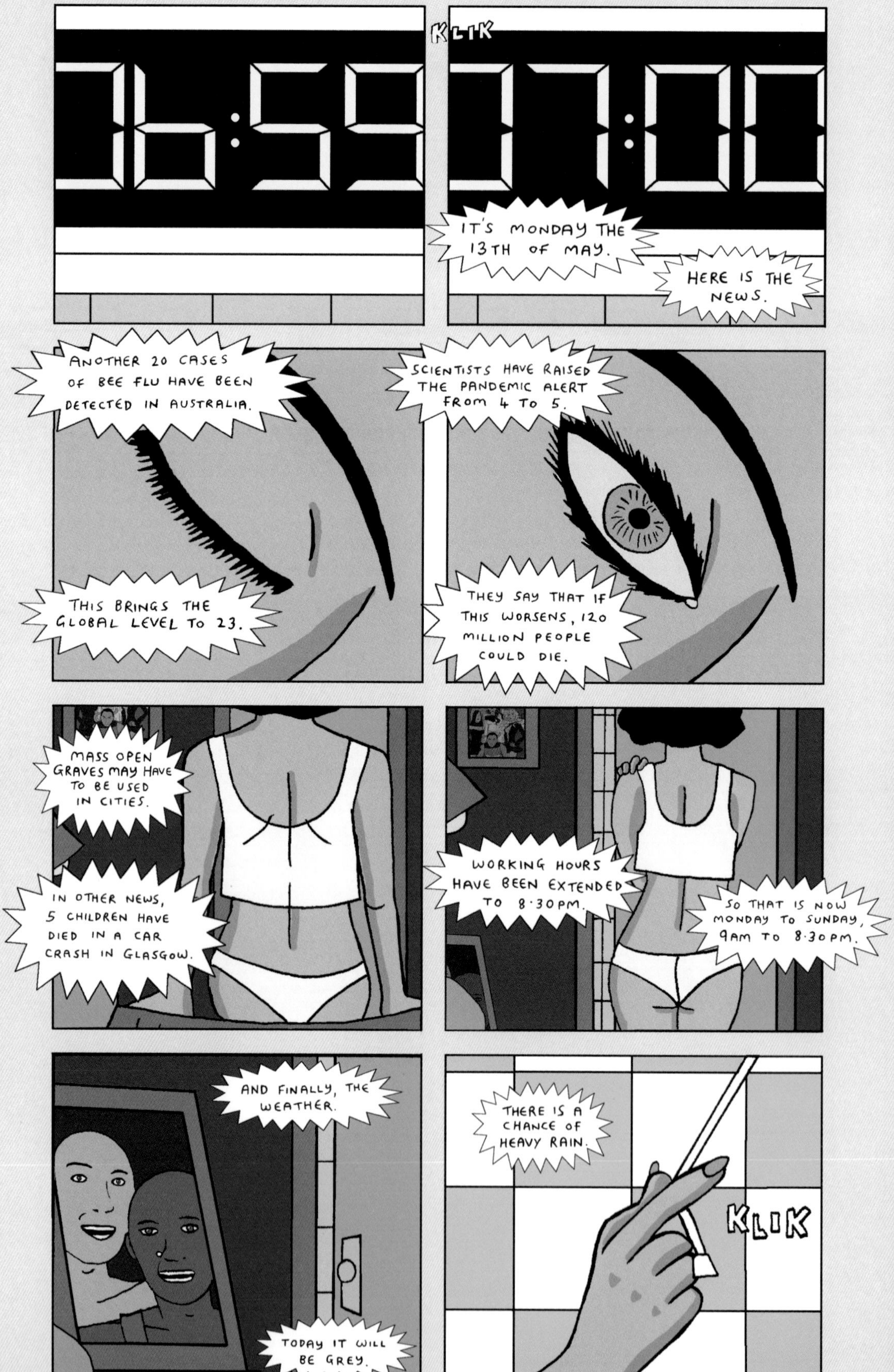
16:59
KLIK
17:00
IT'S MONDAY THE 13TH OF MAY.
HERE IS THE NEWS.
ANOTHER 20 CASES OF BEE FLU HAVE BEEN DETECTED IN AUSTRALIA.
THIS BRINGS THE GLOBAL LEVEL TO 23.
SCIENTISTS HAVE RAISED THE PANDEMIC ALERT FROM 4 TO 5.
THEY SAY THAT IF THIS WORSENS, 120 MILLION PEOPLE COULD DIE.
MASS OPEN GRAVES MAY HAVE TO BE USED IN CITIES.
IN OTHER NEWS, 5 CHILDREN HAVE DIED IN A CAR CRASH IN GLASGOW.
WORKING HOURS HAVE BEEN EXTENDED TO 8·30PM.
SO THAT IS NOW MONDAY TO SUNDAY, 9AM TO 8·30PM.
AND FINALLY, THE WEATHER.
TODAY IT WILL BE GREY.
THERE IS A CHANCE OF HEAVY RAIN.
KLIK

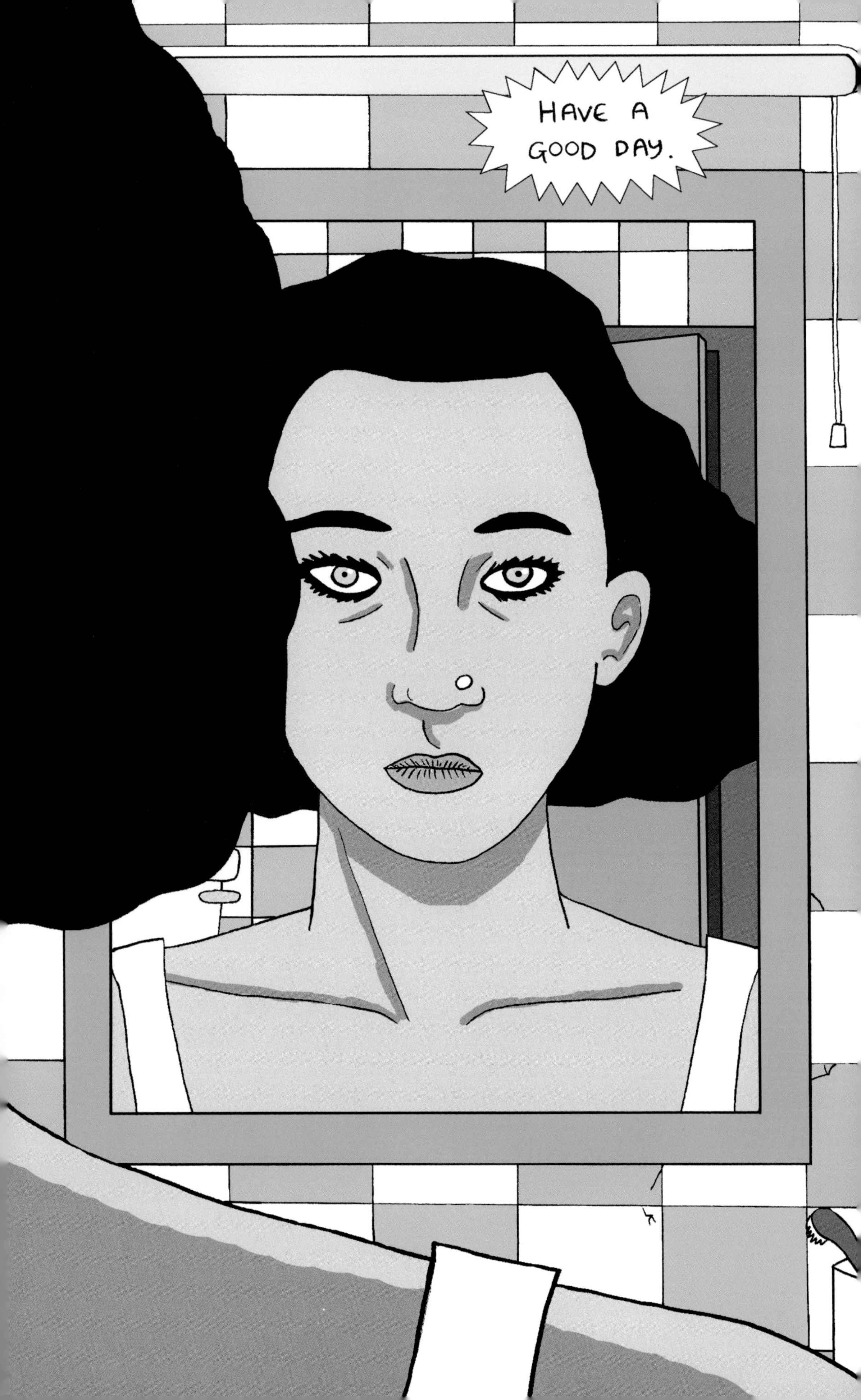
HAVE A GOOD DAY.

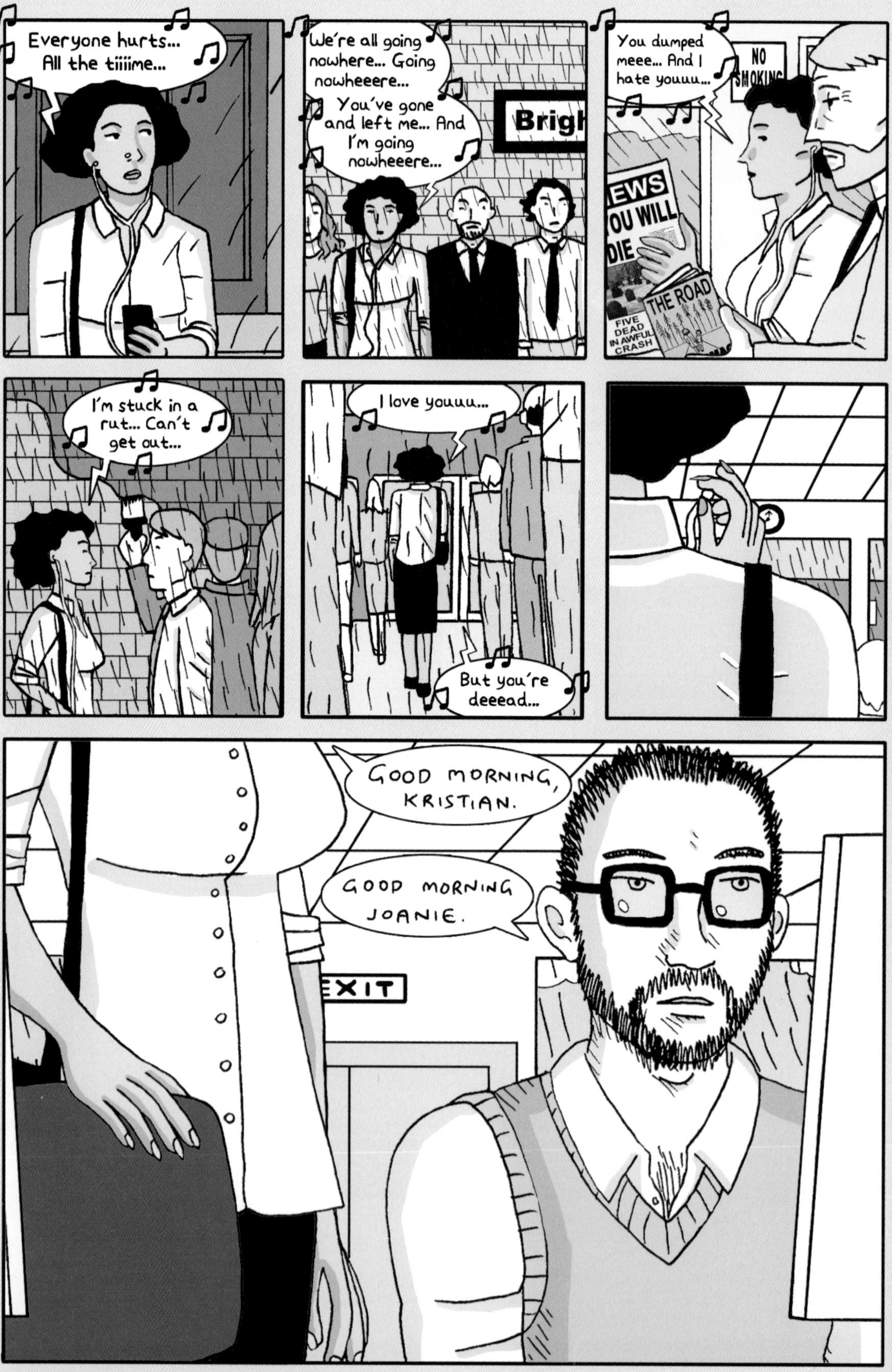
Everyone hurts... All the tiiiime...
We're all going nowhere... Going nowheeere...
You've gone and left me... And I'm going nowheeere...
Brigh
You dumped meee... And I hate youuu...
NO SMOKING
NEWS
YOU WILL DIE
FIVE DEAD IN AWFUL CRASH
THE ROAD
I'm stuck in a rut... Can't get out...
I love youuu...
But you're deeead...
GOOD MORNING, KRISTIAN.
GOOD MORNING JOANIE.
EXIT

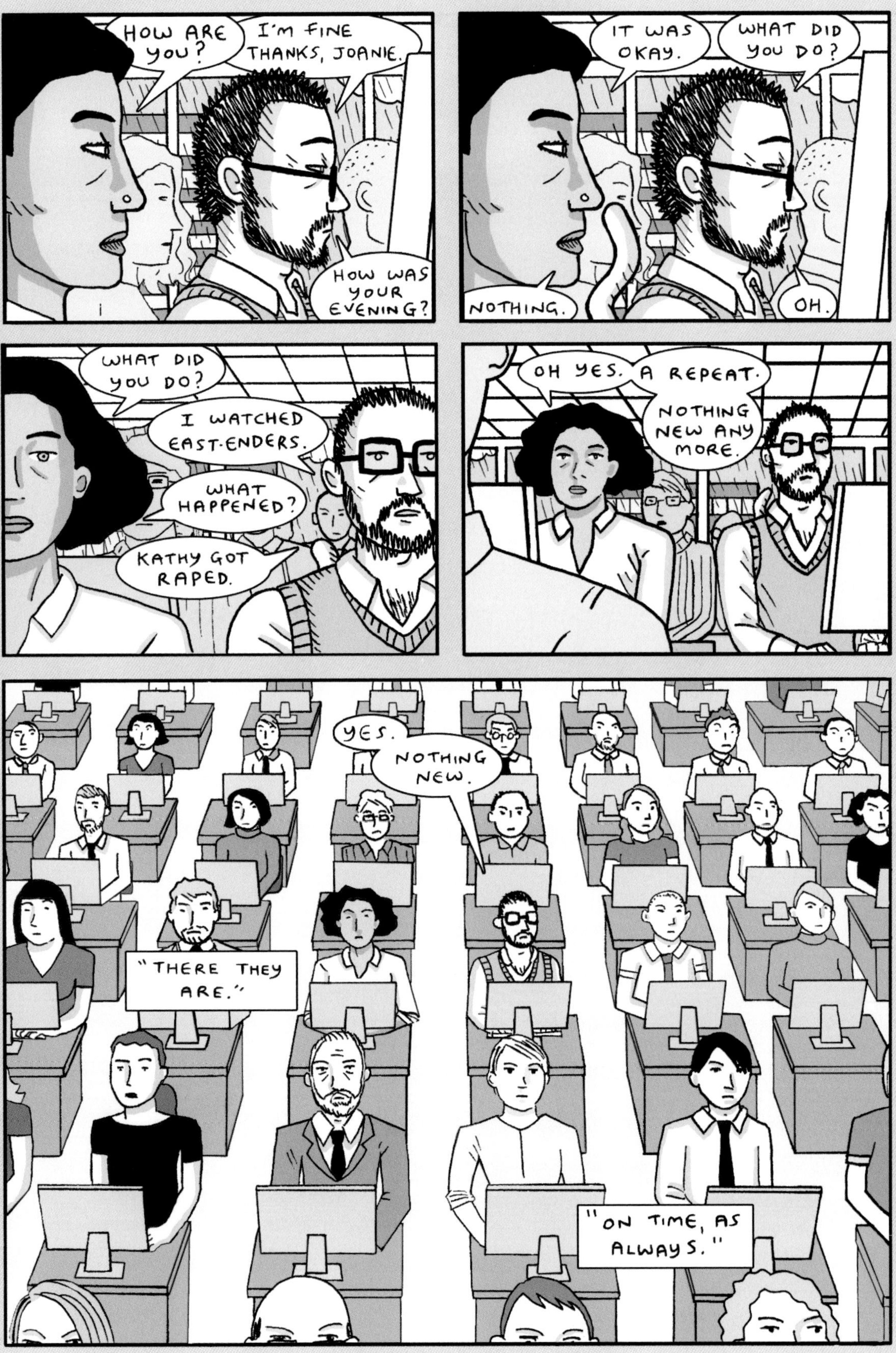
HOW ARE YOU?
I'M FINE THANKS, JOANIE.
HOW WAS YOUR EVENING?
IT WAS OKAY.
WHAT DID YOU DO?
NOTHING.
OH.
WHAT DID YOU DO?
I WATCHED EAST-ENDERS.
WHAT HAPPENED?
KATHY GOT RAPED.
OH YES.
A REPEAT.
NOTHING NEW ANY MORE.
YES.
NOTHING NEW.
"THERE THEY ARE."
"ON TIME, AS ALWAYS."

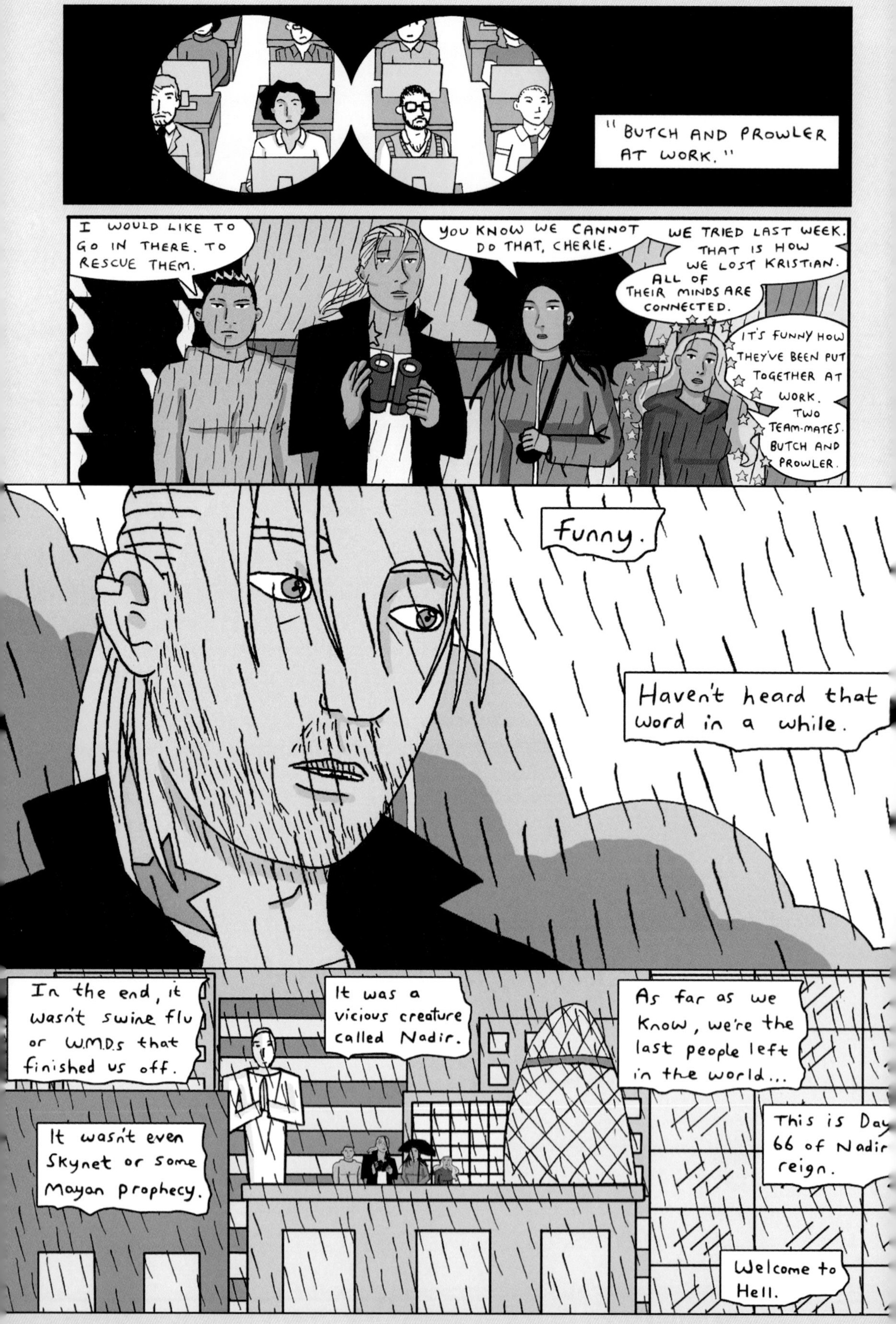
"BUTCH AND PROWLER AT WORK."
I WOULD LIKE TO GO IN THERE. TO RESCUE THEM.
YOU KNOW WE CANNOT DO THAT, CHERIE.
WE TRIED LAST WEEK. THAT IS HOW WE LOST KRISTIAN.
ALL OF THEIR MINDS ARE CONNECTED.
IT'S FUNNY HOW THEY'VE BEEN PUT TOGETHER AT WORK. TWO TEAM-MATES. BUTCH AND PROWLER.
Funny.
Haven't heard that word in a while.
In the end, it wasn't swine flu or W.M.D.s that finished us off.
It was a vicious creature called Nadir.
As far as we know, we're the last people left in the world...
It wasn't even Skynet or some Mayan prophecy.
This is Day 66 of Nadir reign.
Welcome to Hell.

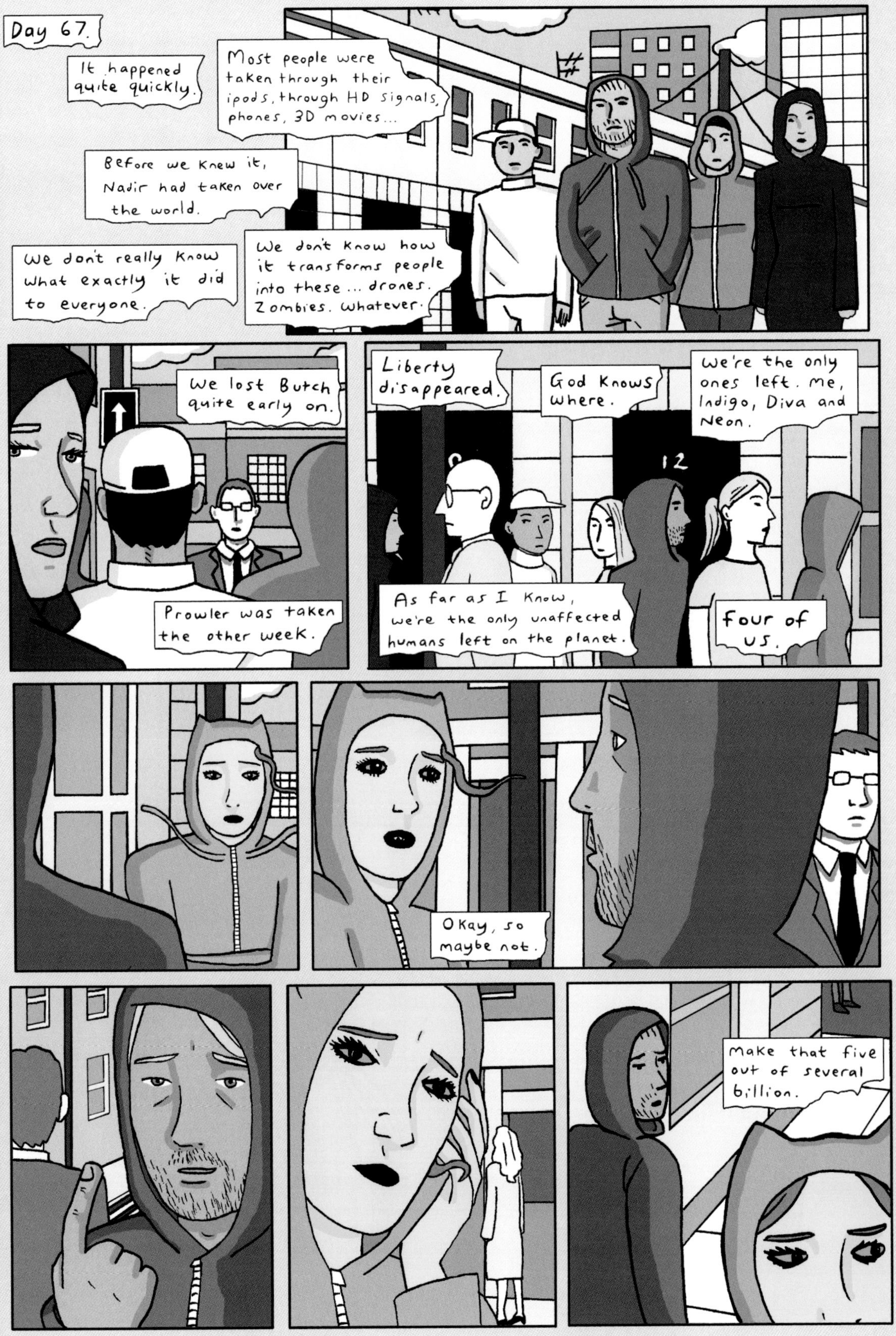
Day 67.
It happened quite quickly.
Most people were taken through their ipods, through HD signals, phones, 3D movies...
Before we knew it, Nadir had taken over the world.
We don't really know what exactly it did to everyone.
We don't know how it transforms people into these... drones. Zombies. Whatever.
We lost Butch quite early on.
Prowler was taken the other week.
Liberty disappeared.
God knows where.
We're the only ones left. me, Indigo, Diva and Neon.
12
As far as I know, we're the only unaffected humans left on the planet.
Four of us.
Okay, so maybe not.
Make that five out of several billion.

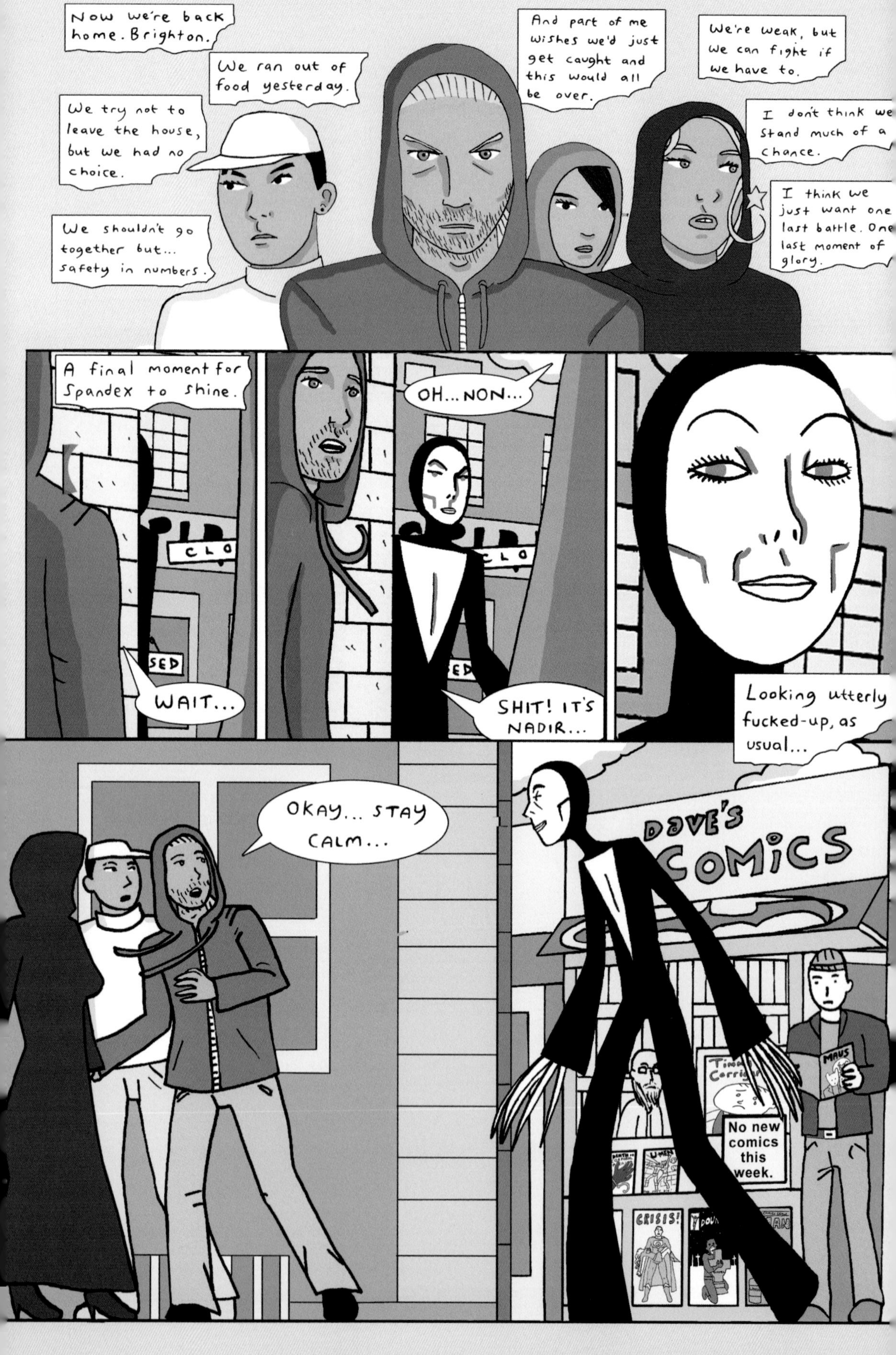

Now we're back home. Brighton.
We ran out of food yesterday.
We try not to leave the house, but we had no choice.
We shouldn't go together but... safety in numbers.
And part of me wishes we'd just get caught and this would all be over.
We're weak, but we can fight if we have to.
I don't think we stand much of a chance.
I think we just want one last battle. One last moment of glory.
A final moment for Spandex to shine.
WAIT...
OH... NON...
SHIT! IT'S NADIR...
Looking utterly fucked-up, as usual...
OKAY... STAY CALM...
DAVE'S COMICS
No new comics this week.
MAUS
CRISIS!

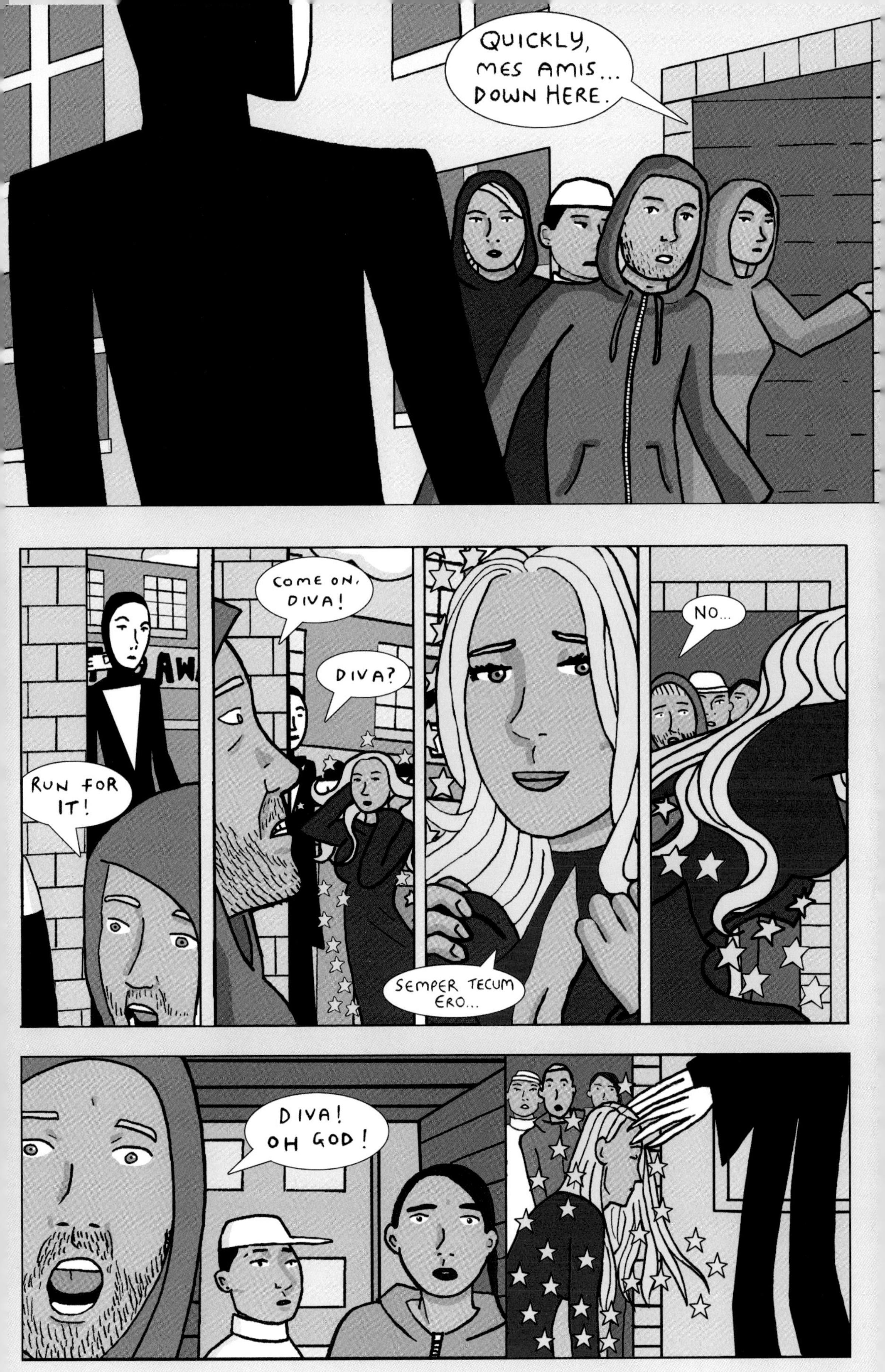
QUICKLY, MES AMIS... DOWN HERE.
RUN FOR IT!
COME ON, DIVA!
DIVA?
SEMPER TECUM ERO...
NO...
DIVA! OH GOD!

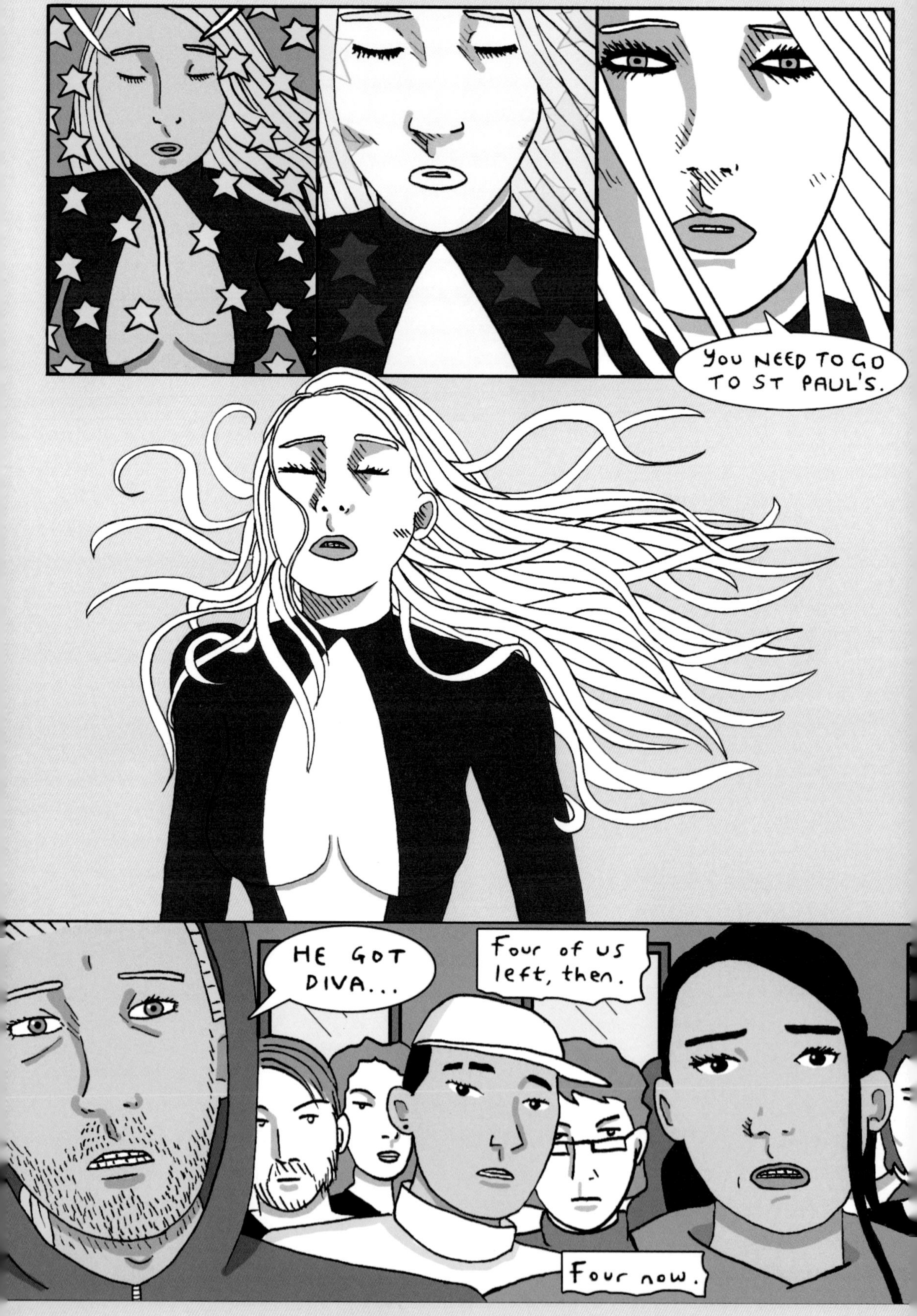
YOU NEED TO GO TO ST PAUL'S.
HE GOT DIVA...
Four of us left, then.
Four now.

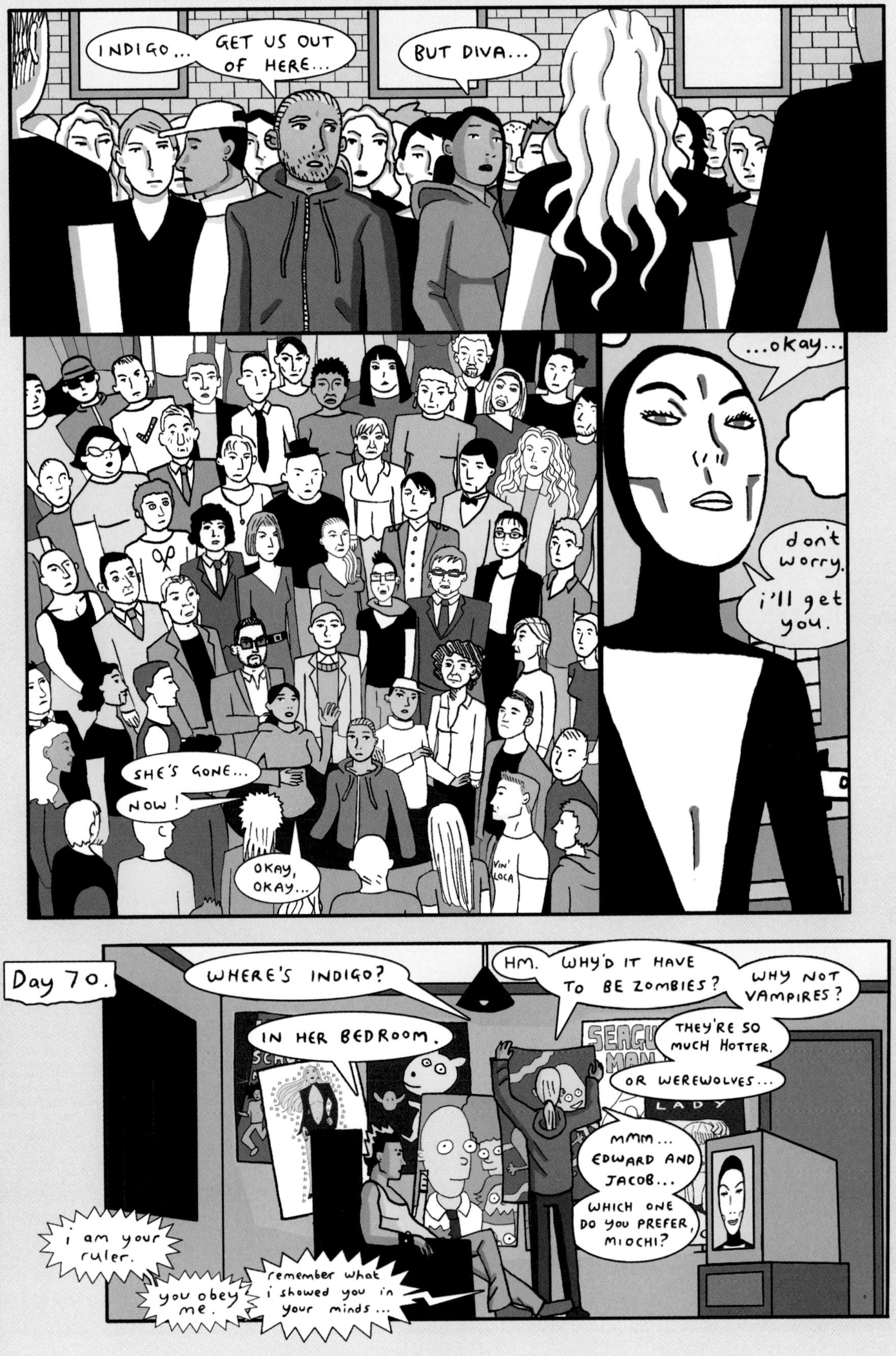
INDIGO...
GET US OUT OF HERE...
BUT DIVA...
...okay...
don't worry.
i'll get you.
SHE'S GONE...
NOW!
OKAY, OKAY...
VIN' LOCA
Day 70.
WHERE'S INDIGO?
IN HER BEDROOM.
HM.
WHY'D IT HAVE TO BE ZOMBIES?
WHY NOT VAMPIRES?
THEY'RE SO MUCH HOTTER.
OR WEREWOLVES...
MMM... EDWARD AND JACOB...
WHICH ONE DO YOU PREFER, MIOCHI?
SEAGU MAN
LADY
i am your ruler.
you obey me.
remember what i showed you in your minds...

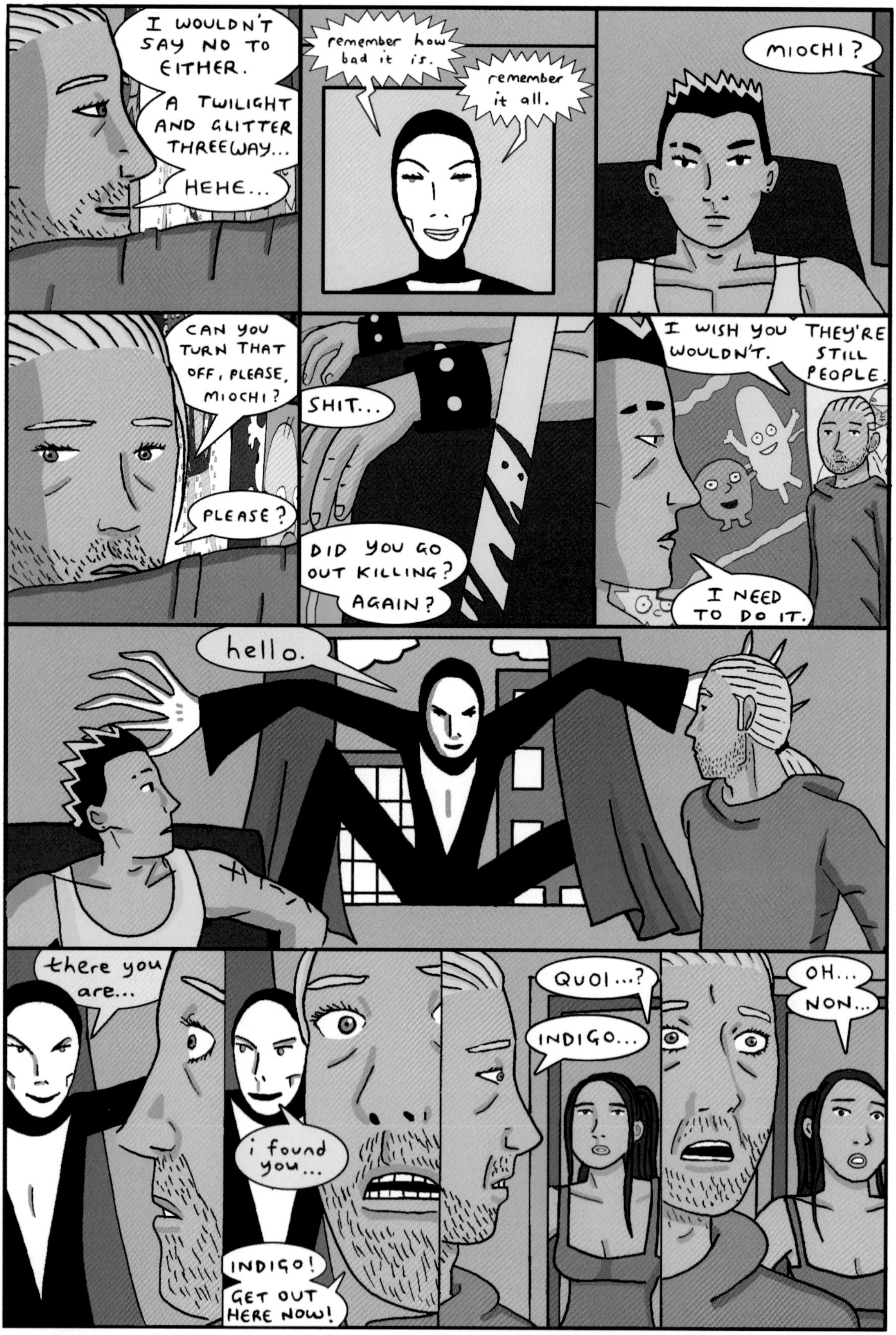
I WOULDN'T SAY NO TO EITHER.
A TWILIGHT AND GLITTER THREEWAY...
HEHE...
remember how bad it is.
remember it all.
MIOCHI?
CAN YOU TURN THAT OFF, PLEASE, MIOCHI?
PLEASE?
SHIT...
DID YOU GO OUT KILLING? AGAIN?
I WISH YOU WOULDN'T.
THEY'RE STILL PEOPLE.
I NEED TO DO IT.
hello.
there you are...
i found you...
INDIGO! GET OUT HERE NOW!
QUOI...?
INDIGO...
OH... NON...

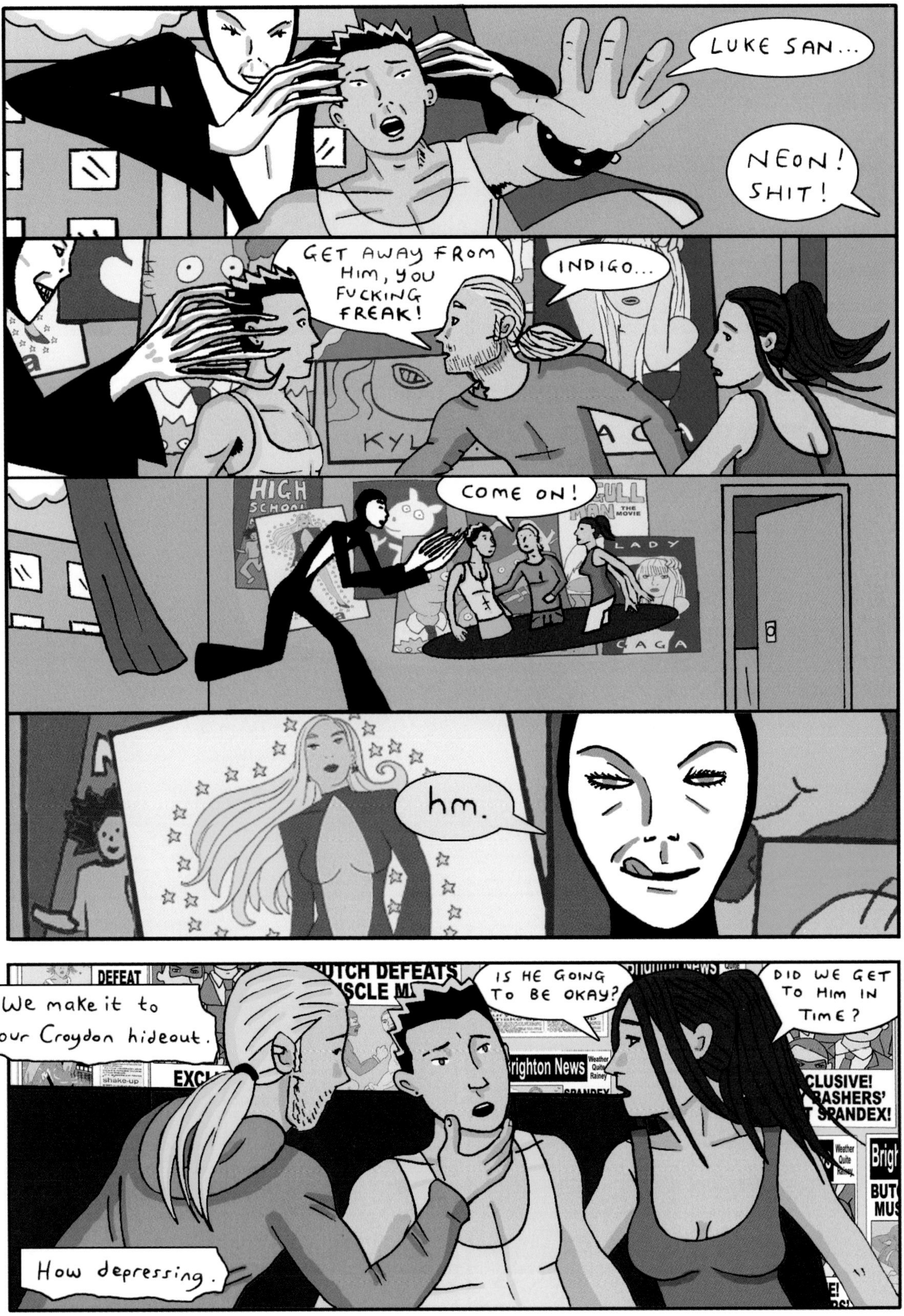
LUKE SAN...
NEON! SHIT!
GET AWAY FROM HIM, YOU FUCKING FREAK!
INDIGO...
COME ON!
hm.
We make it to our Croydon hideout.
IS HE GOING TO BE OKAY?
DID WE GET TO HIM IN TIME?
How depressing.

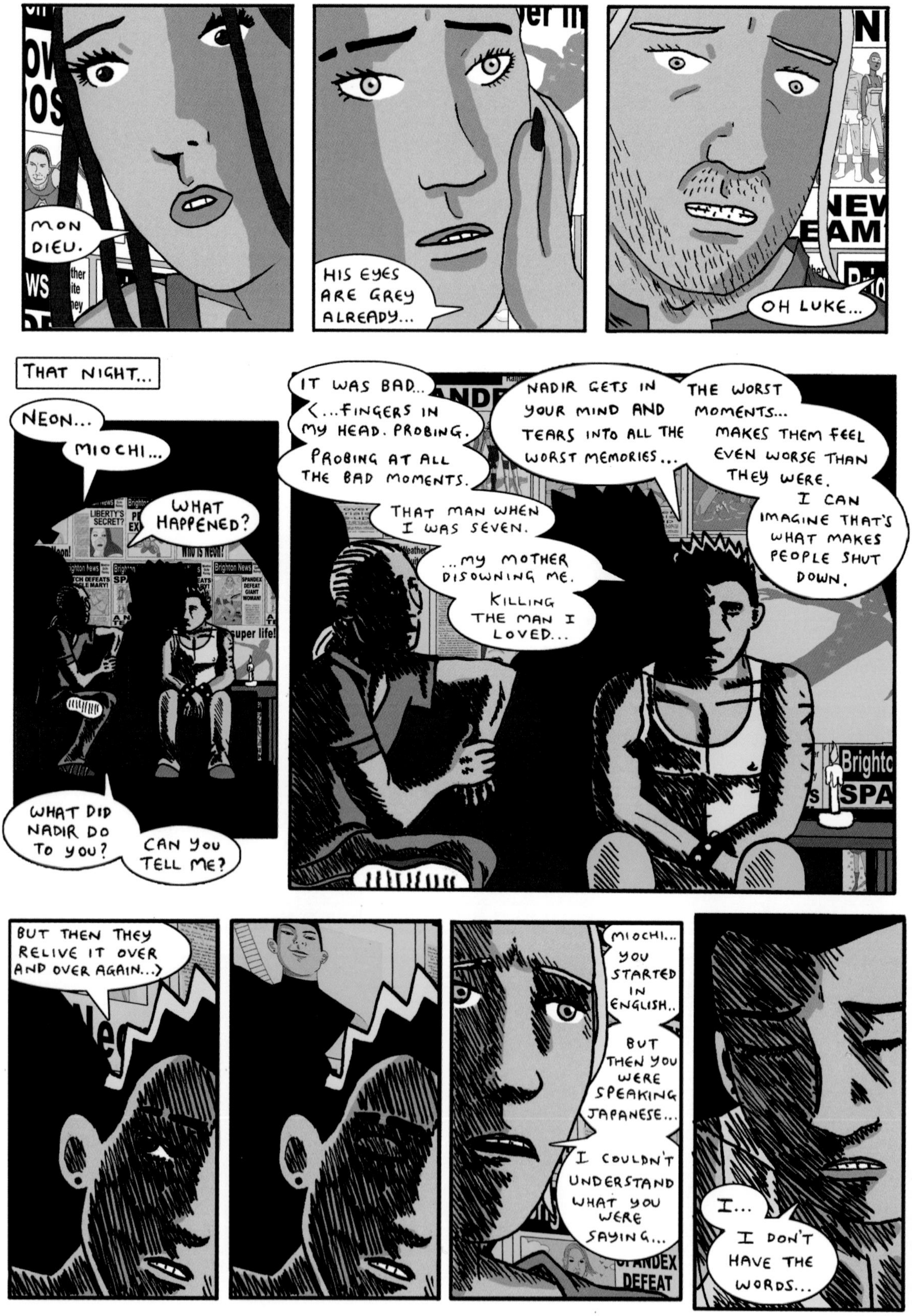
MON DIEU.
HIS EYES ARE GREY ALREADY...
OH LUKE...
THAT NIGHT...
NEON...
MIOCHI...
WHAT HAPPENED?
WHAT DID NADIR DO TO YOU?
CAN YOU TELL ME?
IT WAS BAD...
<...FINGERS IN MY HEAD. PROBING.
PROBING AT ALL THE BAD MOMENTS.
THAT MAN WHEN I WAS SEVEN.
...MY MOTHER DISOWNING ME.
KILLING THE MAN I LOVED...
NADIR GETS IN YOUR MIND AND TEARS INTO ALL THE WORST MEMORIES...
THE WORST MOMENTS...
MAKES THEM FEEL EVEN WORSE THAN THEY WERE.
I CAN IMAGINE THAT'S WHAT MAKES PEOPLE SHUT DOWN.
BUT THEN THEY RELIVE IT OVER AND OVER AGAIN...>
MIOCHI... YOU STARTED IN ENGLISH...
BUT THEN YOU WERE SPEAKING JAPANESE...
I COULDN'T UNDERSTAND WHAT YOU WERE SAYING...
I...
I DON'T HAVE THE WORDS...

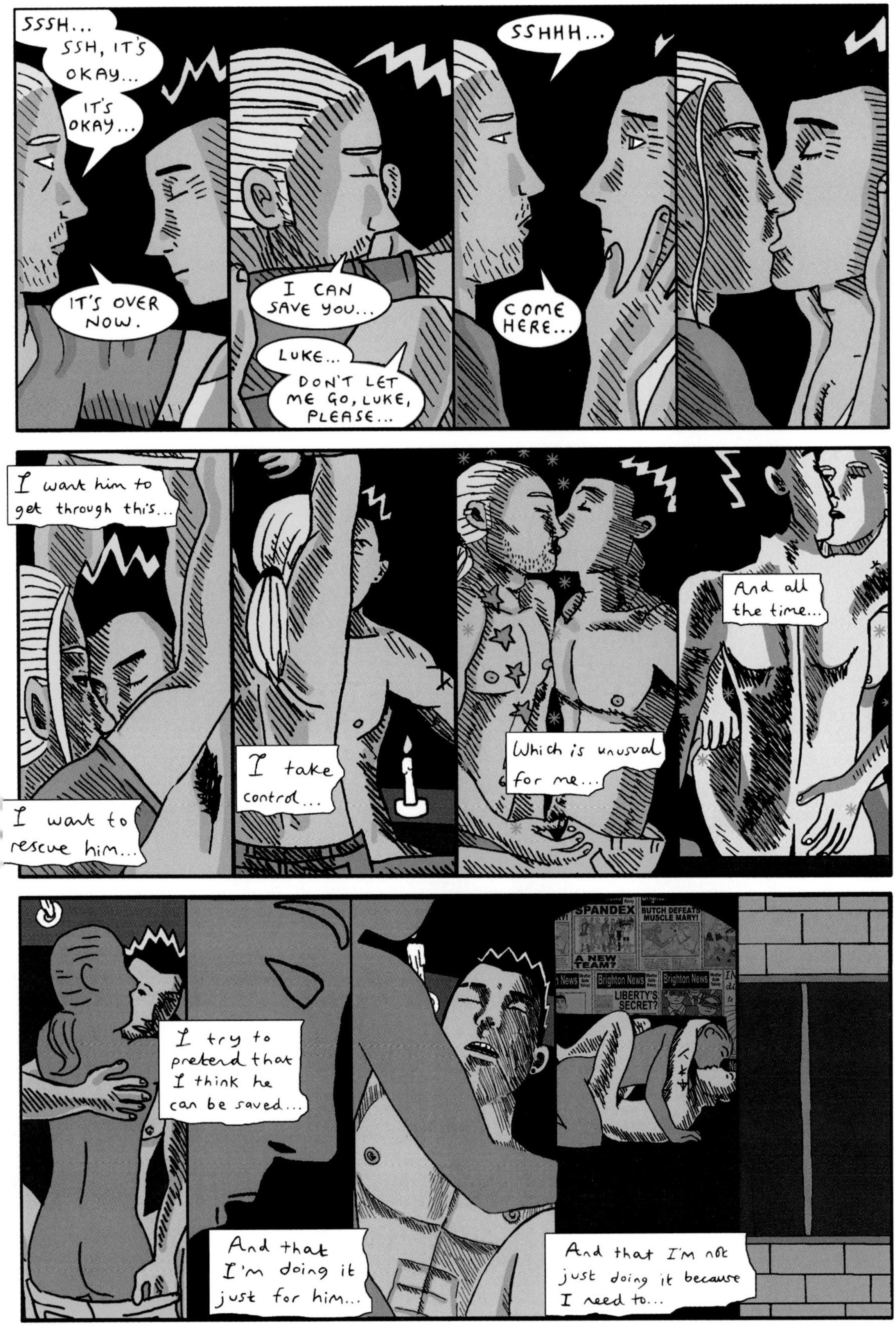
SSSH... SSH, IT'S OKAY...
IT'S OKAY...
IT'S OVER NOW.
I CAN SAVE YOU...
LUKE...
DON'T LET ME GO, LUKE, PLEASE...
SSHHH...
COME HERE...
I want him to get through this...
I want to rescue him...
I take control...
Which is unusual for me...
And all the time...
I try to pretend that I think he can be saved...
And that I'm doing it just for him...
SPANDEX
BUTCH DEFEATS MUSCLE MARY!
A NEW TEAM?
Brighton News
Brighton News
LIBERTY'S SECRET?
And that I'm not just doing it because I need to...

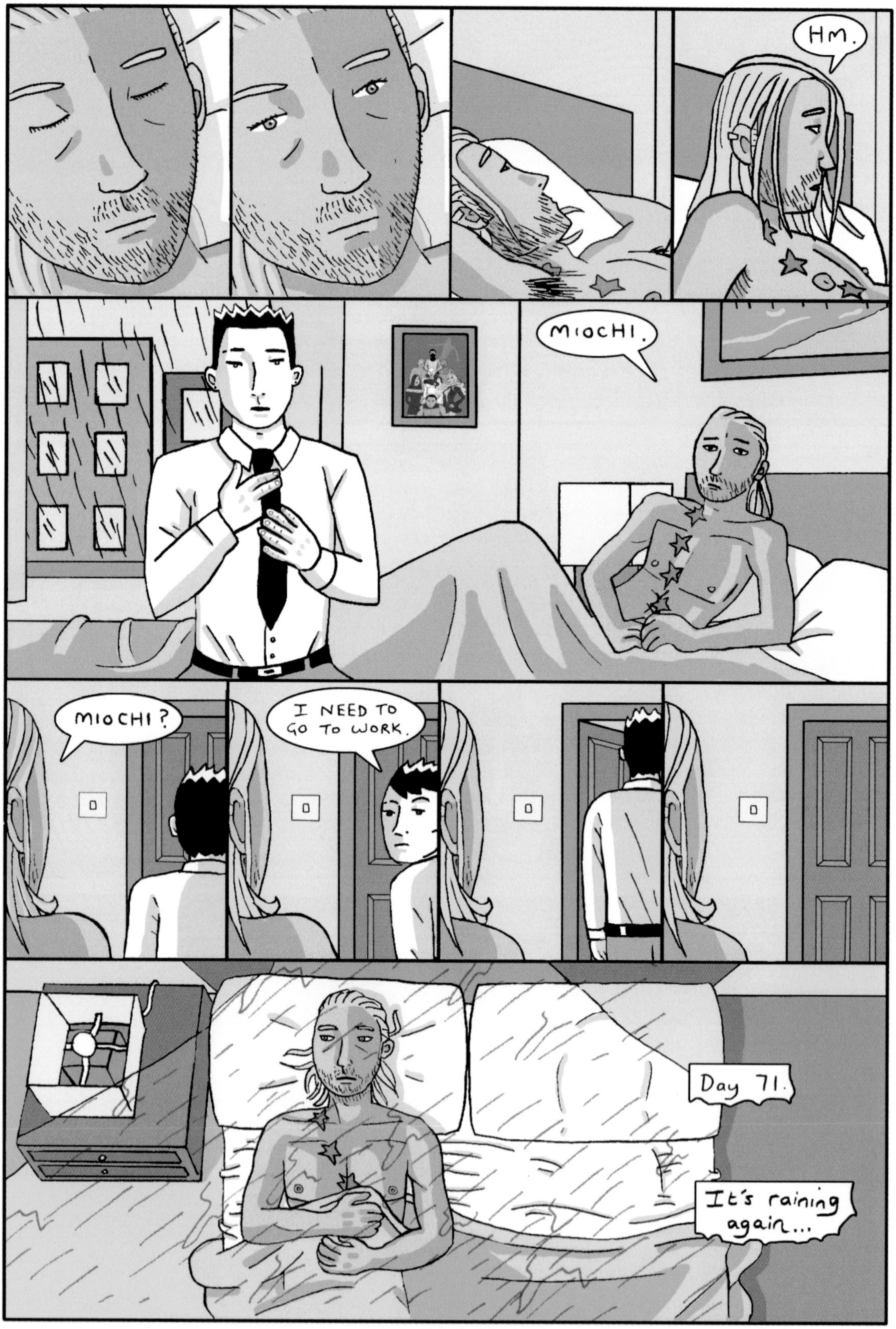
HM.
MIOCHI.
MIOCHI?
I NEED TO GO TO WORK.
Day 71.
It's raining again...

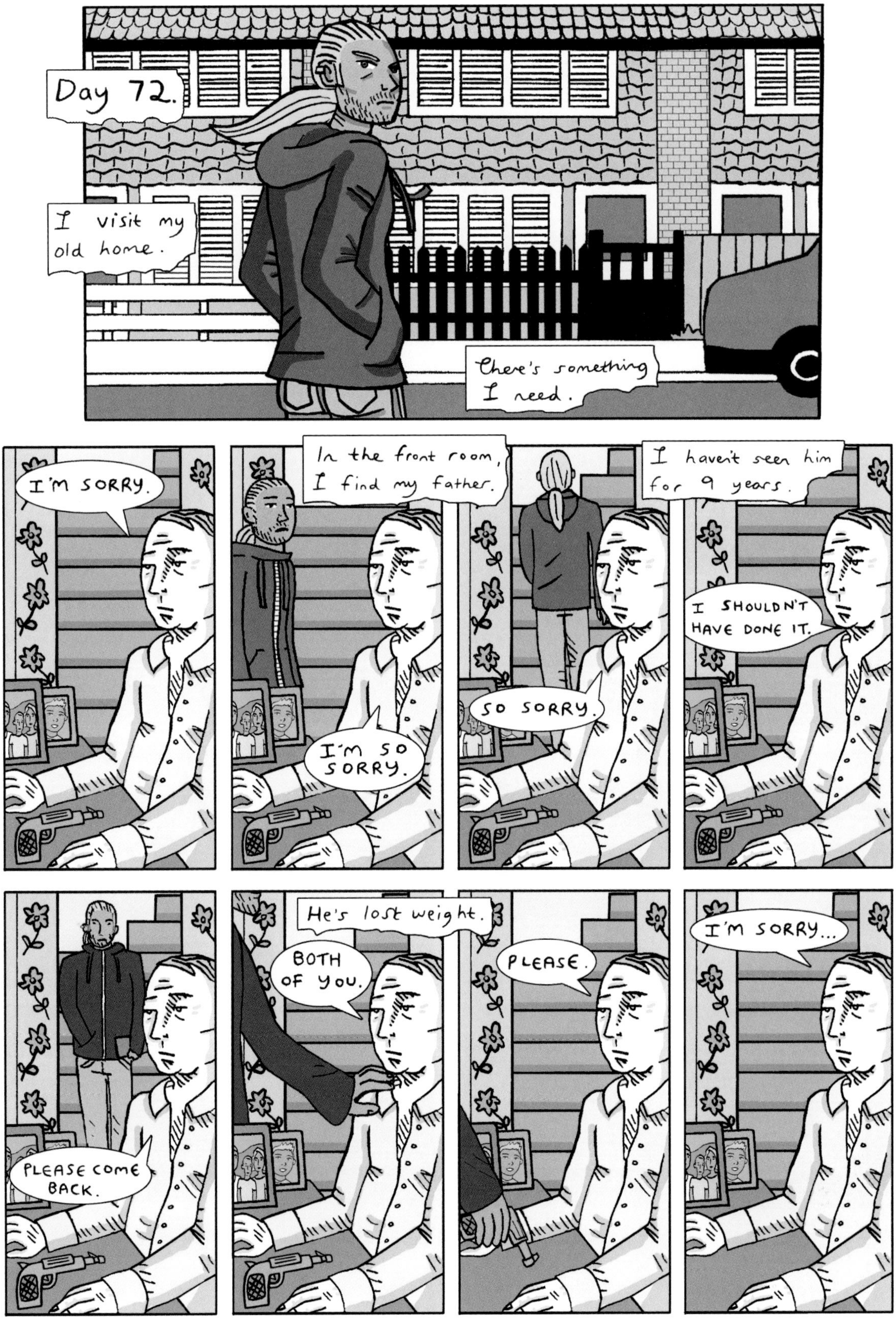
Day 72.
I visit my old home.
There's something I need.
I'M SORRY.
In the front room, I find my father.
I'M SO SORRY.
SO SORRY.
I haven't seen him for 9 years.
I SHOULDN'T HAVE DONE IT.
PLEASE COME BACK.
He's lost weight.
BOTH OF YOU.
PLEASE.
I'M SORRY...

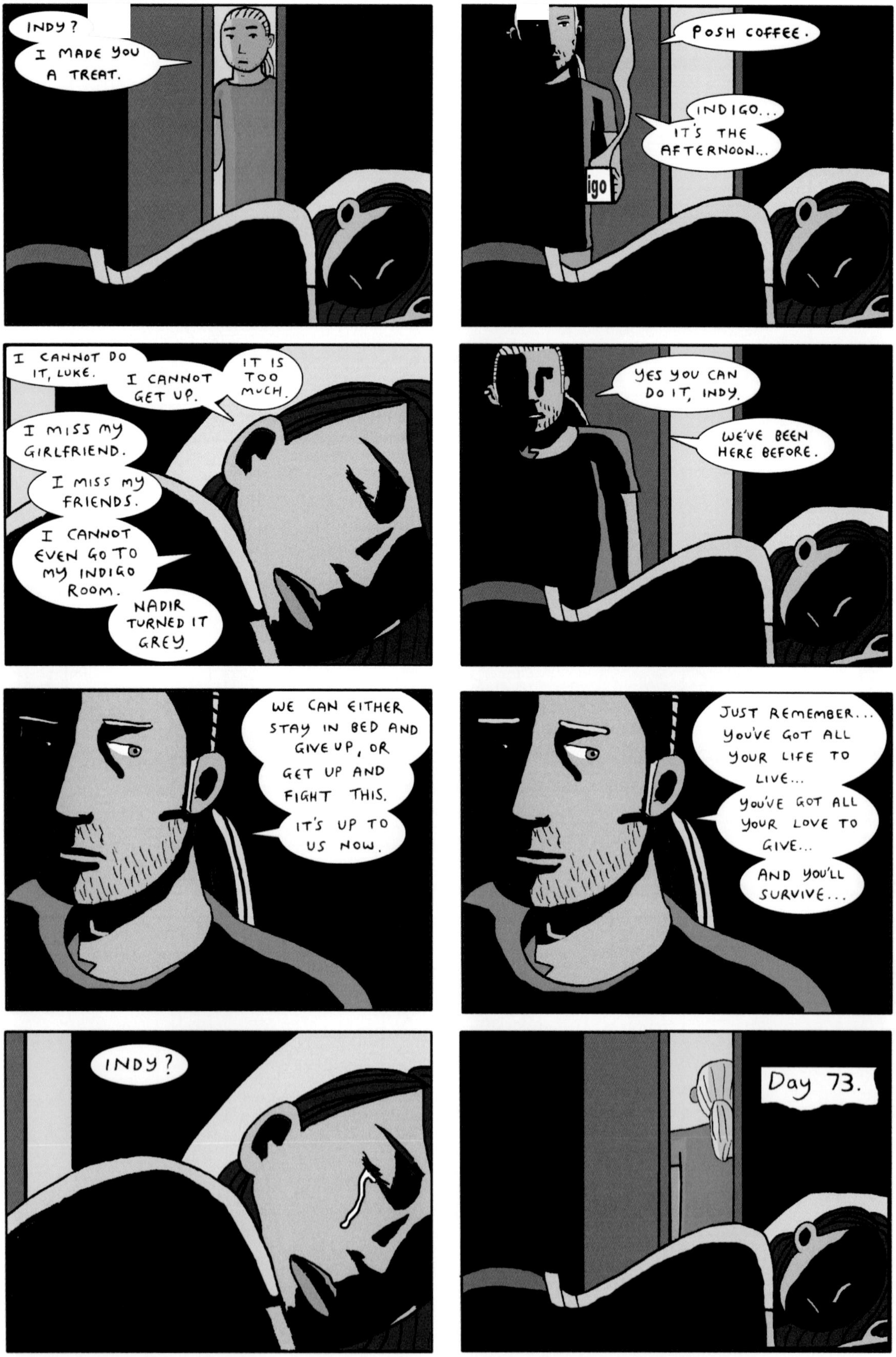
INDY?
I MADE YOU A TREAT.
POSH COFFEE.
igo
INDIGO...
IT'S THE AFTERNOON...
I CANNOT DO IT, LUKE.
I CANNOT GET UP.
IT IS TOO MUCH.
I MISS MY GIRLFRIEND.
I MISS MY FRIENDS.
I CANNOT EVEN GO TO MY INDIGO ROOM.
NADIR TURNED IT GREY.
YES YOU CAN DO IT, INDY.
WE'VE BEEN HERE BEFORE.
WE CAN EITHER STAY IN BED AND GIVE UP, OR GET UP AND FIGHT THIS.
IT'S UP TO US NOW.
JUST REMEMBER... YOU'VE GOT ALL YOUR LIFE TO LIVE...
YOU'VE GOT ALL YOUR LOVE TO GIVE...
AND YOU'LL SURVIVE...
INDY?
Day 73.

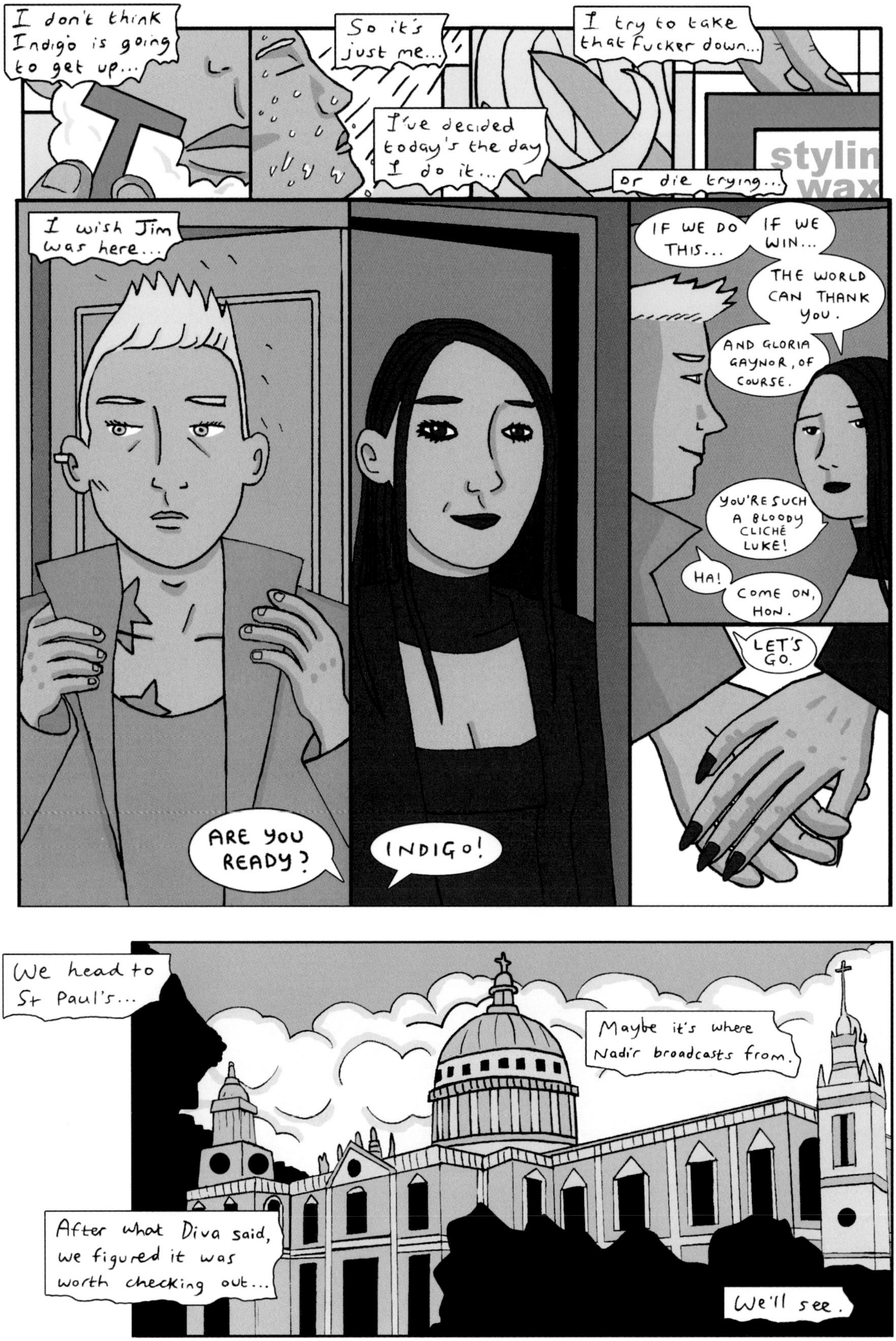
I don't think Indigo is going to get up...
So it's just me...
I've decided today's the day I do it...
I try to take that Fucker down...
or die trying...
stylin wax
I wish Jim was here...
ARE YOU READY?
INDIGO!
IF WE DO THIS...
IF WE WIN...
THE WORLD CAN THANK YOU.
AND GLORIA GAYNOR, OF COURSE.
YOU'RE SUCH A BLOODY CLICHÉ LUKE!
HA!
COME ON, HON.
LET'S GO.
We head to St Paul's...
Maybe it's where Nadir broadcasts from.
After what Diva said, we figured it was worth checking out...
We'll see.

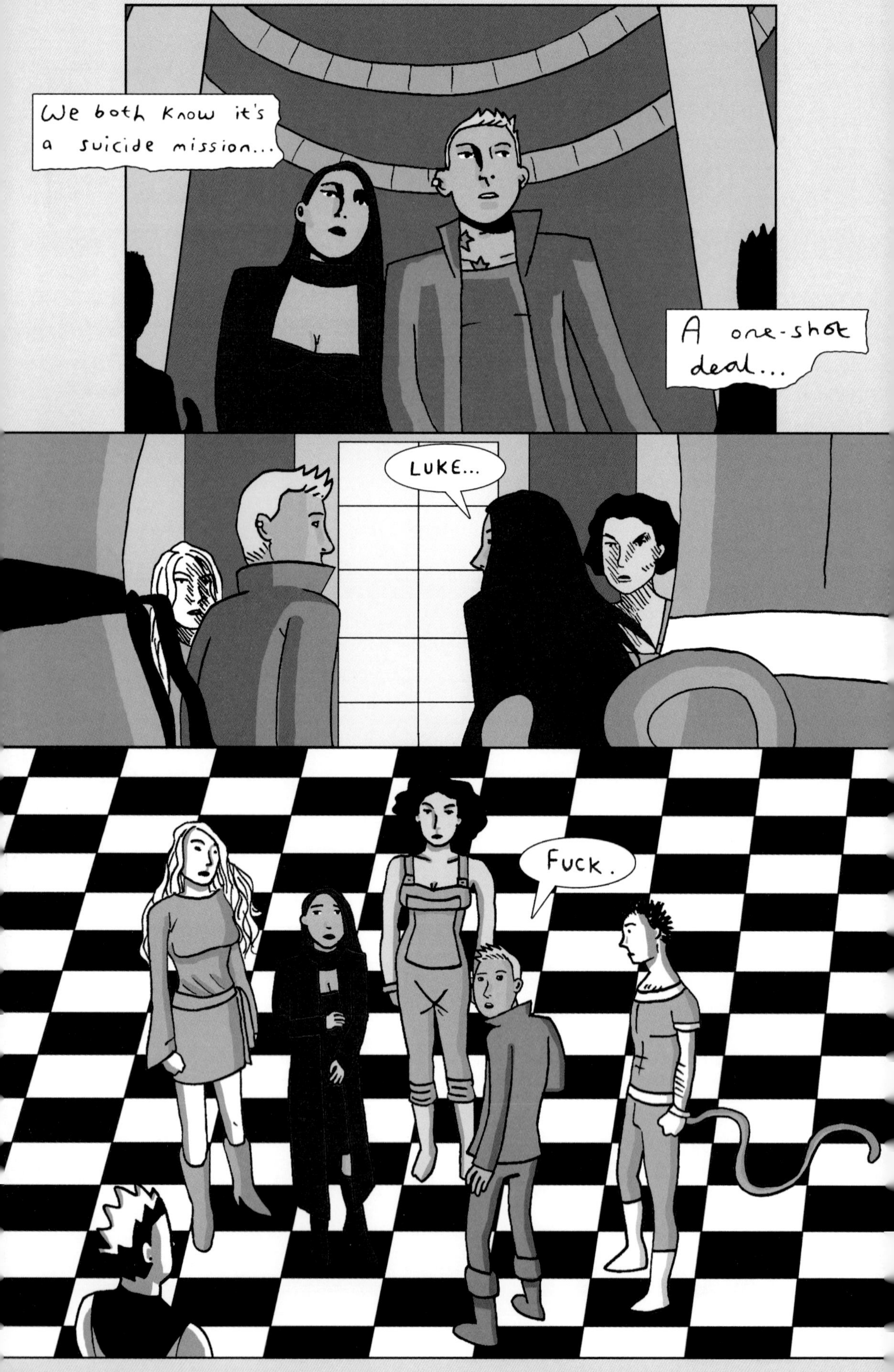
We both know it's a suicide mission...
A one-shot deal...
LUKE...
Fuck.

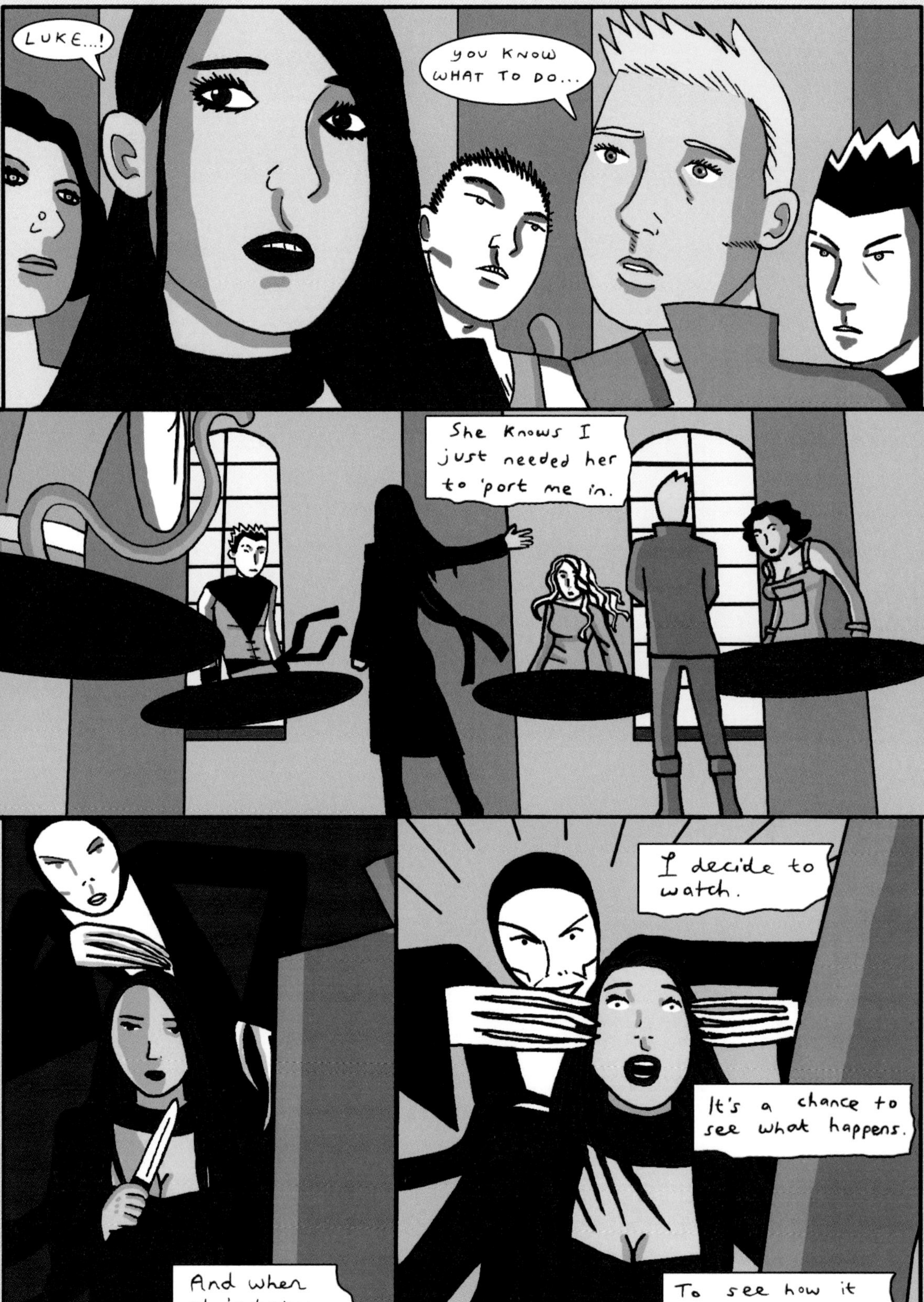
LUKE...!
YOU KNOW WHAT TO DO...
She knows I just needed her to 'port me in.
And when she's taken...
I decide to watch.
It's a chance to see what happens.
To see how it happens for myself...

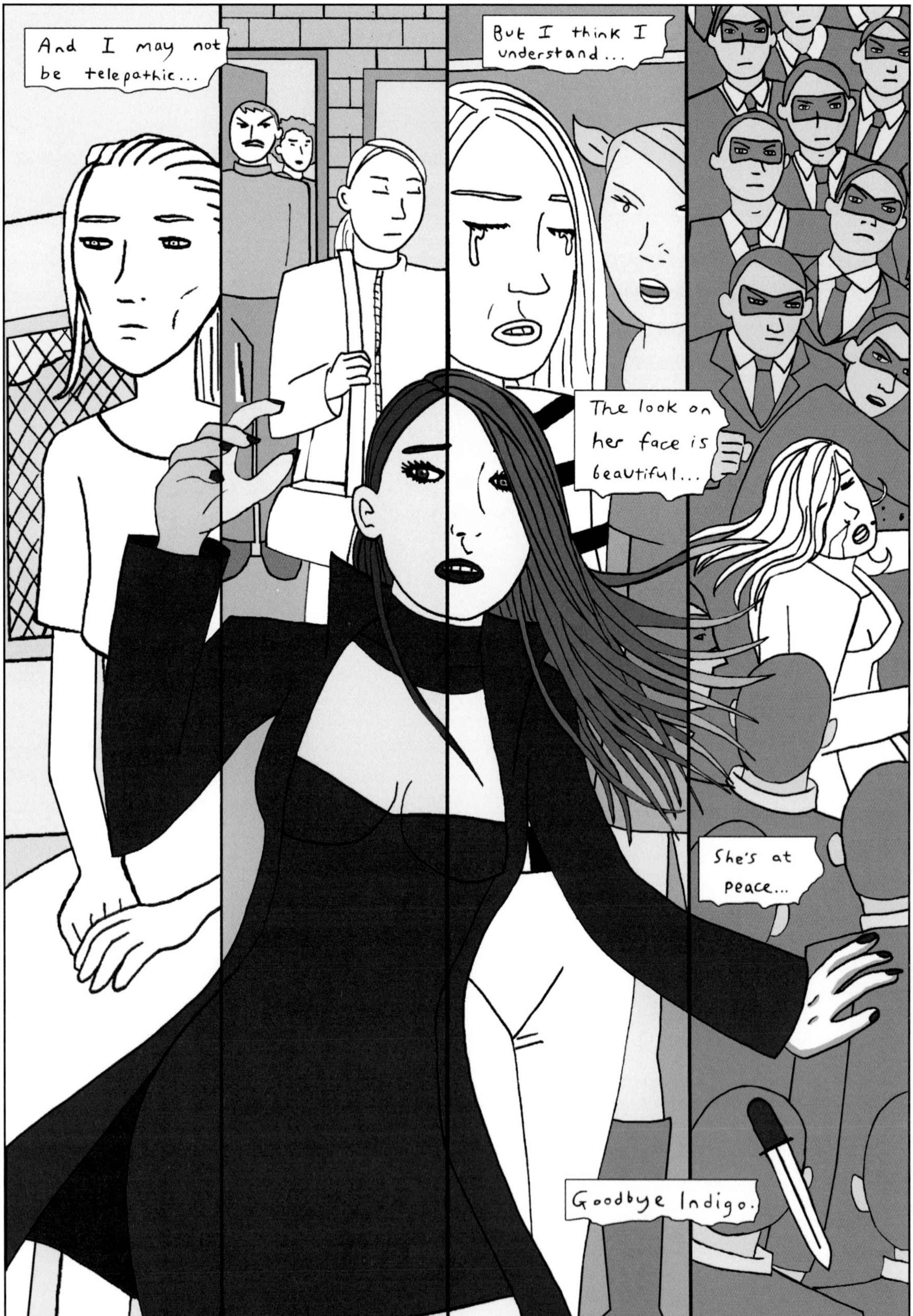

And I may not be telepathic...
But I think I understand...
The look on her face is beautiful...
She's at peace...
Goodbye Indigo.

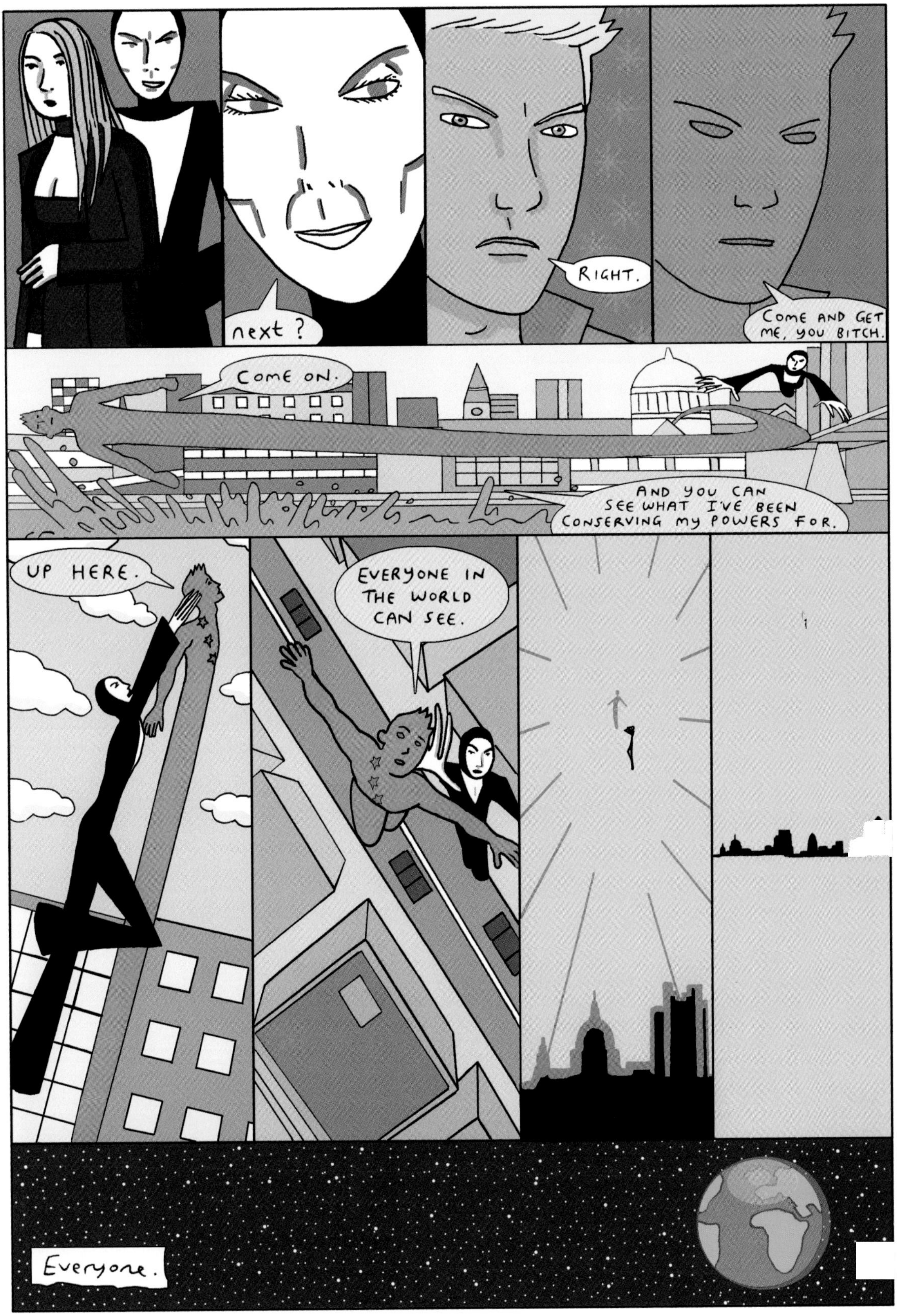
next ?
RIGHT.
COME AND GET ME, YOU BITCH.
COME ON.
AND YOU CAN SEE WHAT I'VE BEEN CONSERVING MY POWERS FOR.
UP HERE.
EVERYONE IN THE WORLD CAN SEE.
Everyone.

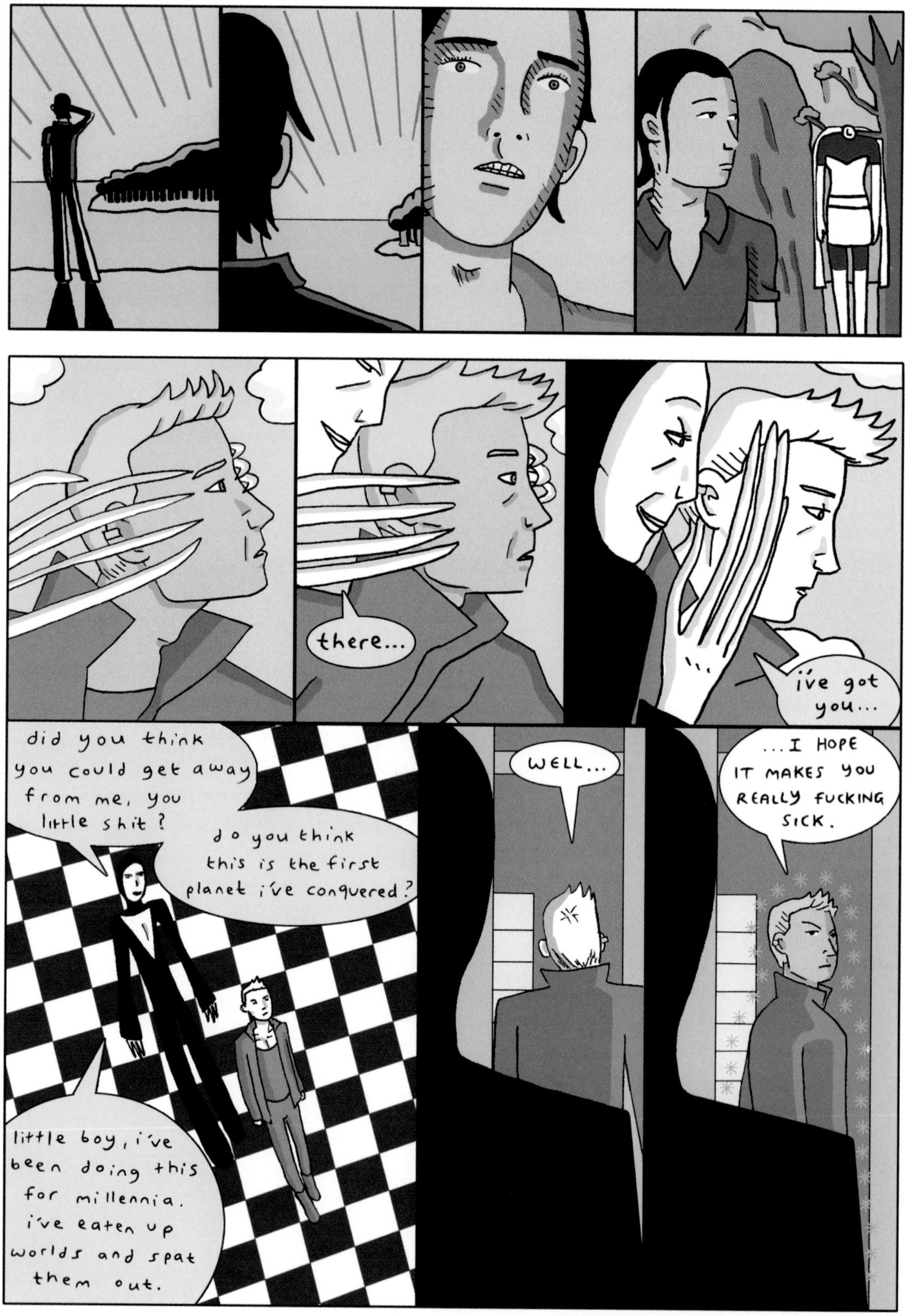
there...
i've got you...
did you think you could get away from me, you little shit?
do you think this is the first planet i've conquered?
little boy, i've been doing this for millennia. i've eaten up worlds and spat them out.
WELL...
...I HOPE IT MAKES YOU REALLY FUCKING SICK.

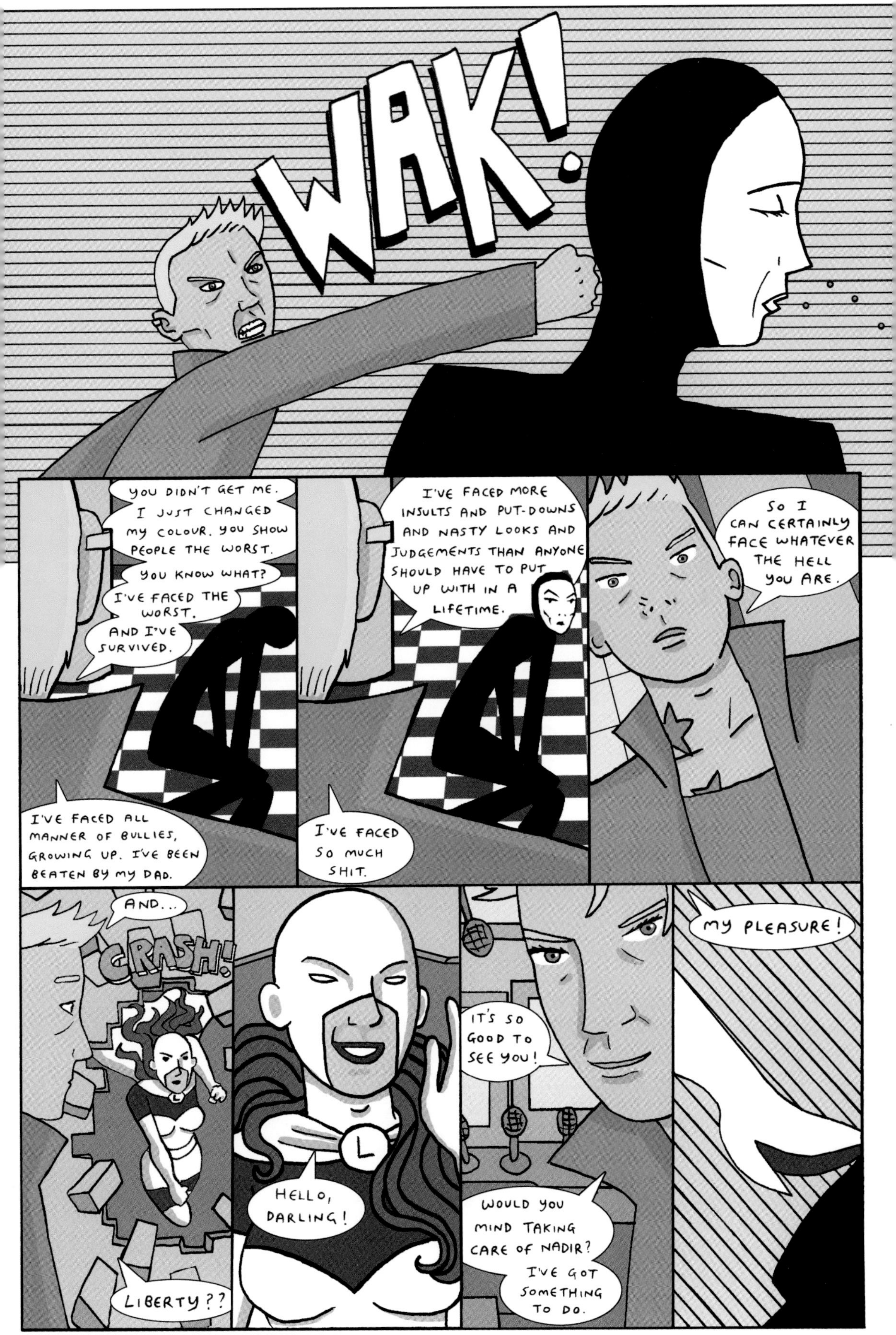
WAK!
YOU DIDN'T GET ME. I JUST CHANGED MY COLOUR. YOU SHOW PEOPLE THE WORST.
YOU KNOW WHAT?
I'VE FACED THE WORST.
AND I'VE SURVIVED.
I'VE FACED ALL MANNER OF BULLIES, GROWING UP. I'VE BEEN BEATEN BY MY DAD.
I'VE FACED MORE INSULTS AND PUT-DOWNS AND NASTY LOOKS AND JUDGEMENTS THAN ANYONE SHOULD HAVE TO PUT UP WITH IN A LIFETIME.
I'VE FACED SO MUCH SHIT.
SO I CAN CERTAINLY FACE WHATEVER THE HELL YOU ARE.
AND...
CRASH!
LIBERTY??
HELLO, DARLING!
IT'S SO GOOD TO SEE YOU!
WOULD YOU MIND TAKING CARE OF NADIR?
I'VE GOT SOMETHING TO DO.
MY PLEASURE!

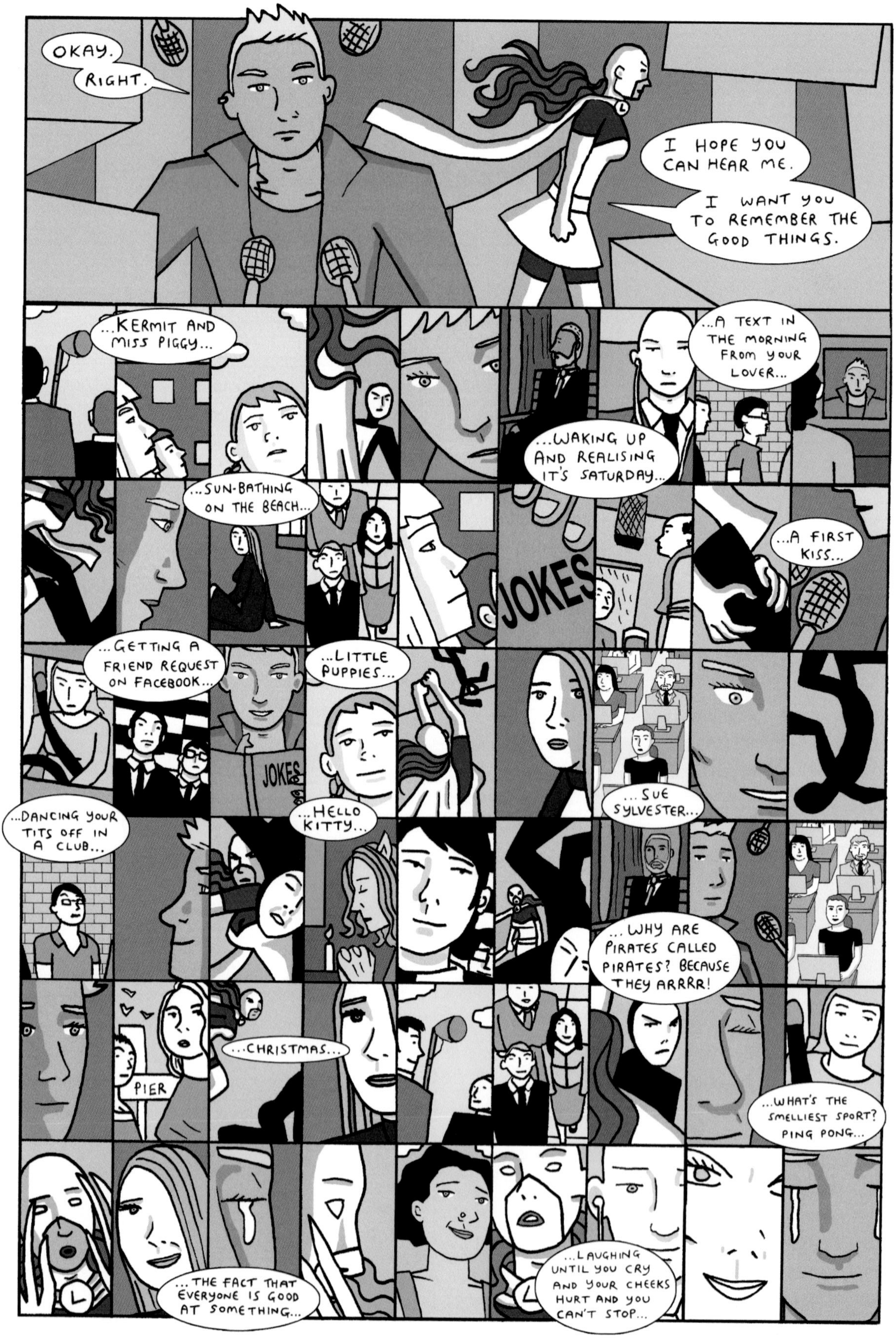
OKAY.
RIGHT.
I HOPE YOU CAN HEAR ME.
I WANT YOU TO REMEMBER THE GOOD THINGS.
...KERMIT AND MISS PIGGY...
...A TEXT IN THE MORNING FROM YOUR LOVER...
...WAKING UP AND REALISING IT'S SATURDAY...
...SUN-BATHING ON THE BEACH...
JOKES
...A FIRST KISS...
...GETTING A FRIEND REQUEST ON FACEBOOK...
JOKES
...LITTLE PUPPIES...
...SUE SYLVESTER...
...DANCING YOUR TITS OFF IN A CLUB...
...HELLO KITTY...
...WHY ARE PIRATES CALLED PIRATES? BECAUSE THEY ARRRR!
PIER
...CHRISTMAS...
...WHAT'S THE SMELLIEST SPORT? PING PONG...
...THE FACT THAT EVERYONE IS GOOD AT SOMETHING...
...LAUGHING UNTIL YOU CRY AND YOUR CHEEKS HURT AND YOU CAN'T STOP...

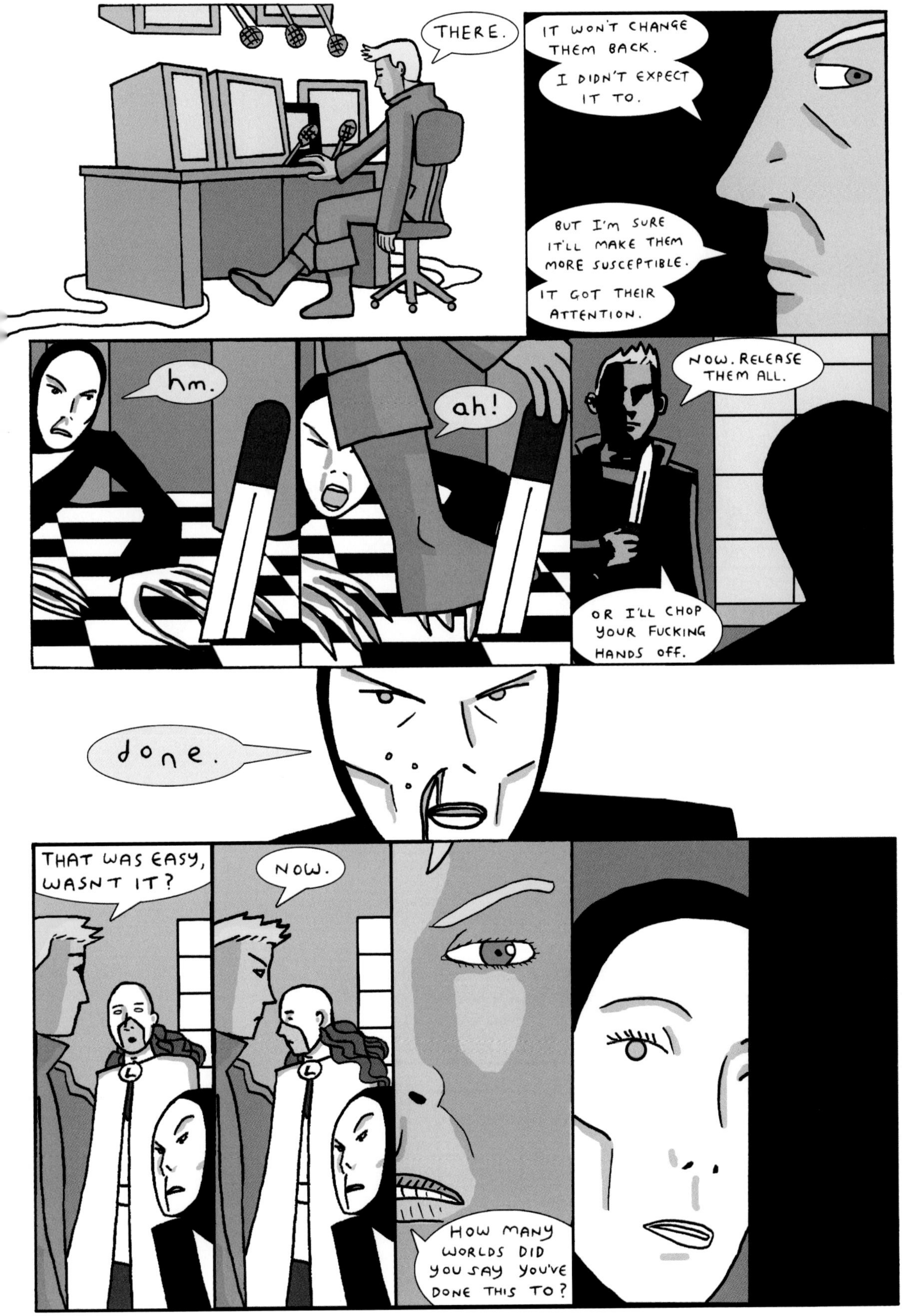
THERE.
IT WON'T CHANGE THEM BACK.
I DIDN'T EXPECT IT TO.
BUT I'M SURE IT'LL MAKE THEM MORE SUSCEPTIBLE.
IT GOT THEIR ATTENTION.
hm.
ah!
NOW. RELEASE THEM ALL.
OR I'LL CHOP YOUR FUCKING HANDS OFF.
done.
THAT WAS EASY, WASNT IT?
NOW.
HOW MANY WORLDS DID YOU SAY YOU'VE DONE THIS TO?

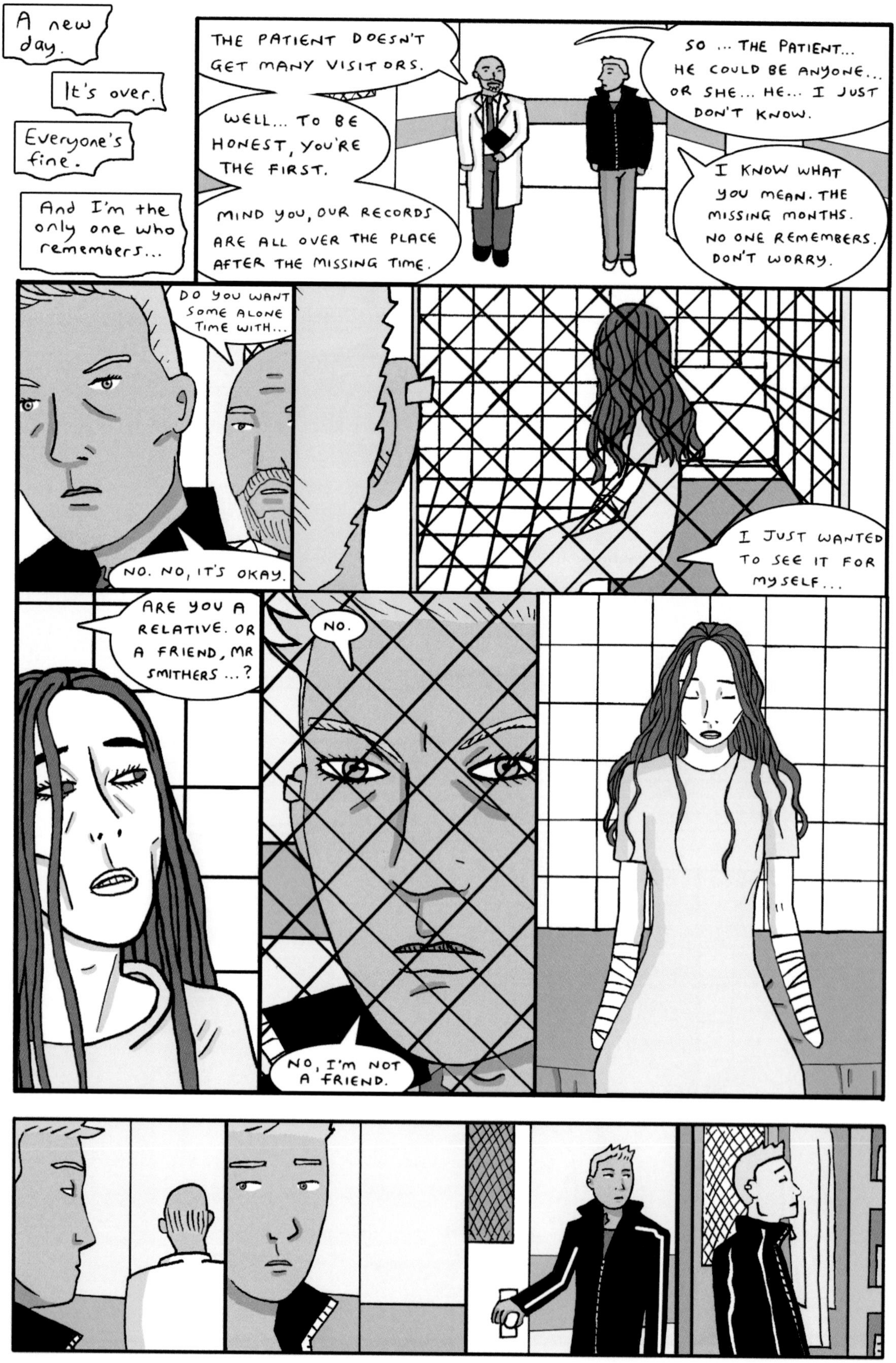
A new day.
It's over.
Everyone's fine.
And I'm the only one who remembers...
THE PATIENT DOESN'T GET MANY VISITORS.
SO ... THE PATIENT... HE COULD BE ANYONE... OR SHE... HE... I JUST DON'T KNOW.
WELL... TO BE HONEST, YOU'RE THE FIRST.
MIND YOU, OUR RECORDS ARE ALL OVER THE PLACE AFTER THE MISSING TIME.
I KNOW WHAT YOU MEAN. THE MISSING MONTHS. NO ONE REMEMBERS. DON'T WORRY.
DO YOU WANT SOME ALONE TIME WITH...
NO. NO, IT'S OKAY.
I JUST WANTED TO SEE IT FOR MYSELF...
ARE YOU A RELATIVE. OR A FRIEND, MR SMITHERS ...?
NO.
NO, I'M NOT A FRIEND.

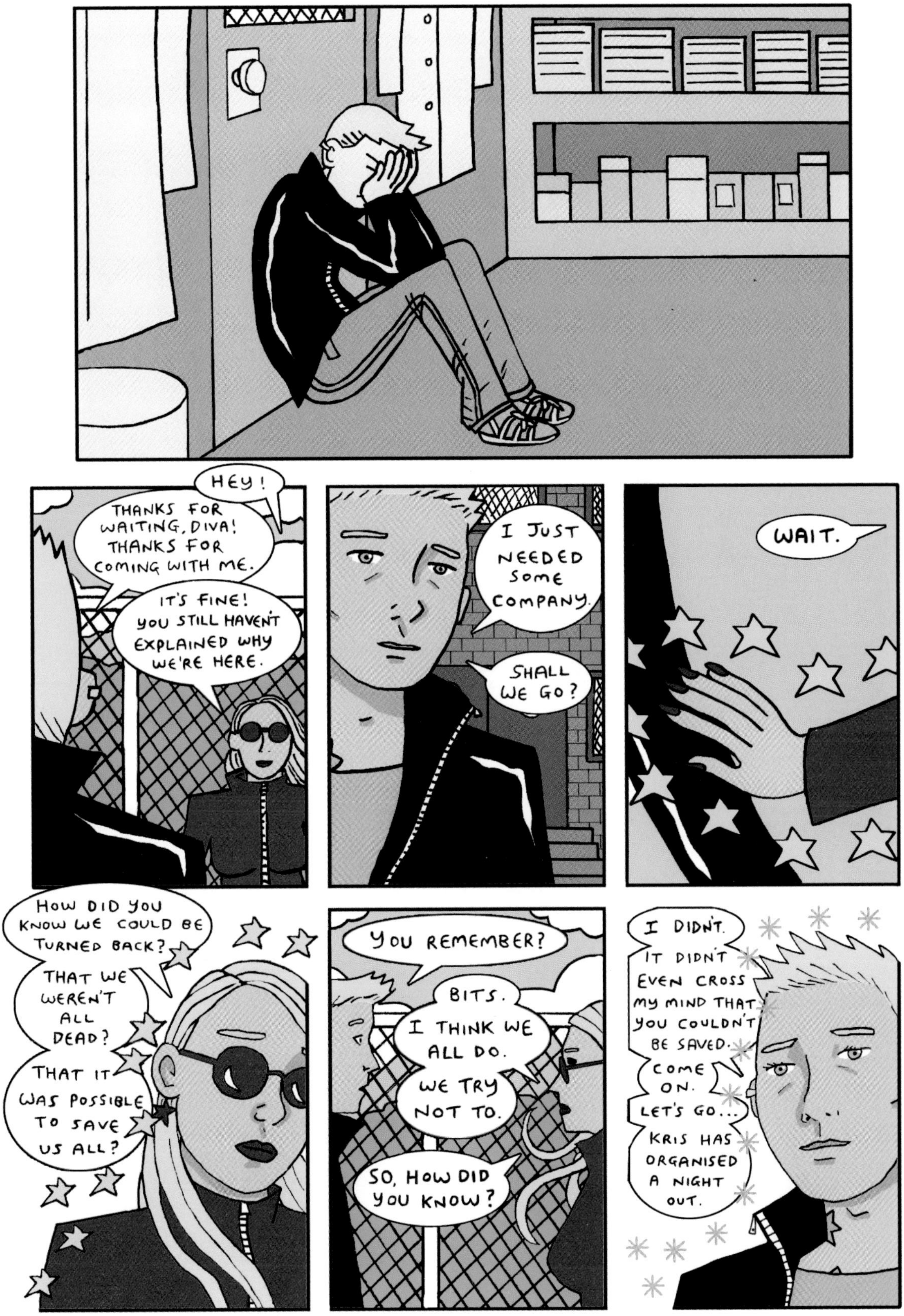
HEY!
THANKS FOR WAITING, DIVA! THANKS FOR COMING WITH ME.
IT'S FINE! YOU STILL HAVEN'T EXPLAINED WHY WE'RE HERE.
I JUST NEEDED SOME COMPANY.
SHALL WE GO?
WAIT.
HOW DID YOU KNOW WE COULD BE TURNED BACK?
THAT WE WEREN'T ALL DEAD?
THAT IT WAS POSSIBLE TO SAVE US ALL?
YOU REMEMBER?
BITS.
I THINK WE ALL DO.
WE TRY NOT TO.
SO, HOW DID YOU KNOW?
I DIDN'T.
IT DIDN'T EVEN CROSS MY MIND THAT YOU COULDN'T BE SAVED.
COME ON.
LET'S GO...
KRIS HAS ORGANISED A NIGHT OUT.

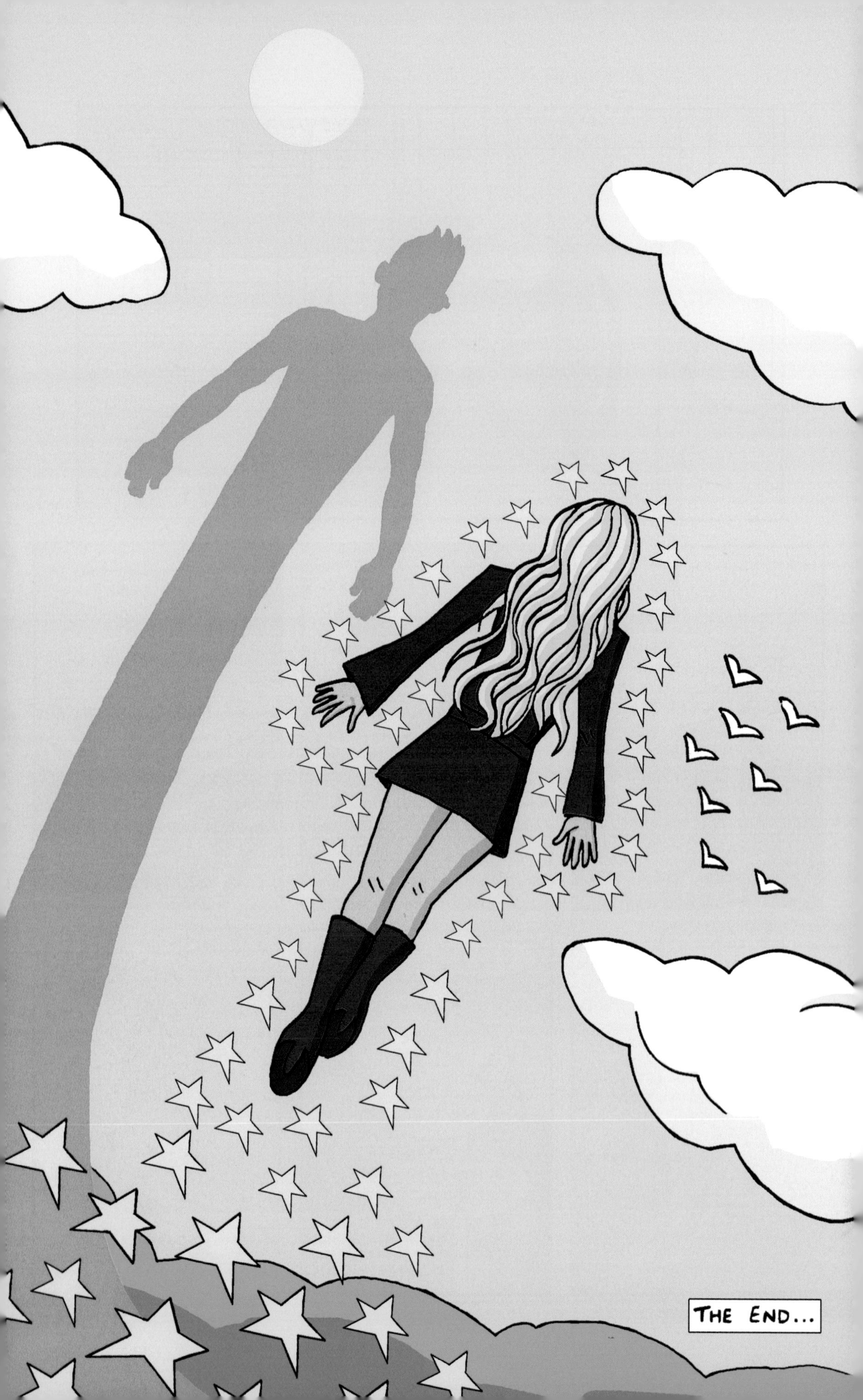
THE END...

A LITTLE NOTE FROM MARTIN

Whether you're gay or straight, sometimes the pressures of day-to-day life can take their toll. This story deals with that (if you read between the lines a bit), and beyond the 'gay zombies' and hermaphroditic villain of this issue, it is a very personal story to me.

If you're currently struggling with problems such as depression, anxiety or stress, or if you're having tough times. don't give up, try not to let it beat you. Things may not get better overnight but they will get better. There are things you can do which can help and there are places you can go to for assistance (check out 'issue 3 notes' at spandexcomic.com where I've put up a list).
Even if you wake up feeling you just can't do it, just remember that the day can improve, and it can actually turn out to be okay— and it often does.
You can do it.

~ Mart x

... And now turn the page for some special 'Spandex Shorts'!

THE J-TEAM in 'Super Evil Giant Kitty Destroys Tokyo!' Part 19327

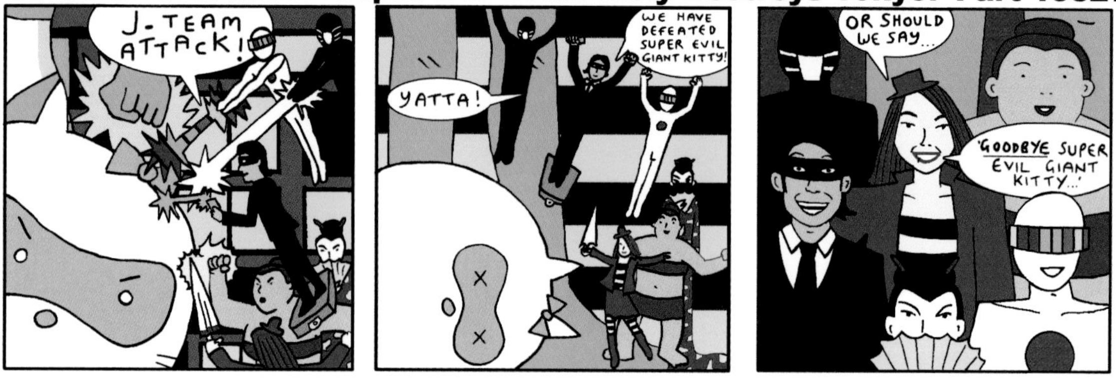
J-TEAM ATTACK!
YATTA!
WE HAVE DEFEATED SUPER EVIL GIANT KITTY!
OR SHOULD WE SAY...
'GOODBYE SUPER EVIL GIANT KITTY...'

BUTCH in 'Lying Here'

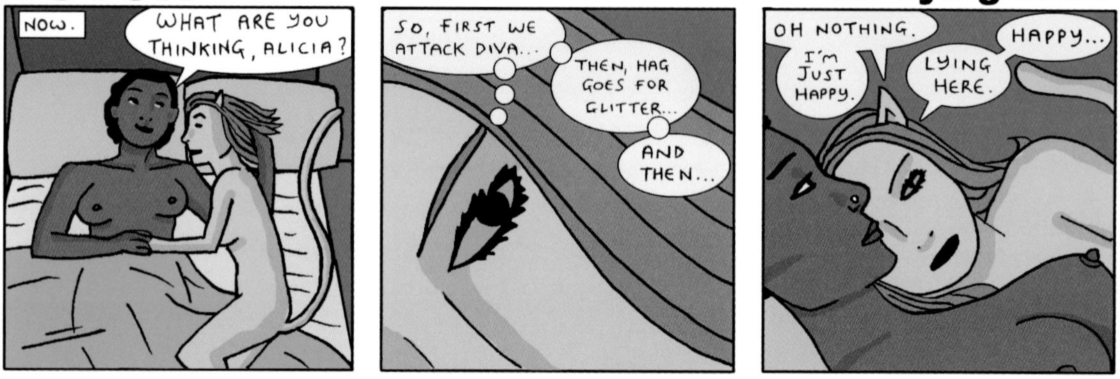
NOW.
WHAT ARE YOU THINKING, ALICIA?
SO, FIRST WE ATTACK DIVA...
THEN, HAG GOES FOR GLITTER...
AND THEN...
OH NOTHING.
I'M JUST HAPPY.
LYING HERE.
HAPPY...

BEAR-MAN & TWINKLE in 'Doctor Stationery' Part 8

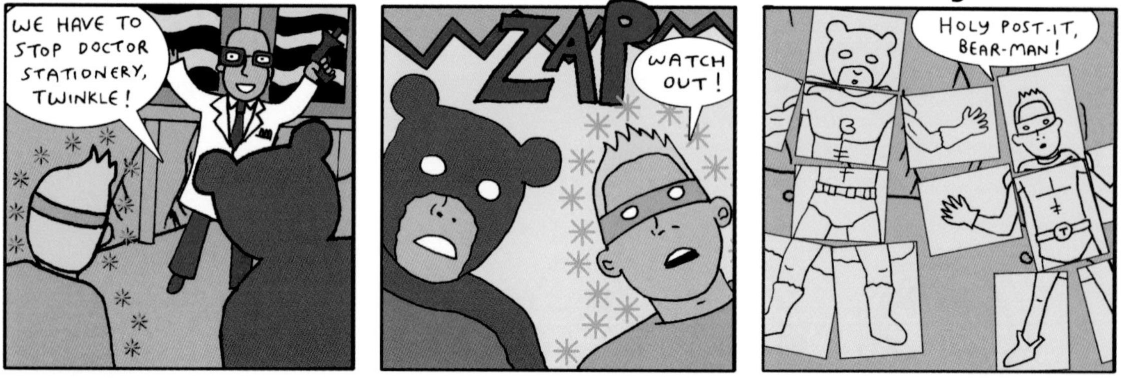
WE HAVE TO STOP DOCTOR STATIONERY, TWINKLE!
ZAP
WATCH OUT!
HOLY POST-IT, BEAR-MAN!

NEON in 'The Origin of Neon' Part 24

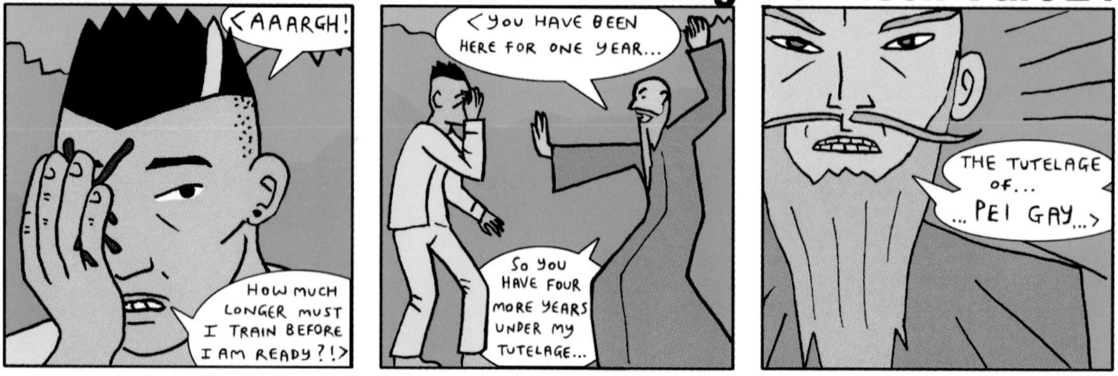
<AAAARGH!
HOW MUCH LONGER MUST I TRAIN BEFORE I AM READY?!>
<YOU HAVE BEEN HERE FOR ONE YEAR...
SO YOU HAVE FOUR MORE YEARS UNDER MY TUTELAGE...
THE TUTELAGE OF... ...PEI GAY...>

PROWLER

in 'Chunk Attacks!' Part 7

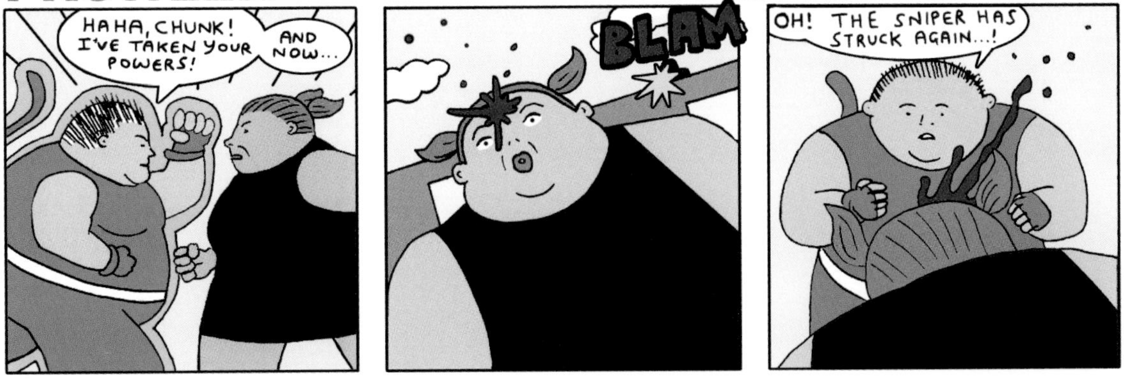
HAHA, CHUNK! I'VE TAKEN YOUR POWERS!
AND NOW...
BLAM
OH! THE SNIPER HAS STRUCK AGAIN...!

DIVA

in 'Trapped'

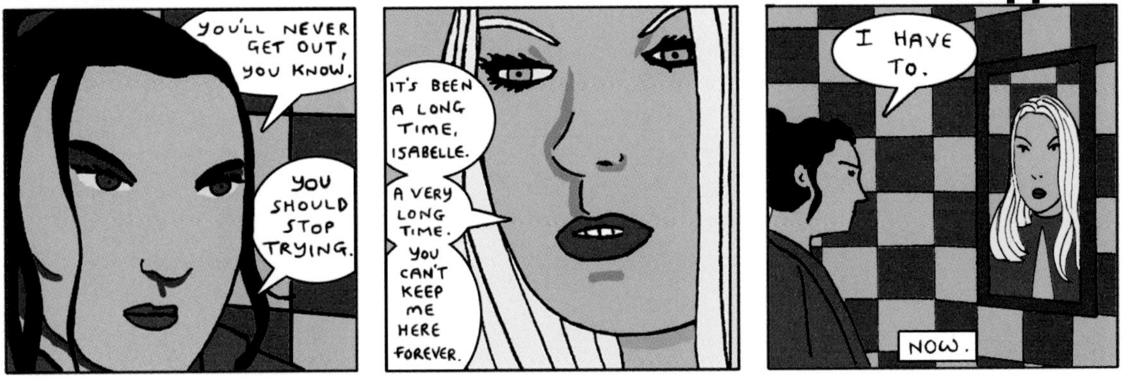
YOU'LL NEVER GET OUT, YOU KNOW.
YOU SHOULD STOP TRYING.
IT'S BEEN A LONG TIME, ISABELLE.
A VERY LONG TIME.
YOU CAN'T KEEP ME HERE FOREVER.
I HAVE TO.
NOW.

ピンクにんじゃだ！

'ピンクにんじゃだ'

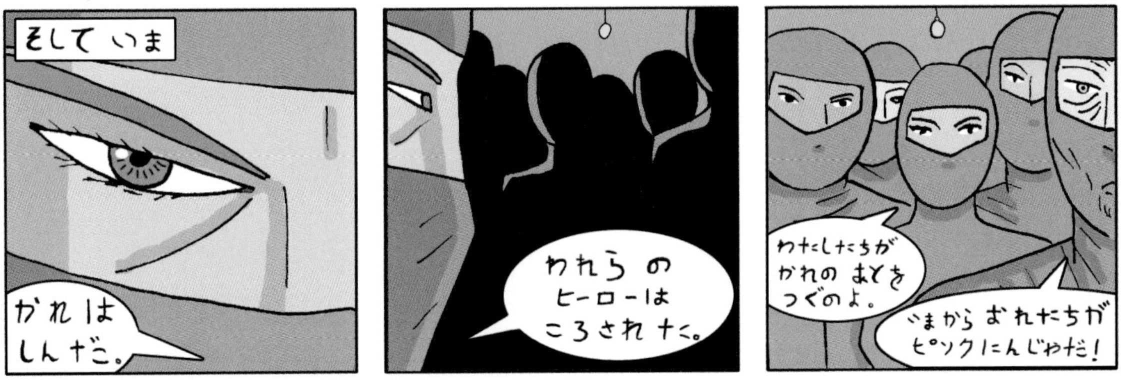
そして いま
かれは しんだ。
われら の ヒーローは ころされた。
わたしたちが かれの あとを つぐのよ。
いまから おれたちが ピンクにんじゃだ！

INDIGO

in 'The Test'

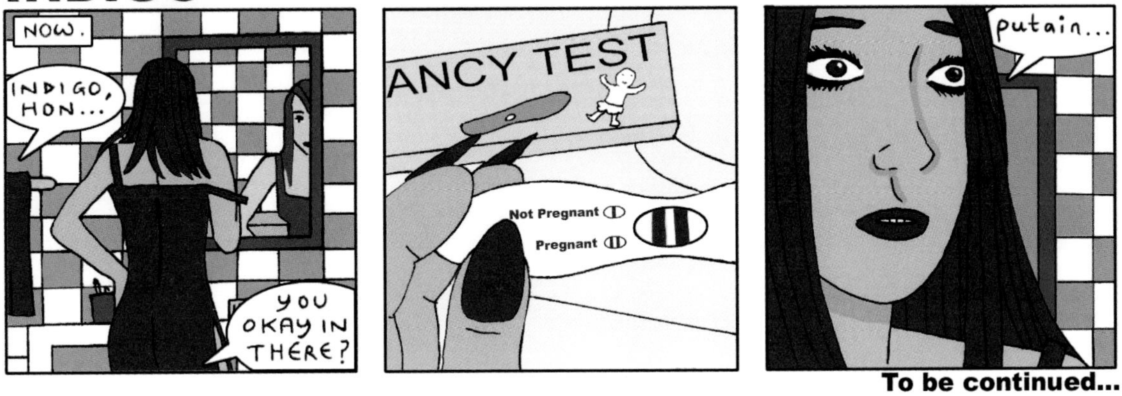
NOW.
INDIGO, HON...
YOU OKAY IN THERE?
ANCY TEST
Not Pregnant
Pregnant
putain...

To be continued...

A BRIEF HISTORY OF SPANDEX

I'd been working on an indie super-soap comic called *The O Men* for around ten years, and I was ready for a break from it... And at the same time, some *O Men* supporting characters – Liberty, Diva and Glitter – started to grab my attention. So one thing led to another and I thought to myself: has there ever been an entirely gay superteam? Well, apparently there has been (are there any original ideas left in the world?), but no real 'household names'. So I decided to go with this idea, and was very anxious to do it before anyone else did in a major way.

So I set about creating a new comic that would be self-contained, and would only last a handful of issues and wouldn't sprawl out of control like *The O Men* did (ironically, *Spandex* has now grown too big for its boots!). I already had Liberty, Diva and Glitter (he hadn't initially been gay in *The O Men* universe, but he kind of headed that way). Next came Butch and Mr. Muscles who were black and white twins (which caused a surprising amount of controversy). Ms. Fantastic had been a member, but I made her a villain instead. Prowler was always there as some kind of cheeky monkey man, but it took me a long time to nail down his powers and name. Indigo took a while to come into my head, but eventually she teleported her way in there.

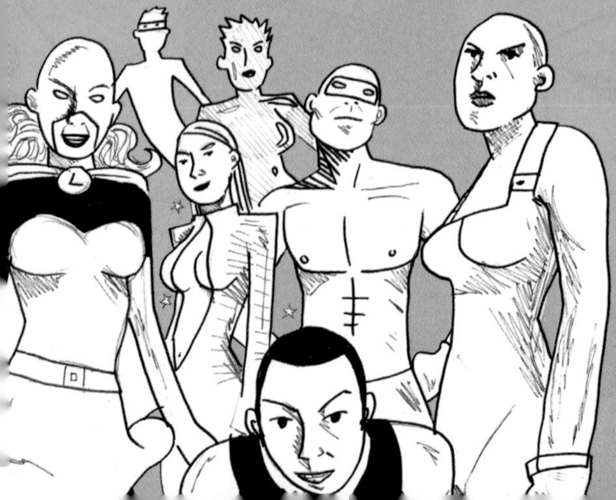

The first issue took me a year to complete. I was getting to grips with Photoshop and it was my first colour comic too. I lettered it all by computer, but then decided to re-letter it all with my own hand-lettering style. I printed up 200 A5 copies of #1, mainly for friends and for a UK comic convention, and the positive response I got was overwhelming.

I toyed with the idea of doing a press release but I didn't have any contacts and I really didn't think anyone would take notice. But then I got chatting to a friend who worked in marketing and he helped me put together a really good press release which we then sent out...

And then suddenly, things went crazy! The UK's *Metro* newspaper picked up on the story, and soon it hit the internet and then went global... I was in shock! I received 1,000 orders for the first issue in a few days, and so I had to reprint it as soon as poss (it took two weeks, argh!).

And my *Spandex* plans changed too. The initial idea was to go straight to a graphic novel containing seven stories which jumped around in the continuity (for example, from #1 to #4, then #8, etc., along with fake covers). But I got too swept up in the excitement, and decided to release the comic on a sequential issue-by-issue basis instead.

So here in your hands, you have the first three issues in one glorious hardback. People seem to like it, and I think the storytelling improves issue by issue – and if there's enough interest, you'll hopefully also get to see the next part of the tale, the very shocking four-part 'O.M.F.G.' storyline!

I really hope you enjoy this volume!

All the best,
Martin Eden

Left: One of my earliest sketches of the Spandex team!

THE SPANDEX TEAM

DIVA

Basically, Diva is a lesbian Wonder Woman – your everyday superheroine, except she dates ladies. Of course, nothing is ever that simple, and later in the series you'll find she's harbouring some very big, very scary secrets. Secrets that are pivotal to the overall storyline. What's going on when she transforms into that dumpy woman, for instance? For some bizarre reason, Diva's costume and look was inspired by an old Britney Spears video, although Diva is older...

GLITTER

Glitter popped up now and then in The O Men (you don't need to read it to understand Spandex). At one point, he was going to suffer Mr. Muscles' fate at he end of #1 and then come back in a Ninja body-suit (!), but it wasn't working for me, so poor old Muscles went as originally planned. I didn't feel all that interested in Glitter at first, and he was a bit snippy and annoying. But I've really enjoyed exploring his character more... and finding out what makes him tick.

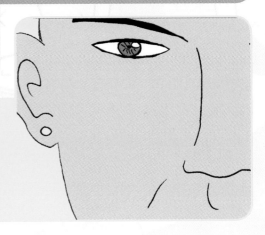

MR. MUSCLES

For some reason, it just seemed natural that Mr. Muscles and Butch were twins. In fact, that caused a pretty big online outcry when I launched the series. We may not have seen the last of Mr. Muscles...

BUTCH

Butch is a female Luke Cage. She's strong and silent. The challenge is making a character like her interesting, and it's been fun trying to convey her personality. She's one of my favourites, definitely.

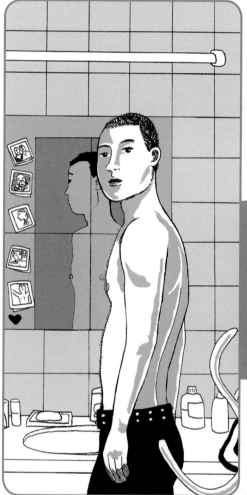

PROWLER

Prowler was the final character I decided on. He took a while to sort out. I knew his powers, but couldn't think up a name. I went through lots of different options – Unity, Origin, Haven, Amalgam... He's got a fun power, very unique, and there's an interesting reason why he's got a tail. That comes up in the next story arc!

INDIGO

Indigo is named after the Indigo Girls, a lesbian folk group. I like her because she reminds me of a sane, calmer Aurora (from the old *Alpha Flight* comic) and I love purple (well, purple/indigo, whatever). I really love her 'Indigo Room' – I don't think that's been done in a comic before.

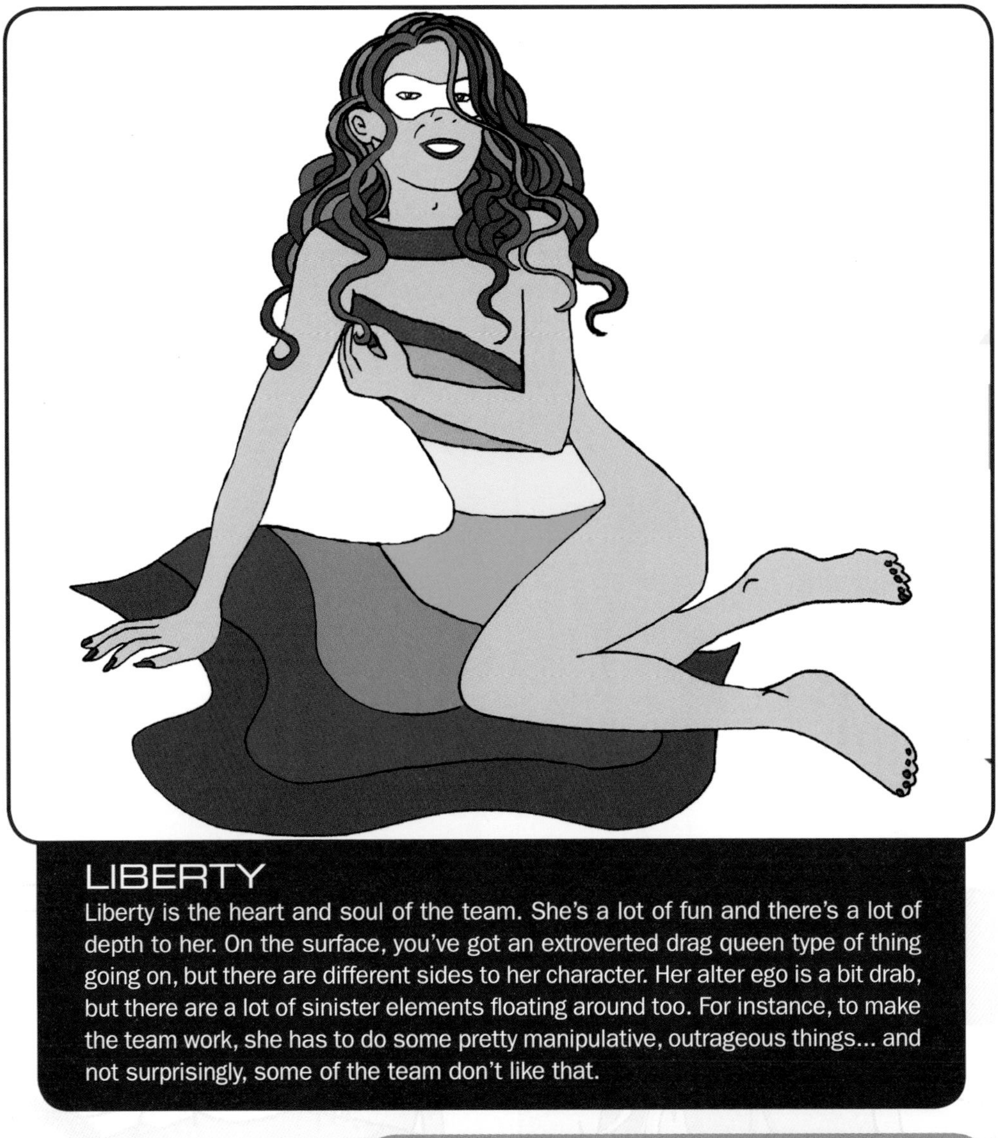

LIBERTY

Liberty is the heart and soul of the team. She's a lot of fun and there's a lot of depth to her. On the surface, you've got an extroverted drag queen type of thing going on, but there are different sides to her character. Her alter ego is a bit drab, but there are a lot of sinister elements floating around too. For instance, to make the team work, she has to do some pretty manipulative, outrageous things... and not surprisingly, some of the team don't like that.

PUSSY

It's been a lot of fun coming up with the villains for *Spandex*, and there are plenty more on the way. I see Les Girlz as the series' main villains, and their presence will build slowly until they really make our poor guys' lives a misery.

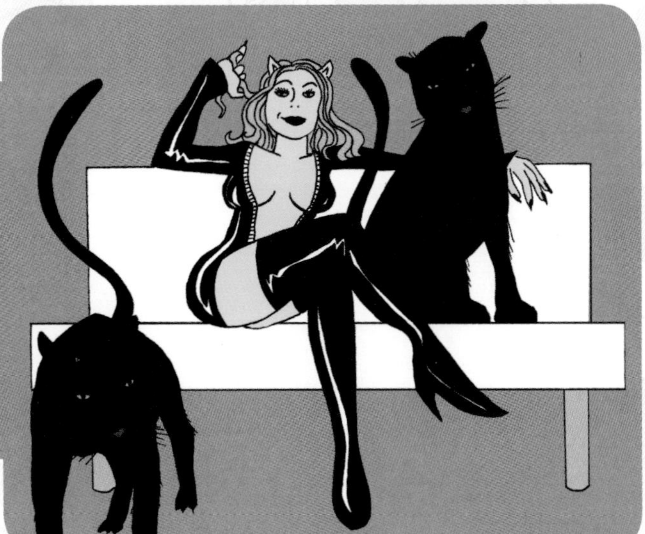

NEON

As you may have gathered, I'm a big fan of all-things Japanese, so I just had to throw in a Japanese character. His hair is loosely based on one of the *Dragonball* manga guys. I thought it was funny to basically have a gay adult *Dragonball* character lookalike in my comic.

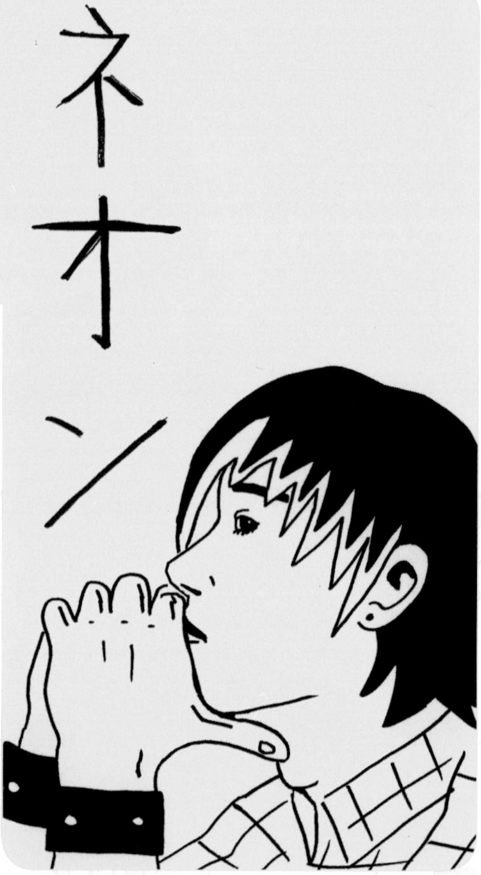
ネオン

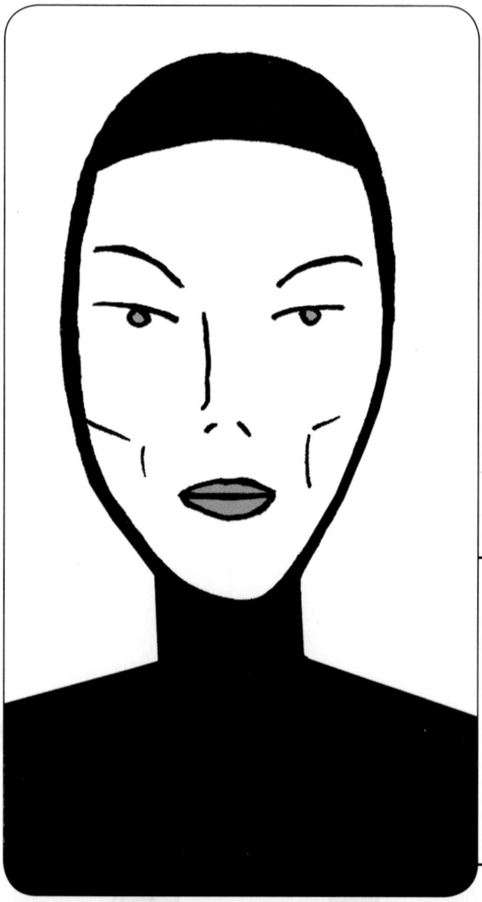

NADIR

I wanted something really creepy for Nadir, and she/he has elements of Michael Jackson and a spider, I think – scary! Plus, to give it the *Spandex* spin, Nadir is kind of sexless – I love it when you don't know if a villain is male or female.

ISSUE #3 COVER

When I was selling Spandex #2 at conventions, I found that some straight readers seemed to be put off by the very pink cover. I really wanted Spandex to be universal, so I made sure this cover had a lot more universal appeal – and huge breasts. I like this cover, because even though the team are all dressed in black, they all shine out with a little bit of colour somehow, each in their own way.

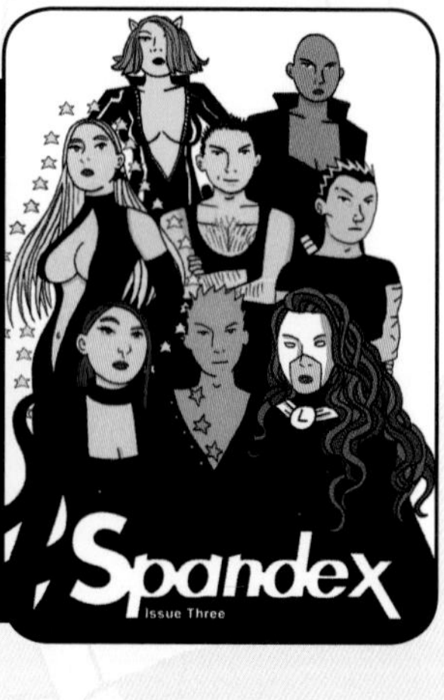
Spandex
Issue Three

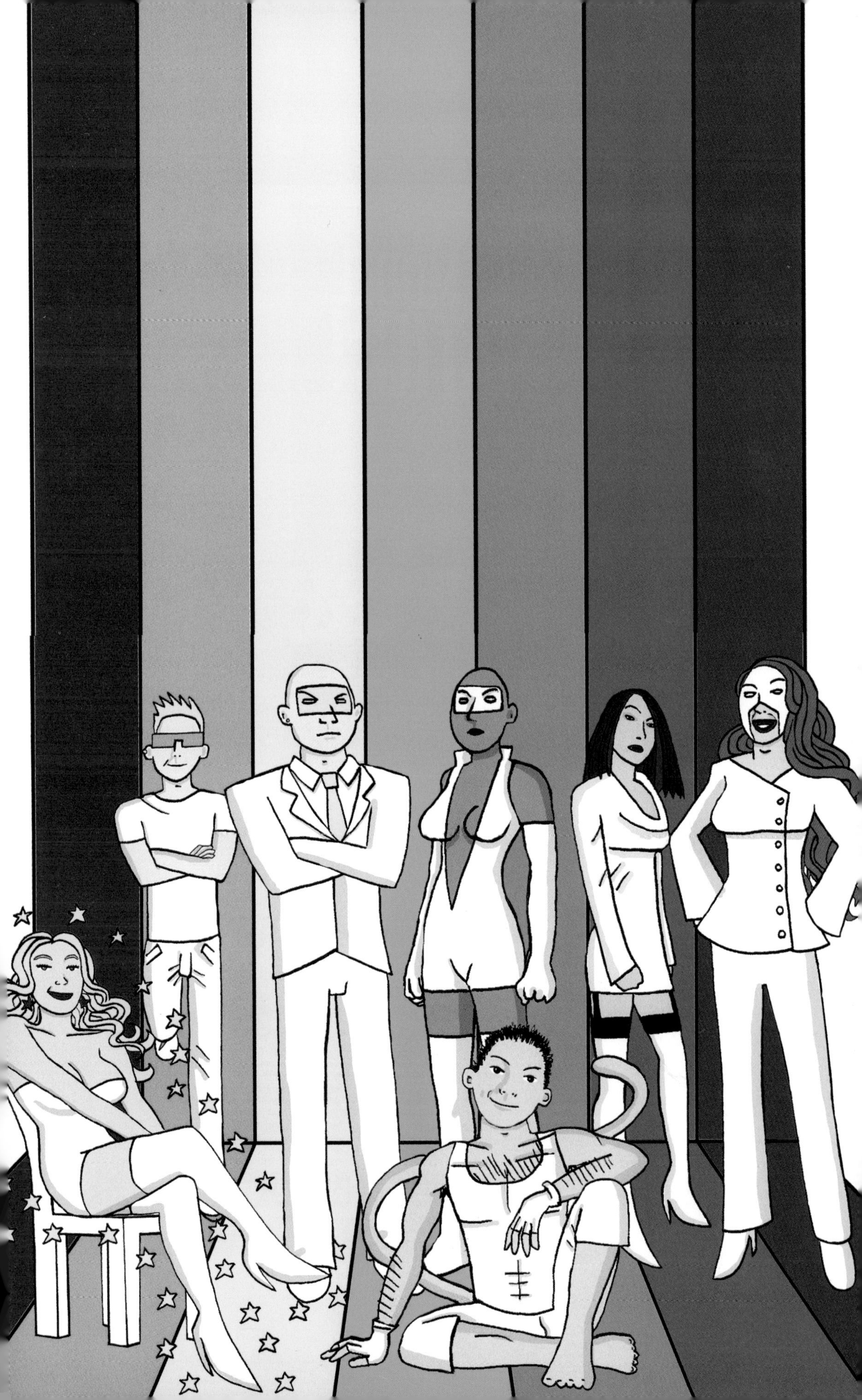

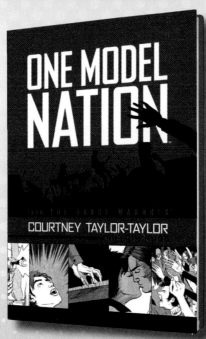

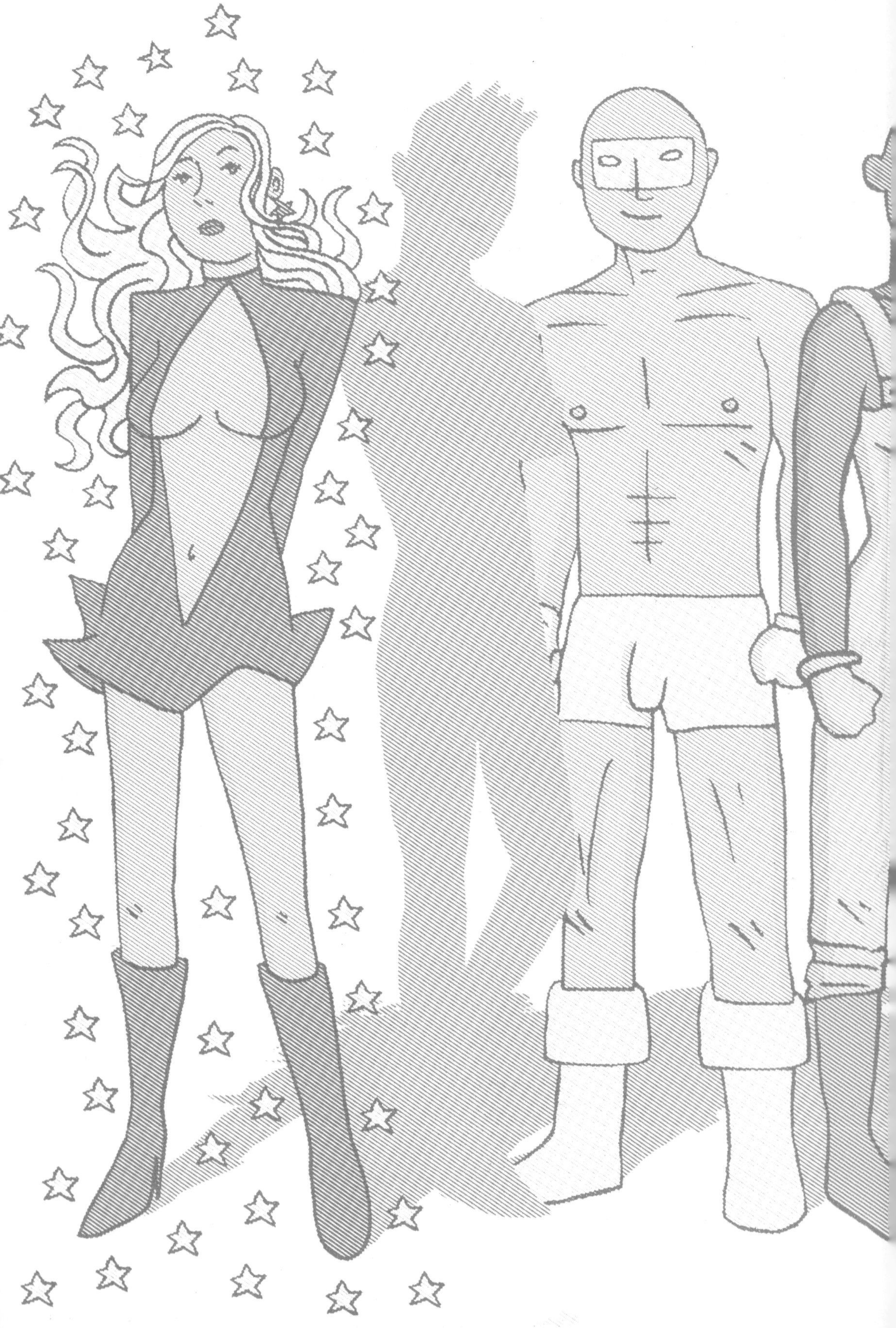